Grant MacEwan Community College:
The First Two Decades
—A RETROSPECTIVE—

Glenn David Ruhl

"...I am prepared to stand before
my Maker, the Ruler of the entire Universe,
with no other plea than that I have
tried to leave things in His Vineyard
better than I found them."

Dr. J. W. Grant MacEwan,
Excerpt from the MacEwan Creed, 1969

Grant
MacEwan
Community
College

Grant MacEwan Community College:
The First Two Decades
—A Retrospective—

Author: Glenn David Ruhl, Ph.D.

Forewords by: J. W. Grant MacEwan & Gerald O. Kelly

Reviewers: Alan Vladicka & Dorothy Gray

Editor: Judith Johnson

Graphic Designer: David B. Cuyler

Cover Design: Jill Murrin

Published by: Grant MacEwan Community College

Canadian Cataloguing in Publication Data

Ruhl, Glenn David.

  Grant MacEwan Community College

ISBN 0-9698554-1-9

1. Grant MacEwan Community College—History.

I.Grant MacEwan Community College II. Title

LE3.5.G522R83 1995   378.7123'34   C95-910705-3

Grant MacEwan Community College recognizes the generous contribution of the Grant MacEwan College Foundation, that made the printing of this book possible.

Contents

A Personal Message

Dr. J. W. Grant MacEwan

I am about to write these lines in Thanksgiving Week, 1993, and I will try to remind myself appropriately of the many occasions of delight experienced during my twenty-year association with GMCC and its distinguished leaders. Nor will I forget at this Thanksgiving season to express gratitude for the rare privilege of sharing my name with the little college that became one of Canada's educational showpieces. The story of a beginning in an abandoned food store followed by a chain of unbroken successes is one that should be told and retold for inspirational value.

It is only fair that those citizens whose imagination and vision brought the College to reality should be remembered with repeated congratulations to them and then that those Albertans in public life who recognize the worth of the educational facility and supported its expansion with the necessary funding should be thanked and congratulated again.

Naturally, I have recalled many times my own thrilling introduction to the proposal to start a college. I was occupying an office in the Legislature Building about twenty-five years ago when two public spirited Edmontonians, Barry Moore and Judge Ed Stack, made an early morning call. They didn't have time for coffee and a muffin but before leaving, Mr. Moore—now an active community college president in Eastern Canada—hinted that they had a plan. "We believe," said Mr. Moore, "that Edmonton should have a community college to accommodate students who are no longer within reach of high schools and not qualified for university." I was impressed and said so but his next remark left me momentarily speechless: "We would like to call it 'Grant MacEwan'." I was puzzled and flattered and didn't overlook the possibility that my guests were indulging in humour. But graciously they explained that they were serious and had already taken the first steps to set their plan in motion. I then hastened to tell my visitors that I liked the idea of a college and was thrilled with their proposal for a name.

Edmonton people received the news of a community college with glee and the plan unfolded quickly. Twenty-five years is not long in the life of a city or nation and it certainly didn't seem long before residents of the northern city were getting the news of the new and handsome home for the City Centre Campus, a three-storey complex covering 65,000 square metres on four city blocks. Members of the teaching and administrative staff, students, and Edmonton residents were pleased and happy. The hope is that it will enrich the lives of young people and older ones. The student populations, the enthusiasm and loyalty of students, and the high public acceptance of graduates tell the rest of what must be one of Canada's best educational stories. Happily it is being written.

J. W. Grant MacEwan
October 1993

Foreword

Dr. Gerald O. Kelly, President

The history of community colleges in Canada has been studied and documented fairly well at the national and, in some cases, provincial levels, but the development of the relatively young institutions called community colleges has not been documented at the level of individual institutions. To a large extent, those involved in the provision of college programming over the last twenty years or so have been too involved in the development of their new institutions, and in meeting the steadily increasing student and community demands for their services, to take the time to reflect seriously on where their institutions have been and how far they have come in their short organizational "lives."

With the publication of this volume, Grant MacEwan Community College is attempting to capture some of the record of its first two decades of development, and to take advantage of the recollections and experiences of many individuals who played major roles in that development. The history is intended to serve several distinct purposes. It will serve as a "source book" for future scholars who may conduct more in-depth study and analysis of the longer term development of the College, and its place in community college education in Alberta and Canada. It can provide a focus for current members of the College community to reflect on the institution's development so far, and to gain a clearer perspective on why the College is the way it is. Finally, the history may serve as a pleasant reminder to past associates of GMCC, of their part in the development of this dynamic and enterprising institution.

It is certainly fitting that the college that bears the name of one of Canada's most prolific historians, Dr. J. W. Grant MacEwan, should pay some attention to documenting and publicizing its own history. Through the efforts of the author, Glenn Ruhl, and the production assistance of the College's Instructional Media and Design department, the College is pleased to offer this work as a contribution to knowledge and understanding of this phase in the development of Alberta's post-secondary education system.

In structuring this book, Glenn Ruhl has chosen to build his story around the position of the College presidency, as reflected by the titles of his third and fourth chapters. I believe that the true MacEwan story could equally well be told from the perspective of the many faculty members, support staff, and administrators who have dedicated their careers to the development of the College we all cherish.

As the President of Grant MacEwan Community College, and someone who has lived at the heart of much of the history described herein, I wish to extend my thanks to all those involved in the production of this volume, and to express my hope that those who read it will find it an interesting and valuable contribution to their understanding of the College.

Gerald O. Kelly
May, 1995

Preface

When the imagery of one's reading is enhanced through personal recognition, a phenomenon author James A. Michener calls "resonance" takes place. This phenomenon, according to Michener, "is to the great advantage of the narrative, when the reader comes upon a phrase, a complete thought, a character or an incident with which he or she is already familiar."[1]

The writing of history has inherent limitations: memories fade, recollections differ, and the "dryness" of the archival record often fails to capture the flavour of a particular event. A major advantage in recounting recent history is that many of the people responsible for the shaping of events are still accessible. But being close to a subject will not guarantee a definitive chronicle. For the people associated with Grant MacEwan Community College, for whom the phenomenon of resonance will have its greatest effect, the College's history will be familiar yet different because, in all cases, it is very personal.

The following historical record is open to debate. What is significant is often relative to an individual's involvement with the topic. Objective interpretation is the goal of the historian and if the present author fails in this quest, it is not intentional. In the case of Grant MacEwan Community College, no historical record can convey the sense of guarded optimism, pioneer spirit, and youthful adventure associated with starting not only a new institution of higher learning, but a type of institution of higher learning with which very few people had any experience. For the people directly involved, the following work may not contain sufficient anecdotal narrative; many of them could embellish the text with "their side of the story." Unfortunately, it is difficult for an outside observer to capture the same feeling as actually "being there."

This means that many areas of the College's history are touched on briefly while others are expanded in areas that some "insiders" will consider trivial. The emphasis given to certain events in the public record, however, such as board notes, annual reports, newspaper coverage, and so on, encouraged the author to assign to them a certain level of significance. The author hopes, therefore, that for those people closer to the topic, this brief history will serve as a "source book" and the beginning of a larger project filled with the personal touches and experiences that make up the true character of Grant MacEwan Community College.

When John Dennison and Paul Gallagher began their work on Canada's community colleges, they noted that "the story of the origins and developments of the colleges and college systems relies heavily on broad but largely unassembled documentation."[2] In preparing this document, therefore, the task at hand was to assemble the documentation and synthesize the historical record concerning Grant MacEwan Community College.

Historical records such as board and committee minutes, planning documents and proposals, personal interviews, and government legislation were systematically reviewed in the course of preparing this history. This involved a critical evaluation of primary and secondary sources using both indirect and direct research methods. Eventually, a level of self-discipline was required to end the investigative process and begin writing. The result of this writing is a paper that is topical and generally chronological. It is not intended to serve as a definitive work; rather, it is a collection and synthesis of material that, in many ways, was far overdue for analysis.

The "official" history of Grant MacEwan Community College spans two decades: a meagre time frame by historical standards. The historical importance of this twenty year period, however, is significant. Recognizing this, the current College President, Dr. Gerald Kelly, initiated this project with the feeling that it was necessary to capture the spirit of the College's origins, describe where it has travelled, and provide some indicators concerning its future.

The body of this history covers the decades of the 1970s and 1980s. The author has chosen to call these two decades the "Haar years" and the "Kelly years," respectively, in recognition of the presidents who led the College during each period. This terminology was used for two reasons: first, because it provided a focal point for the research and writing; and second, because leadership is a critical element in the success of any organization.

Successful leaders create an environment that allows things to happen. John Haar was instrumental in getting the College started, and under Gerry Kelly the College has flourished. Effective programs are now recognized for their value in the community, the College is well-organized and managed, and in the recent development of world-class physical facilities, vision and planning have become reality.

The goal of this document is not to exaggerate the College's strong points or to ignore the weak ones. Edward T. Hall said, "the most difficult task in the world is to know one's self. But knowing others can aid in the performance of that task."[3] An "outsider" writing about Grant MacEwan Community College may, at first glance, appear to be at a disadvantage in writing a comprehensive history; however, an "insider," in Hall's estimation, might face an even greater challenge. Knowing others, in this case the many people I came into contact with while writing this document, most certainly aided in the completion of this task. I am particularly thankful for the help of Gerry Kelly, T. C. (Chuck) Day, Dorothy Gray, Margo March, Sharon Schnell, Andi Pallas, Bert Giles, Alan Vladicka, Sue Couture, Barry Snowden, Dianne Allen, Shirley Graham, Laurene Park, and, of course, all of the College's Learning Resources Centre staff, for putting up with the eccentric work of the historian.[4]

Glenn David Ruhl

[1] James A. Michener, *Journey: A Quest for Canadian Gold* (Toronto: McClelland and Stewart, 1988), pp. 232–233.

[2] John D. Dennison and Paul Gallagher, *Canada's Community Colleges* (Vancouver: University of British Columbia Press, 1986), p. 6.

[3] *Who's Who in America, 1990–91* (Chicago: Marquis Who's Who, 1991).

[4] One final note requires mention. Despite the common convention now employed by journalists that specifies the use of lower-case spellings, the author has deliberately chosen to capitalize the word "college" when it is used in reference to Grant MacEwan Community College. This book, after all, is the College's history, and the College deserves this special attention.

Chapter One

Background

The history of a community college is truly a reflection of the community it serves.[1] No other institution of higher learning is more responsive to the needs of the general population. Grant MacEwan Community College arose out of a specific set of conditions and needs that were defined within the context of the City of Edmonton and the Province of Alberta. "Historians," Gordon Campbell suggests, "have too often written about educational institutions as though they were isolated from the social and economic forces inextricably related to their existence"[2] The Grant MacEwan Community College story will not be relayed in isolated terms; GMCC was established, developed, and continues to evolve as a result of distinct local influences.

Geography, tradition, patterns of immigration, natural resources, and economic growth differentiate the regions of Canada. These factors alone might be seen as the prime influences in creating a distinct educational arrangement; however, early legislation also ensured the unique regional development of educational systems. Regional differences in Canadian post-secondary[3] education are largely the result of the *British North America Act* of 1867, specifically Section 93, which placed Canadian education under the jurisdiction of the provinces. Thus, since Alberta became a province in 1905, post-secondary education has developed under the close scrutiny of the government.[4]

From 1850 to 1950, universities dominated post-secondary education in Canada, England, and the United States.[5] This domination of higher education was marked by conservative ideology and curricula devoted to maintaining the existing class structure. The university's position in post-secondary education, however, was dramatically challenged after World War II by a public that demanded educational reform. Although the university remained the major post-secondary force, the social and economic conditions of this period were perfect for the development of a post-secondary alternative to the university.

In the United States, high schools began to offer advanced work that was referred to as junior college as early as 1901.[6] In American society, public education was viewed as a democratic right. Social mobility and opportunity were open to everyone through higher education. Education in Canada, however, did not develop along the same democratic lines as in the United States. The colleges that existed in Canada by the late 1950s[7] were patterned more after the European model than the American and tended to prepare students for university entrance. According to Dennison and Gallagher, "the entire sector of higher education in Canada was synonymous with academic and professional preparation."[8] Higher education in Canada was attained through a process of elimination and perseverance. A university education was thought of as desirable for the elite, but hardly necessary for the general population.

Faith in the wonder-working powers of education has proved to be one of the most durable and easily assimilated components of liberal ideology.[9] After the Second World War, a new emphasis on social equality, the rapid expansion of the Canadian industrial base, and the concomitant growth of urban centres brought about increasing emphasis on the value of higher education. The growing numbers of people interested in higher education also placed pressure on the universities to offer programs that could accommodate more diverse needs and expectations. Schools at every level, at this time, were expected to provide the solutions for all social and personal problems.[10] In short, post-war higher education was forced to change by pressures that originated in the society, environment, and technology, rather than from within the institutions themselves.

Post-secondary education in western Canada developed without the traditional constraints often associated with eastern Canada. The educational system in western Canada was characterized by equality, stemming from what Dennison and Gallagher refer to as the "enterprising and challenging atmosphere of a more venturesome and individualistic environment"[11] than that found in the rest of the country. Hugh Farquhar, in his examination of the role of the college in Alberta's post-secondary system, notes:

> The basic philosophy, that appears as a continuous thread
> throughout the relevant documents, is based upon the principle
> that individuals differ in their needs, interests, abilities, aptitudes,
> and motivations, and that, in a democracy, every individual has the
> right to educational opportunities that will develop his unique
> talents and abilities to the optimum extent.[12]

Gordon Campbell recognized that a democratic focus has characterized post-secondary education in Alberta since the creation of the first public junior college.[13] From 1910 to 1971, Alberta governments have supported alternative educational institutions through grants, budget assistance, and philosophical consensus.[14]

The industrial growth of the post-war years, the economic affluence from the resource boom, and the challenges to the traditional educational system produced a perfect atmosphere for the development of the college in post-secondary education. By the end of the 1950s, Dennison and Gallagher note, the reluctance to expand post-secondary education in Canada came to an abrupt end, and "the American experience of the previous fifty years was to become a major influence on the way in which Canadian education was to respond to newly felt needs."[15] Thus, as Campbell noted, "democratization of educational opportunity became a theme of educators, planners and politicians alike."[16]

Officially, Grant MacEwan Community College was established in 1971, although its conceptual origins are much earlier. In a sense, the story of Grant MacEwan Community College begins in 1910. In that year, the Alberta provincial legislature passed legislation[17] stating that any institution or college in the province must have an affiliation with the University of Alberta for the promotion of any other useful branch of learning. This act represents the earliest reference to colleges in the provincial legislation. What is particularly noteworthy about the *University Acts* of 1906 and 1910 is that they formed the basis of government policy toward junior colleges for the next half century,[18] and they affirmed the dominant role the University of Alberta would play in the establishment of public and private provincial colleges.

The University of Alberta was the sole provider of post-secondary university-level education within the province until the 1960s.[19] The first government of Alberta gave high priority to the creation of a university and by 1908, only three years after the province entered confederation, university classes were being offered. A single provincial university was considered desirable in order to avoid the regional and inter-institutional rivalries observed in eastern Canadian post-secondary education, while ensuring a high quality of education.[20] This rationalization, of course, was also related to the limited financial resources available in the recently established province.[21]

In 1910 the Royal Commission on Industrial Training and Technical Education was established and a capital grant was directed to agricultural, technical, and vocational education. In addition, federal money was provided for veterans, research programs, and student financial support. The egalitarian nature of these measures was a portent of the democratization that would become significant in Canadian higher education. Although the University of Alberta established a Department

3

Jasper Avenue in the 1930s (photo courtesy Provincial Archives)

of Extension in 1912 "to provide a direct link between the University and the people of Alberta,"[22] decentralized[23] post-secondary education comprised primarily agricultural and pedagogical programs until the 1940s.[24]

The *School Act* of 1931 provided for the establishment of public junior colleges by interested school boards, but only if the Board of Governors of the University of Alberta consented to their establishment and affiliation.[25] The *School Act*, 1952 (Chapter 80) made legal provision, within the public school system, for the establishment of colleges in Alberta, affiliated with the University of Alberta and offering comprehensive programs beyond the high school level. Under this legislation, local school authorities could initiate action for the establishment of a college.[26] It was not until the 1950s, however, that conditions would develop that were conducive to the development of the community college as we know it today.[27] Prior to this time, private colleges,[28] focusing on secondary education and theological training, formed the basis for college-level education in Alberta.[29]

By the late 1950s the post-war baby boom had forced the government to reevaluate its post-secondary policies.[30] This explosion in the number of new students led to the eventual development of three new universities by 1970[31] and an unprecedented demand for post-secondary educational alternatives to university. An increase in retention rates, increased federal funding for technical education,[32] rapid urbanization, and the recognized relationship between workforce training and economic growth were all forces that exerted pressure to establish a more extensive post-secondary educational system in Alberta in the 1960s.[33]

The Lethbridge Community College story marks the beginning of the community college movement in Alberta. Its development was largely responsible for the intense interest in the establishment of community colleges in other provincial jurisdictions. Mount Royal College in Calgary, it should be noted, was established as a Methodist college in 1910 and as early as 1931 offered university courses in affiliation with the University of Alberta.[34] Mount Royal, however, remained a private college until 1966. This gives Lethbridge Community College,[35] established in 1957, the distinction of being the first public community college in Alberta and, arguably, the first in Canada.[36] By 1970, when the minister of education announced that a new community college would be located in Edmonton, colleges were already established at Medicine Hat, Red Deer, and Grande Prairie.

A serious move to establish a community college in Lethbridge was initiated in 1951 when the Lethbridge School District commissioned an American consultant, Dr. S. V. Martorana, to conduct a feasibility study.[37] This study, called *A Community College Plan for Lethbridge*, received considerable attention. As Berghofer and Vladicka point out, "local initiatives, rather than the influence of government policy, played the major role in the establishment of Alberta's first public junior college."[38] In 1955, the Board of the Lethbridge School District No. 51 approached the Board of Governors of the University of Alberta and the minister of education for approval to establish a college in Lethbridge.[39] By 1957 the movement had gained enough support that the provincial legislature passed an act to establish Lethbridge Junior College. In 1958 the *Public Junior Colleges Act* incorporated the Lethbridge events and endorsed the system of university affiliation. The *Cameron Commission Report* of 1959 recommended decentralization of non-university education throughout the province, coordination of services, and regional administration for community colleges. No action, however, was taken on the Cameron recommendations.[40]

While legislation had existed since 1931 that allowed school districts to maintain a junior college, it was the passage of the *Public Junior Colleges Act* in 1958 that heralded the development of Alberta's college system. Under the act, a college could be established by one or more school boards, with the consent of the minister of education and with affiliation approval by the University of Alberta.[41] A college created under this legislation was operated by a board consisting of trustees representing sponsoring school authorities. Colleges could offer first-year level university courses, general vocational courses not already provided in the high school curriculum, day and evening courses of an academic, vocational, or practical nature, and short courses to meet the needs of special interest groups.[42]

The 1959 Royal Commission on Education and the 1961 Survey Committee on Higher Education provided recommendations for community colleges. In 1959, the *Report of the Royal Commission on Education in Alberta*[43] indicated that if the community college were to develop as an integral part of the Alberta educational system, "it must be conceived as an outgrowth or evolution from existing institutions rather than as a radical departure from them."[44]

In 1961, the University of Alberta and provincial government officials formed the Survey Committee on Higher Education in Alberta. This joint committee prepared interim reports in 1961, 1963, 1965, and 1966 that studied the developments occurring in higher education in Alberta. These reports maintained that academic programs should come under the jurisdiction of the universities, but did concede that the pressure on the university to make higher education more accessible should be addressed.[45] The reports for 1961 to 1966 defined three functions for junior colleges:[46]

1. To take pressure off the university in the freshman and perhaps the sophomore year;

2. To provide terminal programs for students not wishing or not qualified to attend university;

3. To provide facilities for much of a community's adult education program.

The 1963 report changed the first function to read: "To increase availability of higher education to people in Alberta and therefore increase the number enroled in post-high-school institutions."[47] The committee also called for an expansion of the junior college system.[48]

Additional recommendations were contained in a study on junior colleges conducted by former University of Alberta president (1950-1959) Andrew Stewart in 1965.[49] In large part, the Royal Commission's recommendations went unheeded. The Stewart study, however, received considerable attention.[50] Stewart proposed dividing the province into college districts distinct from school districts. The proposed system would comprise distinct levels. Primary and secondary school education would be organized and operated locally, with post-secondary education at the college level organized on a college district basis. The Stewart Report separated the school boards from the college district boards. Stewart recommended developing comprehensive community colleges and expanding their role as a valid alternative to university. The junior college, in his view, ought to be a comprehensive institution providing university transfer programs and programs suited to the particular abilities, aptitudes, and interests of different groups of individuals.[51] In addition, college boards would be encouraged to seek funding from additional sources to supplement the provincial funding they would receive. The Stewart Report rejected the Ontario model of colleges of applied arts and technology, suggesting that such an approach would only encourage expensive satellite university campuses throughout the province without addressing the need for college facilities for non-university programs.

In response to the Stewart report, a fact-finding committee was formed to survey post-secondary and continuing education in the province and assess the educational services provided by existing institutions. The committee's report supported the establishment of colleges, regional college boards, "open-door" admissions, and comprehensive programs including university transfer, vocational, general, and adult education courses; in addition, teacher certification was not recommended as a requirement for teaching personnel.[52] As the Stewart investigation was being prepared, draft legislation entitled *The Post-Secondary Education Regions Act* was proposed that organized post-secondary education on a regional basis, with regional boards responsible for a wide variety of post-secondary and continuing educational programs.[53]

Conferences held in 1966 in Banff and Edmonton[54] drew considerable attention to the community college concept. The Banff conference supported the idea of comprehensive, autonomous community colleges with a wide range of academic, vocational, and general programs.[55] At the Edmonton conference, 150 delegates representing provincial organizations directly concerned with education reviewed the *Report of the Fact Finding Committee on Post-Secondary and Continuing Education in Alberta*[56] and the initial draft of *The Post-Secondary Education Regions Act*. The overall conclusion was a strong recommendation to establish some order for junior colleges. T. C. Byrne, co-chair of the Edmonton conference and deputy minister of education at that time, offered an insightful commentary on the state of the community college in 1966:

> "...at the beginning of the decade many people saw it [the community college] as a university campus apart from the university, but throughout the...middle sixties particularly, the idea of the college serving the community more directly, being much more comprehensive in its program,...being more accepting in terms of entrance requirements...this was voiced by more people.... On the other hand, there were very strong traditions of university attachment with the colleges themselves. So these two views were...quite often contradictory in terms of setting objectives for the colleges."[57]

The Edmonton conference suggested that university approval should not be required for a new college and entrance requirements should be lower than for university. The conference recommended that colleges should have a comprehensive curriculum. The conference was responsible for bringing attention to a number of possible directions for post-secondary education in Alberta. The insights and suggestions brought about through the conference did not go unheeded, and resulted in amendments to the *Public Junior Colleges Act*.

The *Public Junior Colleges Act* was amended in 1967 to establish the Provincial Board of Post-Secondary Education.[58] The purpose of this board was threefold: first, to study provincial needs in the field of post-secondary education and make recommendations to the minister; second, to advise the minister on administrative and financial matters; and third, to coordinate the work of the junior colleges.[59] Chaired by Dr. Gordon Mowat, the board examined post-secondary education in Alberta and concluded that it should have two parts: a university system and a college system.[60] With provisions for the university system already in place, "the Board restricted its deliberations to institutions which, collectively, might comprise a college system."[61] As a result of the board's proposals, in 1968 the government rejected local boards of control for all post-secondary institutions, and a single commission for universities and colleges. Resulting legislation—*The Colleges Act*—was passed in 1969.

The *Colleges Act* of 1969 was markedly different from the *Public Junior Colleges Act* of 1958, passed one year after the establishment of Lethbridge Junior College. The 1958 act had legitimized what was already an accomplished fact in Lethbridge.[62] In 1958, colleges were initiated and managed within the framework of the public school system. The finances and curriculum were primarily locally controlled and there was little interaction or coordination between agricultural colleges, institutes of technology, and junior colleges. The university controlled their academic programs through prerequisite affiliation and instructors were regulated depending on their teaching area. There was no provision for academic councils, and local tax support was small and provided through payments by school boards.

When Grant MacEwan Community College was about to be launched in 1969, the college system was distinct from that of the public schools and university. The Alberta Colleges Commission,[63] which evolved from the Provincial Board, had been established by the *Colleges Act* in 1969 with broad regulatory powers independent of the public school and university systems. Local control of colleges was delegated to boards of governors, while the planning, coordination, and control of the system as a whole resided with the commission. The commission enabled the integration of institutes of technology, agricultural schools, and junior colleges under one system. The provincial government now appointed local boards of governors, including faculty and student representatives, and the college president. Although still possible, university affiliation, approval of appointments, examinations, and so on, were no longer required. All faculty were to be included in a single bargaining unit and the provisions of the *Teaching Profession Act* no longer applied.

The most notable contrasts between the legislation of 1958 and that of 1969 lay in the requirements for colleges to form academic councils and the removal of property taxation as a source of local college support. R. C. Clark, then minister of education, strongly supported commission members in their pursuit of the Stewart study's recommendations for a "new kind" of post-secondary institution.[64] Clark stressed the need for colleges to "re-order their priorities, placing terminal, salvage, and community service programs before transfer programs—in keeping with the community college concept."[65]

Briefly, the legislative developments leading to the creation of community colleges in Alberta began with the 1957 order-in-council to establish Lethbridge Community College.[66] The 1958 *Public Junior Colleges Act*, public interest groups, the 1959 Royal Commission, and the "Special Enquiry" conducted by Andrew Stewart, culminating in the *Colleges Act* of 1969, established the context in which Grant MacEwan Community College would develop. Public colleges, with enrolment more than doubling between 1967 and 1971, were the "fastest-growing sector of post-secondary education"[67] and it was only a matter of time until Edmonton developed a college of its own.

The 1960s were truly the "golden age" for public education in Canada. The timing was ideal for the development of community colleges: with public demand and government financial capability coinciding in such dramatic fashion,[68] few people opposed their establishment.

> The movement toward the development of a college system was accelerated by amendments to existing legislation. These had the usual wide consultation and debate prior to enactment. The amendments tended to up-date the legislation while holding in reserve proposals to create a structure for the overall system. The construction of a temporary system—the Board of Post-Secondary Education—was a useful device to bypass certain kinds of official procedures and resistance to change. The board, with its direct access to both the public and the cabinet, helped to generate agreements and establish regulations more rapidly than the processes of government would normally allow. The interaction between the formal interest groups was so effective that when the legislation creating a provincial college system eventually arrived on the floor of the house in 1969, it was approved with little debate.[69]

When Grant MacEwan Community College became a reality in 1970, it was acknowledged that the Alberta college system was in need of coordination. Although many of the steps toward this end had been put into place by this time, the Alberta provincial college system was, ultimately, a product more of evolution than design.[70]

---

[1] John D. Dennison and John S. Levin, *Canada's Community Colleges in the Nineteen Eighties: Responsiveness and Renewal* (Toronto: Association of Canadian Community Colleges, 1989), pp. 4-7, provide an excellent commentary on the influences of federal, provincial, and local factors on the community college.

[2] Gordon Campbell, "History of the Alberta Community College System: 1957–1969" (Ph.D. diss., University of Calgary, 1972), p. 34.

[3] In their definitive work, *Canada's Community Colleges* (Vancouver: University of British Columbia Press, 1986), John D. Dennison and Paul Gallagher distinguish between the terms post-secondary and higher education. According to Dennison and Gallagher, the term higher education was "traditionally restricted to the work of universities and degree-granting colleges," and the term post-secondary emerged at a later date to encompass "all education after secondary school" (p. 11). For the sake of simplicity, and to avoid confusion, the author of this book uses the terms interchangeably.

[4] Desmond Berghofer and Alan Vladicka, *Access to Opportunity 1905–1980: The Development of Post-Secondary Education in Alberta* (Edmonton, AB: Alberta Advanced Education and Manpower, 1980), p. 7.

[5] Murray G. Ross, *The University: The Anatomy of Academe* (Toronto: McGraw-Hill, 1976), p. 51.

[6] In 1886, William Rainey Harper of the University of Chicago coined the phrase "junior" college. Although Joliet Junior College is most often cited as the first junior college, two-year programs were offered in American schools as early as 1835 (Palinchak, 1973). The universities of Georgia and Michigan prepared plans for two-year colleges as early as the 1850s (Brubacher and Rudy, 1976). Lewis Institute, later the Illinois Institute of Technology, was the first American private two-year college (Ferrier, 1937). Eells (1941) suggests that Lasell Female Seminary, established in 1851, was the first junior college (its name was changed to Lasell Junior College in 1932).

[7] Dennison and Gallagher, *Canada's Community Colleges*, p. 2.

[8] Ibid.

[9] Christopher Lasch, *The Culture of Narcissism* (New York: Warner Books, 1979), p. 221.

[10] Arthur M. Cohen and Florence B. Brawer, *The American Community College* (San Francisco: Jossey-Bass, 1982), p. 2.

[11] Dennison and Gallagher, *Canada's Community Colleges*, p. 2.

[12] Hugh E. Farquhar, "The Role of the College in the System of Higher Education in Alberta" (Ph.D. diss., University of Alberta, 1967), p. 97.

[13] Campbell, "History," p. 34.

[14] John C. Clarke, "Alberta Community Colleges: Ten Years in Review" (M.Ed. thesis, University of Alberta, 1983).

[15] Dennison and Gallagher, *Canada's Community Colleges*, p. 15.

[16] Campbell, "History," p. 20.

[17] *University Act*, 1910.

[18] Berghofer and Vladicka, *Access to Opportunity*, p. 6.

[19] *Report of the Committee of Inquiry into Non-Canadian Influence in Alberta Post-Secondary Education* (Edmonton, AB: Minister of Advanced Education, 1972), pp. 4–5.

[20] Berghofer and Vladicka, *Access to Opportunity*, p. 3.

[21] Ibid., p. 5.

[22] Ibid., p. 3.

[23] The decentralization trend was noted as early as 1910. See Guldbrand Loken, *An Analysis of the Junior College in Alberta: Progress, Programs and Prospect* (Edmonton, AB: University of Alberta Printing Services, 1966).

[24] Berghofer and Vladicka, *Access to Opportunity*, pp. 5–6.

[25] Ibid., p. 12.

[26] The University of Alberta had strict conditions for affiliation. *The University of Alberta Calendar, Forty-Third Session 1950–51* (Edmonton, AB: University of Alberta, 1950), states the following guidelines:

> 1. A minimum staff of six teachers giving the major part of their time to junior college work must be maintained. The members of the staff must be university graduates with special training in their particular fields and have at least one year of post-graduate study.
>
> 2. Junior college work may be associated with the work of the high school, but must be dissociated both in organization and in buildings from the work of the primary grades.
>
> 3. Library and laboratory equipment must be reasonably adequate in the subjects taught in the junior college.
>
> 4. The examinations of the junior college will be the regular university examinations of the first year. The conditions of entrance and of advancement to junior college will be those which obtain in the university.
>
> 5. Except in the case of high schools which may obtain junior college affiliation and receive the regular department grant, junior colleges will be affiliated on a basis of private financial support only.

In fairness to the university, the dilution of university level studies was a serious concern, hence its determination to exercise control. Dennison and Gallagher may be somewhat harsh in their assessment that "the U of A was prestigious, influential, and determined to see the post-secondary universe unfold as it felt it should" (*Canada's Community Colleges*, p. 22).

[27] Among these conditions was the Department of Education's 1954 decision to provide grants to school boards in support of adult continuing education.

[28] These private colleges were: Calgary College, Alberta College, Alberta Industrial Academy, Mount Royal College, Camrose Lutheran College, Concordia College, College Saint-Jean, and Robertson College.

[29] Berghofer and Vladicka, *Access to Opportunity*, p. 6.

[30] The *Report of the Committee of Inquiry into Non-Canadian Influence in Alberta Post-Secondary Education* (Edmonton, AB: Minister of Advanced Education, 1972), p. 4, suggests: "The University of Alberta remained static for a period of twenty years because of the great depression commencing in 1929 and the second world war."

[31] The three new universities were Calgary (1966), Lethbridge (1967), and Athabasca (1970).

[32] The expansion of post-secondary education in Canada was viewed as an important component of economic growth. A series of studies, especially Canada's Economic Council Report of 1964, indicated post-secondary expansion was imperative. (See Dennison and Gallagher, *Canada's Community Colleges*, p. 13.) Dennison and Gallagher also point out that "Federal support was a common boost throughout Canada but the individual responsibility for education resting with the provinces as granted by the British North America Act gave an individuality to the development of the Canadian community and junior college" (*Canada's Community Colleges*, p. 16).

[33] Campbell, "History."

[34] Mount Royal later transferred its affiliation to the University of Calgary.

[35] In 1957 it was known as Lethbridge Junior College.

[36] See Dennison and Gallagher, *Canada's Community Colleges*, Appendix D, for further debate on the first community college in Canada.

[37] A community college for Lethbridge was first suggested in 1949, largely due to the urging of Gilbert Paterson, Q.C., who was then the Chairman of the Board of the Lethbridge Public School District. Paterson visited community colleges in California and became very excited about the prospects of such an institution in Lethbridge. Assistant superintendent L. H. Bussard, on the direction of the Lethbridge School Board, investigated the feasibility of a Lethbridge community college and commissioned Martorana to undertake this study in 1951. James M. Small, *College Coordination in Alberta: System Development and Appraisal*, Research Studies in Post-Secondary Education, no. 18 (Edmonton, AB: Alberta Colleges Commission, 1972), p. 66.

[38] Berghofer and Vladicka, *Access to Opportunity*, p. 19.

[39] Alberta Colleges Commission, *First Annual Report: 1969–70*, p. 11.

[40] Berghofer and Vladicka, *Access to Opportunity*, p. 29.

[41] Alberta Colleges Commission, *First Annual Report: 1969–70*, p. 14.

[42] Ibid.

[43] *Report of the Royal Commission on Education in Alberta* (Edmonton, AB: The Queen's Printer, 1959).

[44] Ibid.

[45] The *University and College Assistance Act* of 1964 legislated annual grants for junior college students enroled in university-level courses.

[46] P. G. Stewart, "Grant MacEwan Community College: The Period Prior to April, 1970," unpublished paper, Grant MacEwan Community College Archives, 1970.

[47] Ibid.

[48] Ibid.

[49] Andrew Stewart, *Special Study on Junior Colleges* (Edmonton, AB: L. S. Wall, The Queen's Printer, 1965).

[50] Although public reaction to the Stewart Report was generally favourable, the University of Alberta expressed reservations.

[51] Stewart, *Special Study.*, p. 2.

[52] *Report of the Fact Finding Committee on Post-Secondary and Continuing Education in Alberta* (Edmonton, AB: Conference on Post-Secondary and Continuing Education, 1966).

[53] Alberta Colleges Commission, *First Annual Report: 1969–70*, p. 14.

[54] J. E. Seger and G. L. Mowat, eds., *The Junior College: Banff Regional Conference of School Administrators, 1966* (Edmonton, AB: Department of Educational Administration, Faculty of Education, University of Alberta, 1966); and the Conference on Post-Secondary and Continuing Education, November 1966, Edmonton, Alberta.

[55] The Banff conference did not formally consider the Stewart proposals; nevertheless, "basic questions similar to those Stewart had been asked to answer were discussed and on the general issue of what guides should govern development of the junior-community college." John C. Long, *An Historical Study of the Establishment of College Systems in Ontario and Alberta in the 1960's*, Research Studies in Post-Secondary Education, no. 20 (Edmonton, AB: Alberta Colleges Commission, 1972).

[56] *Report of the Fact Finding Committee on Post-Secondary and Continuing Education in Alberta* (Edmonton, AB: Conference on Continuing and Post Secondary Education, 1966).

[57] Long, *An Historical Study*, p. 111.

[58] Long suggests that establishment of the Provincial Board of Post-Secondary Education "is one of the strongest indications that the Alberta government looked favourably upon the Stewart proposals of a year previous" (Ibid., p. 117). Long calls the creation of the Provincial Board of Post-Secondary Education, "undoubtedly the most important government initiative in the eventual establishment of a public college system in Alberta" (Ibid., p. 134).

[59] Alberta Colleges Commission, *First Annual Report: 1969–70*, p. 15.

[60] Ibid., p. 16.

[61] Ibid.

[62] Ibid., p. 14.

[63] *Colleges Act*, Chapter 14, Statutes of Alberta, 1969.

[64] P. G. Stewart, "Grant MacEwan Community College," p. 3.

[65] Ibid.

[66] Gordon Campbell's doctoral dissertation (1972) provides an extensive review of the various elements involved in the establishment of Alberta's community college system. In addition, works by Loken (1965), Markle (1965), Farquhar (1967), Kolesar (1968), McIntosh (1971), Small (1972), Long (1972), and Clarke (1983) are useful resources for anyone interested in exploring the development of the community college in Alberta in greater detail.

[67] Berghofer and Vladicka, *Access to Opportunity*, p. 35.

[68] Dennison and Gallagher, *Canada's Community Colleges*, p. 11.

[69] Campbell, "History," pp. 38–39.

[70] James M. Small, *College Coordination in Alberta*, p. 71.

Chapter Two

The Edmonton College

The Edmonton Separate School Board made the first real effort toward establishing a community college in the city of Edmonton[1] by commissioning J. A. Macrae, O.M.I., to examine this issue. Macrae's study, dated January 30, 1965, recommended the establishment of a public junior college under the auspices of the Edmonton Separate School Board. Macrae felt additional opportunities for undergraduate university education in the Edmonton area were needed, and that Roman Catholics could make a valuable contribution to ecumenism and the field of higher education by establishing a public junior college.[2] Macrae argued:

> "It is possible that a junior college could be founded upon a positive Christian intellectual spirit, in keeping with what is best in the long tradition of Hebrew-Christian humanism construed in a broad ecumenical sense, and alive to the needs of contemporary society. Its aim would be to build bridges not walls, to work in close harmony with all other interested groups and agencies for the further development of higher education in this community. Such an institution will provide a unique opportunity for Catholics to meet more fully their responsibilities towards higher education and to work with Christians in a spirit of unity in the pursuit of common educational objectives: 'quaecumque vera.'

> "Such a junior college would be public, not private. It would be open to all qualified matriculants and have the same admissions requirements as the University of Alberta. There would be no formal religious services. The college would be administered by a lay board. It would be staffed by fully qualified academics, some of whom might be priests or religious, not all of whom would be

Catholic. It would have proper instructional, social and recreational facilities, the focal point of which would be the library. It would seek to work in close co-operation with the University of Alberta in all areas of mutual interest. There would be no effort to duplicate facilities unnecessarily or to provide competition with the University; rather, it would supplement and support the University. The aim of the junior college would be to provide some positive assistance in meeting the growing responsibility of the community in offering adequate opportunities for all who wish to pursue higher education by the establishment of an institution dedicated to the ideals of academic excellence."[3]

Macrae believed that a junior college would be attractive to the community as a whole and, under the grant structure for junior colleges, financially realistic.[4] The Edmonton Separate School Board's proposal was refused. The government, acting within the authority of the *Public Junior Colleges Act*, turned down the proposal based on financial considerations.[5]

Harold A. MacNeil, superintendent of Edmonton Catholic Schools from 1961 to 1978, recalled that looking into this matter involved consultation with Walter Johns, then president of the University of Alberta. Johns supported the California model of "colleges within the city."[6] In 1964, Johns described Lethbridge Community College as "the best example of a public junior college in Western Canada, if not in the whole country."[7] Johns recognized the need for local campus facilities and junior colleges: as dean of arts and science for the University of Alberta, he had strongly supported the Lethbridge College movement.[8]

The Edmonton Separate School Board's singular attempt to establish a junior college ended with an amendment to the *School Act*. MacNeil recalled:

The major metropolitan school boards, with the Alberta School Trustees Association, organized a tour of select California colleges in June of 1965. The feasibility study was accepted by the board and a dean for the college was hired. After the School Act was changed in June of 1965, the dean was compensated and the board's involvement stopped.[9]

The idea of a community college for the Edmonton region received tacit support from both the public and separate school boards. The Separate School Board's notion of a community college was not unlike the commonly held public perception of community colleges, as expressed by Dennison and Gallagher:

Public preference was primarily for academic, university-like junior colleges, which would, in the anticipation of many, eventually become degree granting institutions in their own right.[10]

The conventional view of the junior college was counterbalanced by the government's thinking at this time. Dennison and Gallagher report:

The government wanted the new colleges to be primarily educational centres which would concentrate on occupational preparation, while also providing access to educational opportunity to a broader segment of society—in fact, to democratize post-secondary education.[11]

Indeed, the *Report of the Public Expenditure and Revenue Study Committee* in 1966 urged the junior college to offer a "somewhat broader service to its community."[12]

The expansion of post-secondary opportunities throughout the province and the increased demand for access among the general populace made the development of an Edmonton community college an obvious and logical response to expressed needs. In 1968 the Edmonton Public School Board joined the Separate School Board to request the establishment of an Edmonton community college.[13] The joint school board proposal emphasized the fact that the University of Alberta and the Northern Alberta Institute of Technology (NAIT) served only half the students leaving Edmonton schools. It noted that workers in 50 percent of job classifications could benefit from education beyond grade twelve and that existing vocational and training programs required consolidation in one institution for sound growth and development.[14] In short, "the Boards agreed to sponsor whatever steps were necessary to establish a community-service oriented college which would offer a diversified program to meet the needs of Edmontonians and surrounding communities."[15]

The Post-Secondary Board responded to the joint Edmonton Public and Separate School Board proposal and to public interest in an Edmonton community college by requesting in September 1968 that a study be done by a planning committee concerned with "the establishment of an Edmonton college."[16] The Edmonton Planning Committee to the Board of Post-Secondary Education, comprising members from the University, the Northern Alberta Institute of Technology, public and separate school boards, and the Alberta Colleges Commission,[17] completed its study, *The Edmonton College*, in April 1969. The report stated that there was an immediate need for a college in Edmonton to serve the northern part of the province.

The committee recommended that the nature of the Edmonton College should be determined by "those who will actually be administering the College and providing its programs."[18] The college, it was presumed, would complement the work already being done by the Northern Alberta Institute of Technology and the University of Alberta.[19] "The proposed college," the committee urged, should "be developed as an institution in its own right and not as a means of relieving enrolment pressures at existing institutions."[20] It is interesting to note that the report indicated a full-time student enrolment of 10,000 was expected within ten years of the college's inception.[21]

The Edmonton College was a well-prepared and thorough report. Ultimately, this document, as Campbell points out, was the final step required for the approval of a community college for Edmonton:

> It made full use of the experience of earlier colleges, and the assistance made available by the post-secondary board. In a policy statement issued by the Honourable Robert Clark, minister of education, in January 1970, the government announced the establishment of Alberta's sixth college. Subsequently, a board was chosen, a president appointed, and the college opened its doors to its first class of students in September, 1970, as planned.[22]

On May 4, 1970, Minister of Education R. C. Clark recommended to Lieutenant Governor in Council Grant MacEwan, pursuant to section 19, subsection (1), and section 31 of the Colleges Act, that the public college be established with the name "Edmonton College," and that a board of governors be established with the name "The Board of Governors of Edmonton College." *The Colleges Act* (1969)[23] defined the college board as a corporate body with the power to establish the functions to be served by the college; to establish procedures and bylaws required to conduct its business; and to authorize other activities normally pursued by such a corporate body, such as the employment and dismissal of staff members and the appointment of a president.

The New College

In February 1970 the Alberta Colleges Commission announced it would be seeking nominations for members of the Board of Governors for Edmonton College. The board selected by the commission held its first meeting on April 29, 1970. Chaired by Barry Moore,[24] it also included Winnifred Ferguson, Fort Saskatchewan housewife; Robert Guebert, Leduc businessman and school trustee; Fred Kurylo, Edmonton realtor; and Edward Stack, Edmonton barrister and solicitor. The commission also made provisions for the board to include the president of the College and representatives from the faculty and student associations.[25]

The early board meetings were concerned, as might be expected, with defining the duties of the board, relationships with the government, and the selection of a president. As previously mentioned, members of the Board of Governors for the College were treading on new ground. The first priority of board members was to identify their purpose and relationship with the Colleges Commission. The critical path they defined included recognizing the board's responsibilities for locating offices, personnel, and students. The Colleges Commission, on the other hand, addressed admission requirements, tuition fees, and capital development involving the purchase of land and erection of buildings.

The Colleges Commission's chair, Dr. Henry Kolesar, indicated to the board that its philosophy should follow the college system's policies. The College was not to provide courses already being offered adequately by other institutions. Kolesar recommended that the College implement the first phase recommended by *The Edmonton College*. With the appointment of the board, he pointed out, "the College commenced functioning."[26]

The guidelines established for the board's next course of action were clear—appointing a president was a priority, to be followed by hiring the administrative personnel that would make the College functional. One of the board's first actions was to hire a secretary. The Edmonton Planning Committee to the Board of Post-Secondary Education suggested that the administrative officials for the College should initially include the following:

1. Vice-president–instruction, responsible to the president for the instructional program and student affairs.

2. Business manager, responsible to the president for the financial and business management of the college.

3. Director of plant, responsible for site development and physical facilities.

4. Program deans, responsible for the major program areas: academic, vocational, remedial instruction, and continuing education.

5. Director of research and planning, responsible to the president for institutional research and long-range planning.

6. Instructional media coordinator, responsible for the acquisition, maintenance, and control of all instructional materials, and the library.

7. Program development consultant, a staff position responsible to the vice-president–instruction, whose function would be to assist the program deans and faculty in the development of programs and courses.

8. Dean of students, responsible for all non-instructional activities related to students: admissions, guidance and counselling, student government, and student activities.[27]

The original board considered the possibility of university transfer courses, but these were not a primary concern: "...the College would not be, to any large degree, concerned with university transfer credits, nor would it pattern itself after existing institutions in Canada or the United States, but would strive to achieve the filling of educational needs presently not met, stress Canadian studies, community services, et cetera."[28] The major recommendations taken from *The Edmonton College* included the following:

1. We are to offer courses of varying degrees in length. For example, it may be that many of our courses would be of a two-year diploma granting variety.

2. The function of the college should be to provide programs and courses complementary to those offered at the University and NAIT, and other existing organizations.

3. Major program offerings of the college will be in the areas related to career development, particularly in the services sector, remedial educational programs for youth and adults, general post-secondary education, and continuing education.

The concept of the "open door" also received some attention. According to early admissions policies:

1. Students were to be 18 years of age or older.

2. Admissions practices were to be flexible. In some courses people with very little education could be admitted and in some courses background would be needed.

3. A tuition fee would be charged.

4. No student should be prevented from attending due to lack of funds.

The subject of tuition fees generated an interesting debate. The decision to charge fees was not made for cost-recovery purposes but rather, to quote from the board minutes of May 20, 1971, was based on the premise that, "If anything is worth anything it must cost you something—some tuition fee should be charged."

Original space for the board was provided by the Colleges Commission, then housed on the sixth floor of the Devonian Building. These temporary quarters would be used until September 1, 1970, or until alternative space became available. The board decided that a downtown location for the College would be preferable if feasible. Some suggested locations included the old RCMP barracks, the Omniplex, CNR trackage (from 116 Street west to 97 Street east), Clairview, west Jasper Place (from Highway 16, 1 1/4 miles south to 107 Street), Riverbend, southeast Edmonton (in the area of 45 Avenue), and an old Safeway building (95 Street and Jasper Avenue). R. C. Clark was asked to support the RCMP site as the initial location.

Dr. Walter H. Worth informed the board that an estimated two-thirds of the people in rural towns would be moving to the larger centres in approximately ten years.[29] Worth felt the College's decision to participate in urban renewal was a good one and that the College's overall plans were sound.

Securing a president and naming the College were important considerations for the new board. The board wanted the term "community" in the name of the College in order to distinguish the institution from what was commonly referred to as the "junior" college. Two possible names were originally considered: Community College of Edmonton and Edmonton Community College. The board directed its secretary to ask the Names Commission to provide a list of names for consideration.[30] Edward. Stack convinced the board that naming the College after an individual was a meaningful approach. Two names were submitted of people who "held the interests of the community in top priority"—John Michaels[31] and J. W. Grant MacEwan. Dr. MacEwan, then lieutenant governor of Alberta, the author of eighteen books, past mayor of Calgary, educator, and conservationist, was well known for his involvement in and services to community groups. It was agreed on July 15, 1970, "that the Honourable Dr. J. W. Grant MacEwan be selected because of his availability to perhaps lay the cornerstone and otherwise participate in the opening of the College."[32] An Order-in-Council was required to change the name, since "The Edmonton College" was identified in the act. Barry Moore and Edward Stack met with Dr. MacEwan and were received very warmly, although his initial reaction was the comment: "This isn't one of them funny religious groups, is it?"[33]

With his fears assuaged, Dr. MacEwan even expressed an interest in teaching in the College. Dr. MacEwan formally granted permission to use his name in a letter dated July 24, 1970, in which he said:

Lieutenant Governor Dr. J.W. Grant MacEwan & Mrs. MacEwan with guest, 1970

I repeat my very great delight in the proposal which you made on behalf of your Board and I can only repeat that the adoption of my name in connection with the College will bring me lasting joy and satisfaction. You certainly have my permission as well as my blessing.[34]

Commenting informally on the honour of having a community college bear his name, Dr. MacEwan said, "I don't know why they did it and still don't. But I'm not going to ask any questions in case they change their minds."[35] Naming the College in honour of Grant MacEwan would prove to be a source of considerable pride. Dr. MacEwan was an Alberta resource and, for GMCC, his name was and is a treasured distinction.

The board then concentrated its efforts on hiring a president. At its June 10, 1970, meeting, guidelines were set out. The board began by identifying the college as an institution that was not interested in becoming a university. It was described as a new venture, not bound by existing institutions or practices, with an open-door policy. It would fill the gaps in the educational process. The board defined itself as a a policy-making body that would not interfere in administrative details. Construction was to occur late, rather than early, and the College would initially operate out of temporary quarters. The College was interested in courses of varying length that would not compete with those offered by existing institutions, but would be complementary to them. Courses would focus on career development and general education (education for education's sake). It was undecided if this multipurpose institution would comprise several campuses or only one, but it would be flexible and place great importance on counselling, and would not be a residential school.

The president the board sought was to be genuine, outgoing, and flexible; a scholar who would be respected by staff and the community as a whole; someone who was in sympathy with the philosophy of the community college, and had good public relations skills.[36]

Advertisements were placed in western and eastern papers and Canadian and American community college publications. The College was described as "a new venture in non-university post-secondary education, with the possibility of a multi-campus approach." The person wanted for the job needed "…imagination and flexibility and a concern for relating a college to the community. A doctorate preferred."

As the search for a president began, the board entered into considerable discussion regarding the role that the College would play in the community. Reno Bosetti's report, "Community Involvement in Public Colleges,"[37] stressed the importance of community participation. This report urged the College to make an effort to reach unorganized groups, since the "strong and organized are in a position to make their needs known." Henry Kolesar cautioned against getting too involved with the other existing institutions, but suggested that course offerings like business administration (for which NAIT was unable to meet the demand) and nursing technology (not offered elsewhere) could be provided at the outset. The government supported the rapid expansion of colleges.

The board invited Dr. Kristjanson, a member of the Alberta Universities Commission and coordinator of the Task Force on Post-Secondary Education for the Commission on Educational Planning, to address its August 5, 1970, meeting. Kristjanson was asked to provide his assessment of the post-secondary needs of the community that could be served by the College. The board minutes relate that he "described the community college as a 'second chance' or a 'first chance later' institution, serving a broad age spectrum, whose value or success should be measured by what it accomplishes." Kristjanson's observations were a portent of what was in store for the College. He envisioned possibilities that included a college centre with four peripheral locations, an institution that offered general programs of its own, serving real needs but "in addition should have programs like—Freedom and Responsibility—Decision Making—Man, the Meaning Maker, et cetera." Kristjanson pointed out there was a general lack of good counselling and guidance available and that if the College accomplished nothing other than the provision of good guidance and counselling services, thereby indicating the real deficiencies in the post-secondary area, it would have served its purpose. The College could become recognized in the community as a convenient and reliable source of information "to whom the community can turn for advice on their educational needs."[38]

Board members noted with considerable satisfaction that Dr. Kristjanson's observations were in agreement with the original guidelines for the College. The board concurred with Kristjanson's opinion that the College must be flexible and function as an institution whose role is to determine those educational needs not being met for a large segment of the community and to establish programs that would provide opportunities in terms of ideas and access for these people. The consensus was that, initially at least, the new college ought to concentrate its efforts on identifying problems, developing potential, and responding to community needs, rather than focusing on the construction of new buildings.

Dr. Gordon McIntosh of the University of Alberta offered to chronicle the development of the College. He felt that his work might be helpful to others planning to begin a college. The board approved McIntosh's request to be an observer and to study the board's proceedings on the condition that any written material would receive board approval before publication.[39] McIntosh suggested that the College could be patterned after the University's Extension Department and follow the same staff hiring practices, starting with a small core of staff and adding people as the need arose. A board member added that classes for the College need not be restricted to classroom instruction.[40]

Barry Moore and Gordon McIntosh met John Haar, president of Centennial College of Applied Arts and Technology, Scarborough, Ontario, at a meeting in Banff in 1970. Both were very impressed with Haar and his reputation and felt that he should be approached to apply for the College presidency. From an applicant pool of 135,[41] four people were interviewed for the post. Haar was offered the position and formally accepted the board's offer on October 16, 1970. Barry Moore said that Haar "personifies the kind of college we want to build, a college concerned with a wide variety of educational experiences."[42]

The First Decade: A Preview

For Grant MacEwan Community College, the next ten years would be a challenging, exciting, but also nervous decade. A variety of factors contributed to the direction taken by the new college. The community college was largely an untested entity. Few if any educators within the system or elsewhere had had any experience with it. Putting theory into practice that would incorporate the rhetoric concerning open admissions and community responsiveness was easier said than done. Nevertheless, public and government support was highly favourable. This was something new, daring, and for the ultimate betterment of society. If mistakes

24

were made, there were few benchmarks against which to judge them and, certainly, any shortcomings could be attributed to youthful enthusiasm and naïvety. Criticism and comparisons would be difficult to make, for the community college was not a university or institute of technology.

Grant MacEwan Community College was a "community" college in the true sense of the word. The origins and original intent of the College set it apart from its Alberta contemporaries. It differed from the colleges established in the 1960s[43] in one major aspect. While the other colleges followed, essentially, the Lethbridge model, Grant MacEwan Community College, from the outset, did not focus on university parallel programs. Thus it "began life as a full-fledged community college."[44] John Clarke observed:

> The government and governing boards of the other five colleges watched the progress of Grant MacEwan Community College with interest as a result of this. The success of this college by 1971 resulted in the change in orientation of the other five colleges towards rather than away from community orientation.[45]

It is helpful to touch briefly upon the period from 1971 to 1981 from a legislative perspective to understand the context in which Grant MacEwan Community College operated during the early years of its history. As mentioned previously, colleges grew more during this period than at any other time. By 1971, many colleges were requesting permission to add a second year to their university transfer programs.[46] The University of Alberta continued to dominate university transfer issues, although the newly formed universities in Calgary and Lethbridge began to challenge this dominance. Regardless, the University of Alberta continued its resistance to any affiliation with the community colleges except on a transfer basis.[47]

After 1970, the Alberta Colleges Commission was no longer as effective as it had been in coordinating the non-university system.[48] This was partly due to its isolation and irregular contact with related government agencies such as the Universities Commission. In the summer of 1972, the government announced the dissolution of the Alberta Colleges Commission as of March 31, 1973, with its authority and responsibilities assigned to the Department of Advanced Education. The change was motivated by the government's desire to continue to improve "coordination in post-secondary education by eliminating intermediary authorities including both the Colleges and Universities Commissions."[49] During the Colleges Commission's existence, full-time equivalent enrolments in day programs for the college system had grown from 3,200 to 6,600. Participation in continuing education and community service programs increased from approximately 2,000 to more than 10,000 during the same period.[50]

Little long-range planning occurred between 1971 and 1981. *A Future of Choices: A Choice of Futures*, also called the Worth Report, and *System Integration—Coordination—Growth, The Alberta System of Post-Secondary Non-University Education: Master Plan Number One* are the only substantial documents pertaining to this area. The Worth Report was the most influential document of the period. It made a solid attempt to apply institutional research models to education and emphasized the importance of planning:

> ...educational planning must take lifelong learning as a basic assumption. Through the process of recurrent education, learning must become a chosen way of life and not merely occupy a specific period of a lifetime.[51]

The Worth report received some criticism. The minister of education called it "a mishmash of catch phrases and piecemeal conglomeration of educational management ideas."[52] However, it did help colleges to focus on the community:

> In the case of the community it means providing leadership services in the solution of special regional problems, and in the anticipation and direction of future events. Through such interaction with a much wider constituency each college also establishes its own special identity of mission.[53]

Grant MacEwan Community College was one of the first public community colleges to incorporate the philosophy of the Worth Report. What has been called an "experimental situation"[54] developed into a pattern other colleges would follow in their attempts to incorporate responsiveness to community needs into their basic philosophies.

Prior to 1971, issues and trends such as population growth and institutional change had not been discussed in what could be called an organized way. *Master Plan Number One*[55] called for the government and colleges to look closely at system integration and coordination, including institutional roles, service parameters, program development and instruction, allocation of funds, operating expenses, and other planning issues. The importance of long-term planning was eventually recognized in 1978–1979 when, almost simultaneously, the six public colleges created five- to ten-year master plans.

From 1971 to 1981, college administrative procedures changed from a traditional pyramid structure to a system characterized by flows of communication in many directions.[56] A liberal management group concept was adopted, along with the orientation toward human values and community needs. As Clarke noted, "Colleges began to focus on being student-oriented teaching institutions rather than teaching-re-

Logo Chronology

THE EDMONTON COLLEGE

Used until Grant MacEwan Community College name established, 1970.

Used from 1970 until its replacement in 1980.

One of several variations of the logo used from 1980 until its replacement in 1992.

GMCC

The current Grant MacEwan Community College logo as it appears on the towers on the City Centre Campus.

search institutions."[57] Thus, since 1971, community colleges have committed themselves to being teaching institutions responsive to their communities.

[1] A number of unpublished Grant MacEwan Community College sources, in particular an historical summary by P. G. Stewart, mention a proposal by the Separate School Board as early as 1957. The author's research could not confirm this proposal. Dr. H. MacNeil did not recall ever seeing the alleged 1957 proposal and suggests that the 1965 proposal was the first by the Separate School Board. In his history of Alberta community colleges, Gordon Campbell refers only to the 1965 proposal. For this reason, the present study confines itself solely to the 1965 reference.

[2] Gordon Campbell, "History of the Alberta Community College System: 1957–1969" (Ph.D. diss., University of Alberta, 1970), pp. 220–222.

[3] Ibid.

[4] Ibid.

[5] Harold A. MacNeil, personal interview, March 10, 1993.

[6] Ibid.

[7] Guldbrand Loken, "An Analysis of the Junior College in Alberta" (Ph.D. diss., University of Alberta, 1965), p. 44.

[8] Johns was a strong advocate of the community college. He had earlier suggested establishing a branch of the University of Alberta in Calgary, the affiliation of private institutions such as Mount Royal College with the University, and the establishment of a college under a local authority which the university might or might not recognize. He strongly recommended that the best course of action would be to establish a two-year junior college, primarily academic, under the aegis of the university. Public financial support, he noted, would only be available if the college would offer vocational training in addition to university transfer courses. John D. Dennison and Paul Gallagher, *Canada's Community Colleges* (Vancouver: University of British Columbia Press, 1986), p. 18.

[9] Harold A. MacNeil, personal interview, March 10, 1993.

[10] Dennison and Gallagher, *Canada's Community Colleges*, p. 22.

[11] Ibid.

[12] *Report of the Public Expenditure and Revenue Study Committee* (Edmonton, AB: The Queen's Printer, 1966), p. 55.

[13] P. G. Stewart, "Grant MacEwan Community College: The Period Prior to April, 1970 (unpublished paper, Grant MacEwan Community College Archives, 1970).

[14] Ibid.

[15] Ibid.

[16] Campbell, "History," p. 221.

[17] Committee members included W. D. Neal (chair), University of Alberta; R . G. Fast, Alberta Colleges Commission; R. W. Jones, Superintendent, Edmonton Public School Board, W. A. B. Saunders, President, Northern Alberta Institute of Technology; E. D. Stack, Edmonton Separate School Board; and P. J. Husby, Executive Assistant.

[18] Campbell, "History," p. 221.

[19] Ibid.

[20] Edmonton Planning Committee to the Board of Post-Secondary Education, *The Edmonton College: Report of the Planning Committee to the Board of Post-Secondary Education* (Edmonton, AB: Author, April 1969), p. iv.

[21] The report anticipated the need for a major educational facility on a permanent site. The need for a 200 acre site with a planned space of more than 1,500,000 square feet was foreseen. Ibid., p. v.

[22] Campbell, "History," p. 222.

[23] Alberta Colleges Commission, *First Annual Report*, p. 18.

[24] As a note of interest, Barry Moore was a chaplain at the University of Alberta at the time. In 1971, he enroled in the U of A's Ph.D. program in Educational Administration. One of his classmates was Gerry Kelly, who had worked with Paul Gallagher at Dawson College in Montreal. Ten years later Kelly was to become the second president of Grant MacEwan Community College.

[25] The *Colleges Act* [Part 3–32 (1) (b)] stated: "A College board shall consist of the president of the college and the following members appointed by the Lieutenant Governor in Council, namely: (b) a member of the student body of the college nominated by the students' council."

[26] GMCC Board Meeting Notes, Volume One: 1970–71.

[27] Edmonton Planning Committee to the Board of Post-Secondary Education, *The Edmonton College*, p. 40.

[28] Board Meeting, November 10, 1970.

[29] Board Minutes, September 16, 1970.

[30] Contacting the Names Commission appears to be a curious decision. This body generally deals with the naming of streets and avenues and provides guidance concerning appropriate name usage.

[31] John Michaels was a well-known Edmonton figure at the time and is still fondly remembered by many people. He was a long-time newsboy on the corner of Jasper and 101 Street and the eventual owner of Mike's Newsstand. He is also remembered for initiating the Newsboys' Band and contributing a great deal to minor baseball in the community.

[32] Board Minutes, July 15, 1970.

[33] Grant MacEwan, quoted by Barry Moore at GMCC's 10th Anniversary Convocation, November 13, 1981.

[34] Grant MacEwan, GMCC Archives.

[35] Grant MacEwan, undated quotation, GMCC Archives.

[36] In the College's early history the language used reflected an assumption that the president would be male.

[37] Distributed at the Board Meeting of July 15, 1970.

[38] Board Minutes, August 5, 1970.

[39] Dr. McIntosh was appointed special assistant to the president from July 1, 1971, to June 30, 1972, on a cross-appointment basis between the Department of

Educational Administration at the University of Alberta and GMCC, to assist in instructor training during July 1971 and for ongoing instructor training and development.

[40] Fred Kurylo, Board Minutes, August 5, 1970.

[41] Alberta applications numbered 28.

[42] Barry Moore, quoted in *College Comment: Alberta Colleges Commission Newsletter,* vol. 1, no. 1 (1970), p. 3.

[43]The following community colleges were established in the 1960s: Red Deer (1964), Medicine Hat (1965), and Grande Prairie (1966).

[44] John C. Clarke, "Alberta Community Colleges: Ten Years in Review" (M.Ed. thesis, University of Alberta, 1983), p. 22.

[45] Ibid.

[46] The transfer issue was a major challenge for the college system during the 1971 to 1981 period.

[47]James M. Small, *College Coordination in Alberta: System Development and Appraisal,* Research Studies in Post-Secondary Education, no. 18 (Edmonton, AB: Alberta Colleges Commission, 1972), p. 100.

[48] Ibid.

[49] *College Comment,* vol. 2, no. 3 (1973), p. 1.

[50] Ibid. The author cautions the reader with respect to enrolment statistics. Various counting formulae and methods have been employed over the years and comparative evaluations are difficult, if not misleading. The enrolment figures contained in this document should be viewed cautiously.

[51] Alberta Commission of Educational Planning, *A Future of Choices: A Choice of Futures* (Edmonton: The Queen's Printer, 1972), p. 38.

[52] L. D. Hyndman, November, 1972.

[53] Clarke, "Alberta Community Colleges," p. 55.

[54] Ibid.

[55]*System Integration—Coordination—Growth, The Alberta System of Post-Secondary Non-University Education: Master Plan Number One* (Edmonton, AB: Alberta Colleges Commission, 1972) was developed by a three-member committee chaired by R. A. Bosetti, former high school inspector and executive assistant to the Alberta Colleges Commission. The other members were R. G. Fast, director of instructional services, and Neil Clarke, recording secretary, then a graduate student at the University of Alberta serving an internship with the commission.

[56] Clarke, "Alberta Community Colleges," p. 35.

[57] Ibid.

Chapter Three

The Haar Years

John Haar became the College's first president in April 1971. As the founding president of Centennial College, Haar had community college experience few of his contemporaries could match. At the time of his appointment, Haar was vice-president of the Association of Colleges of Applied Arts and Technology of Ontario and a member of the Senate of York University. He was also a member of the National Commission on Community Colleges and the Canadian Association for Adult Education. The board minutes described Haar as an individual who knew industry, understood students of every description, was able to "pull his weight in political areas," and understood the community college concept.

Born in Vancouver, Haar received his early education in Woodfibre, British Columbia. He served with the RCAF during World War II in Iceland, Britain, and North Africa. He graduated from the University of British Columbia in 1950 with a bachelor of arts degree in history, German, and international affairs. Although he never earned a post-graduate degree, he undertook additional studies at Rice University, Long Beach State College, and the University of British Columbia.

Haar was assistant director of the UBC Department of Extension between 1952 and 1954 and shortly afterward worked in private industry in Edmonton. He was assistant director of the Banff School of Advanced Management from 1957 to 1958, served as director of the UBC Alumni Association from 1958 to 1959, and from 1959 to 1964 was director of International House, student activities, and residences and housing at UBC. He was director of the Centre for Continuing Education at Elliot Lake, Ontario, from 1965 to 1966 and had been president of Centennial College since September 1966.

John L. Haar
GMCC President, 1971-1981

Barry Moore described Haar as "very innovative in designing curriculum and in seeking out means of financing. He is well respected by a wide spectrum of students and, at Centennial College, teaches a course in Canadian politics to stay in touch with the kids."[1] Moore would discover the term "kids" was slightly inappropriate when applied to the student population about to descend upon Grant MacEwan Community College.

With the hiring of a president, GMCC began to implement policies and direction. In anticipation of a September 1971 opening, Haar presented a proposal to the board outlining basic courses for consideration. He strongly recommended a trimester system for "maximum utilization of expensive facilities and staff."[2] This implied a college that would be operational 12 months of the year, from 8:00 a.m. to 10:00 p.m. Haar believed in a community college concept that brought educational opportunity to the community, rather than requiring the community to come to the college. He was convinced, and very capable of convincing others, that the concept of the community college was growing in acceptance and public awareness.

Initial programming for the College was based on calculated risk and what Haar felt would be attractive to the community. Haar proposed instructional divisions and programs for the College at the November 26, 1970, board meeting. Essentially copied from those at Centennial College, these five divisions were technician/technology, applied arts, business, academic, and continuing education.

As proposed, the technician/technology division would include science-based programs such as engineering technician and technologies and allied health programs. The applied arts division would have a humanities base, including community service and applied arts techniques programs. The business division would offer secretarial science, computer, and administrative and business programs.

The academic division comprised academic support courses, student study services, educational services such as a learning resources centre, and self-study programs (special projects). The fifth, and final division, continuing education, incorporated evening and extension classes, teacher training (professional development), worker retraining programs, and community services and developmental projects.

T. C. (Chuck) Day
Vice President, Academic

Staffing was a prime concern. Instructors would be drawn from business, industry, and professional agencies, as well as the secondary and post-secondary educational systems. This meant that particularly strong candidates for an instructional position might not require a degree if they were considered to be authorities in their field. The term instructor was chosen instead of teacher or professor to avoid confusion and comparison to other institutions. Teacher, in Haar's estimation, was an authoritarian term and he saw the expression "education consultant authority" a more apt description for the educator of the future.[3] Instructors were to be hired on a probationary basis for two-year terms, with a cyclical tenure then offered.

Initially, it was felt that enrolment would be approximately 400 to 500 students in 30 course offerings. It was suggested at this time that advisory committees of five to seven people be established comprising members from the community, business, and industry, to assist in the development of the various programs.

Legislation was amended to permit GMCC, and any other new college, to institute its own employment agreement with staff for the first year, following which an agreement between the College Board and the Faculty Association of the College would be binding. Administrative staff were not covered by the legislation.

T. C. (Chuck) Day was completing his doctoral degree in educational administration at the University of Alberta when he started his career at Grant MacEwan Community College. Like that of many other people involved with the College in its early development, Day's employment experience included the secondary school system. He was educated and had taught school in his native Saskatchewan, and had attended Stanford and Oregon State Universities. He was prepared to launch an academic career at Queen's University when the GMCC offer was presented. The challenge of starting something new, youthful con-

Old Scona Campus

fidence, and a desire to stay in the West, began for Chuck Day a career that would span the first twenty years of Grant MacEwan Community College. He would experience the College's growth and development and share in its accomplishments and tribulations.

Day's career at Grant MacEwan Community College was largely concerned with academic and curricular administration. Course content and staffing have always presented a challenge, but never more so than in the initial start-up period. Commenting on the GMCC staff, Day noted, "we went after teachers...the early staff had few Ph.D.s, nor did it need them."[4] The first programs used curriculum "borrowed from other sources, mostly Centennial College," Day noted, "or anywhere else we could get it." Day recalled that when GMCC opened, "very few people in Canada knew anything about community colleges."[5]

Grant MacEwan Community College was now a reality; all that remained before the start of classes in September 1971 was to find suitable classroom space and hire appropriate faculty and staff. In its first year of operation, 16 two-year programs were offered.[6]

The RCMP barracks at 9542-101A Avenue were proposed as the original site for the College. Haar requested Dr. Milton Fenske of the Alberta Colleges Commission to undertake a survey to provide data about potential student enrolments, use of space, and cost of renovations for the RCMP site. The proposal of the RCMP site led to considerable debate. The status of its acquisition depended on its being officially declared surplus property. First choice of purchase was given to federal, provincial, and municipal governments, in that order. Haar contacted the Alberta Colleges Commission to suggest that GMCC place before the minister of advanced education a request that confirmed the College's interest in acquiring this property at the provincial level. Eventually, and after a great deal of board discussion, the acquisition of the RCMP site was dropped when the provincial government informed the College in March 1972 that the location would not become available.

Negotiations for acquiring a number of campus locations occurred simultaneously. Working with the Colleges Commission for the acquisition of campus property involved a series of negotiations and compromises. A central administration building at 400, 10150-100 Street and Strathcona School (10523-84 Avenue) became the first "official" College locations. The latter became known as "Old Scona Campus," since the building, a former school, was commonly referred to as "Old Scona," and was so steeped in tradition and history that to call it anything else would have been awkward. Later, the College purchased the Dominion Store at 8020 -118 Avenue for $400,000. The College required a permit from the city to use this facility, which became known as the Cromdale Campus, for educational purposes. A proposal to purchase the McLeod Building (CIBC) at 100 Street and 101 Avenue was rejected by the owners, who claimed the area was for commercial purposes only. It seemed that the "business" of education was still an unaccepted concept.

The College negotiated an arrangement with Allarco Developments Ltd. to acquire 5,145 square feet of vacant space on the west side of the ground floor of the old Workmen's Compensation Building (10048-101A Avenue) to accommodate the department of student affairs. President Haar informed the board that the directors of the divisions were offered the choice of moving their offices to the Cromdale or Old Scona campuses of the College. They elected to remain at the central administration location, but the chairs of the various divisions relocated to the academic facilities. Finally, after a pragmatic and expeditious search for suitable facilities, the College officially opened its doors on September 7, 1971, with facilities that included Old Scona School, space in the Workmen's Compensation Building, the Dominion Store, and central administration offices in the Canada Trust Building, 10150-100 Street.

The search for new facilities would dominate the early, and in some ways entire, history of Grant MacEwan Community College. An institution attuned to the needs of the community required planning and foresight. Soon after the original facilities were announced, discussion began in December 1971 regarding the availability of land for possible construction of facilities in the then proposed developments of Mill

Woods and Terwillegar Heights. If GMCC was to become Edmonton's community college, the planning process should ensure that it would eventually have a presence in every area of the city.

As might be expected, staffing a new college involved the recruitment of staff and intuitive appointments that were often the result of educated guesswork. Haar suggested hiring three people from Centennial College, including Ron Skelton as manager of computer operations and Kay Puil as director of student affairs. The board accepted the recommendations and additional appointments rapidly followed. By May 3, 1971, staff had increased to 51.[7] Staffing was not without difficulty; indeed, in some cases, appointments were terminated. Nevertheless, most initial appointees were capable professionals whose lack of experience and prior affiliation with existing colleges allowed them to develop and nurture a vision for a community college unfettered by preconceived ideas. Student services counsellor Bert Giles, one of the first employees of the College, remembered the "high expectations Haar had for everyone, and the enthusiasm for getting involved with the innovative kinds of things being discussed."[8] This thinking resulted in a college that was flexible and dynamic. Wilbur Collin, an early appointee, commented on the different approach to college education he experienced at GMCC:

> When I first came to GMCC a mere 2 1/2 years ago, I didn't understand the spirit of GMCC. Thankfully, those whom I came into contact with during my orientation to GMCC forgave me for my nearsightedness and narrow-mindedness. Gradually I learned that because a practice, policy, or system was used, tested, tried and true somewhere else, didn't mean it was appropriate, acceptable, etc. at GMCC. I not only support that concept or approach, I relish it; I think it is appropriate and defensible. There is a need for such a college in Alberta.[9]

In the early years, all instructors received one level of pay which, as Chuck Day remembers, "may have hurt, in that it lacked incentives for further training."[10]

Faculty met to form an academic staff association on July 29, 1971. A proposal for the Faculty Association was submitted dated August 10, and a constitution was approved on September 16, 1971. John S. Scharf was named the first president of the Faculty Association.

GMCC and the Alberta Vocational Centre

It was far from clear to the other post-secondary institutions what the establishment of Grant MacEwan Community College would mean. Because both GMCC and the Alberta Vocational Centre (AVC) offered remedial work, the Alberta Colleges Commission requested the GMCC board chair to provide information about the relationship between the two institutions.[11]

The Department of Advanced Education was to undertake a study of advanced education in Alberta. The minister of advanced education toured the AVC in Calgary before deciding on the integration of the colleges and AVCs in both Edmonton and Calgary. In a letter to GMCC dated July 7, 1971, Milton R. Fenske, director of administrative services for the Alberta Colleges Commission, requested the Department of Education, the Alberta Colleges Commission, and the staff involved to begin discussions regarding the transfer of the Alberta Vocational Centre, Edmonton, to Grant MacEwan Community College. A working committee was set up to negotiate the transfer. On November 3, Haar attended a meeting with the deputy minister of advanced education, Dr. Fenske, Dr. Stan Souch, J. P. Mitchell, and L. S. Villett to discuss the rationale of the transfer of the AVC to GMCC. It was recommended that the transfer should occur soon, since the growth potential of GMCC was seen as being good for the AVC students and the physical facilities at AVC could be put to more effective and economical use.

Concerned about the status of their positions and how both staff and program integration would take place, the faculty associations of AVC Calgary and Edmonton made a concerted effort to avoid such a merger. It is not clear from the historical record available what level of influence the AVC faculty associations' concern had with government officials, but on December 31, 1971, Dr. R. E. Rees, deputy minister of advanced education, informed the College "that the AVC building will be used to capacity, at least during the daytime, by the fall of 1972" and that "under the circumstances, I suggest you (GMCC) would be wise to plan on the basis that space will not be available for your use in the AVC building."[12]

Despite efforts to coordinate Edmonton's post-secondary educational offerings, NAIT, AVC, and GMCC worked more in isolation than cooperation.[13] Chuck Day recalled:

GMCC was viewed with some skepticism by NAIT and the U of A in the early years. In particular, AVC was unsure how GMCC would impact its operation. There was an overlap in the remedial area and it made sense that this might be a concern. The resources for GMCC were not sufficient to handle this area and AVC maintained its role in remedial education.[14]

Nursing Adds to GMCC's Credibility

Nursing is an example of the process GMCC had to follow in order to gain approval for new programs. First, a broad curriculum outline was prepared by the Curriculum Committee. This was followed by the preparation of a brief to request approval from the Alberta Colleges Commission. The curriculum was then refined and completed, along with course outlines and content. Also needed were consultations with advisory committees and visits to various agencies in order to identify the clinical experience requirements.

In response to a request from the Edmonton General Hospital to assist in the development of a two-year nursing program, the executive director of the Edmonton General Hospital, Gordon Pickering, and the hospital's director of the school of nursing, Sister C. Leclerc, met with the GMCC representatives. GMCC Board Chair Barry Moore, President Haar, and Applied Science Director Clark R. Tingley had met in the later part of 1970 to discuss the transfer of the Edmonton General Hospital nursing program to the College. A chair for the GMCC nursing program was appointed in September 1971. With the director of the applied science division, the Advisory Committee, and the Ad Hoc Curriculum Committee, the new chair prepared a brief for submission to the Committee on Nursing Education of the Universities Coordinating Council. This submission was presented on October 30, 1971, and final approval for the program was granted by the council on February 2, 1972. The last step was to hire instructors and determine admission procedures. Long-range planning was essential, as it was apparent from the beginning that the program would be required to respond to constantly changing needs and facilities requirements. The Board of Governors approved the change of the name of the Nursing Program to the Nursing Department in August of 1972.

The Nursing Advisory Committee held a total of five meetings between October 1971 and June 1973. These meetings produced the following recommendations:

> Because of the uncertain future of hospital-based nursing programs, there may be a tendency for the better qualified teachers to move to other jurisdictions outside the province. It was recommended that the College should consider itself under an obligation to take on qualified staff from a hospital-based program if the hospital-based program was being phased out and the College program was expanding.

> If the Department of Health and Social Development should require the present hospital-based nursing programs to phase out, the Board of Governors of Grant MacEwan Community College

should state that it is prepared to supply all nurses required in the Edmonton area.[15]

Other early programs notwithstanding (such as the social care worker program at NAIT that was transferred to GMCC), the nursing program was a great advantage to the young college. It drew a high level of immediate respect from the community and contributed a great deal to the image of GMCC.

The College Goes Public

The 1971 preliminary announcement for Grant MacEwan Community College contained the following message from President Haar:

> A need was felt in the community for a broader educational base, easier re-entry into the educational system, and a new kind of educational thinking combining general education and sub-professional skills. The programs which have been established were designed to meet the challenge of change in the "70s", and will reflect such areas of change as occupational outlook, environment, urban and rural patterns of living, together with the realization that education is a "life long" process.

Haar believed that the vocational and general educational needs of the community were reflected in the programs themselves:

> The City is our campus, and all students will be participating in projects utilizing resources in the community. It is hoped that by this practical involvement with community life we will serve the needs of the individual, the community of Edmonton, and the province.

The College operated on a system that made it possible for students to gain admission at three times during the year. Admission was granted on the basis of an Alberta Grade 12 high school diploma or through an "open door" policy that permitted students 18 years of age or over with some experience in the workforce to continue their education as "mature" students. Tuition and fees for students were $100 per semester for each program.[16]

By June 7, 1971, over 800 inquiries had been received by the admissions office, 87 applications from prospective students had been received, and one student had been fully enroled. By July 14, approximately 240 students were either fully enroled or in the process of enroling and the child care worker, psychotechnician, and social care worker programs had reached their enrolment quotas.

Figures, of course, can be deceptive, and different methods of funding have often produced figures that defy comparison. "Block funding," Chuck Day admonished, "was used in the early years and we never really knew how many students we had, as our registration system was far from what it would eventually become."[17]

Early promotional material called Grant MacEwan Community College "a new kind of college for a new kind of world":

> Have you heard about Edmonton's Grant MacEwan Community College? Do you know why it is being called "a new kind of college for a new kind of world"? Do you know how it is different from other colleges, institutes of technology and the university?
>
> Have you heard that as Alberta's newest College it began classes in September in two locations.... Were you aware that it has 21 day class programs.... Have you heard that the College is now offering these Programs....[18]

A January 1971 issue of the *Edmonton Journal* reported that Grant MacEwan College filled a new need. GMCC was called "a post-secondary institution that has no central monolithic headquarters, operates in a former high school on the south side and a converted supermarket on the north side." The *Edmonton Journal* noted the College's future plans included "in-depth involvement with the community in an assessment of its as yet unmet and undefined needs in an attempt to fulfil the true 'community' dimension of the College." John Haar's message to the College's first students in the 1971 *Student Handbook*, the College's first publication, establishes "responding to change" as a lasting focus for the College:

> Education is undergoing constant change: taking on new directions. It must meet the needs of people who face a world of changing technology, values and self-interests.
>
> Grant MacEwan Community College was founded to try to meet the needs of life-long education; in order to enable students to re-enter the educational process at various stages of their own development and that of society....
>
> We trust that you will develop flexibility of thinking, skills with which to master your environment, and competence to deal with the ever-changing pattern of living.[19]

At the October 5, 1971, special meeting of the Board of Governors, a date of February 14, 1972, was tentatively set for the official opening of the College. The board agreed that the Jubilee Auditorium would be an appropriate setting for the official opening ceremonies. Special

Cromdale Campus, formerly a supermarket

invited guests included Lieutenant Governor Grant MacEwan, the rector and dean of College Saint-Jean, the mayors of Edmonton and surrounding towns such as Fort Saskatchewan, Leduc, St. Albert, Stony Plain, and Spruce Grove, original members of the Edmonton College Committee, Deputy Minister of Advanced Education R. E. Rees, and the presidents of the University of Alberta and Athabasca University.

At the official opening, the board entertained the lieutenant governor at a dinner at the Edmonton Inn. Other guests included the minister of advanced education, the former minister of education, the chair of the Student Council, and the president of the Faculty Association. A platform party was assembled at the Cromdale Campus. The parade marshall was personnel officer Art Parker, and a piper escorted the procession. The procession was led by the chair of the Student Council, who was followed, according to protocol, by the academic staff, senior officers, and the platform party with the lieutenant governor and president entering last. Opening ceremonies were chaired by Barry Moore. President Haar closed the ceremonies by inviting everyone to a reception and the procession left the auditorium, led by the president and lieutenant governor. A twenty-piece orchestra entertained the guests at the reception.

A great deal of thought was involved in determining the first programs to be offered by the College. Obviously, trial and error were necessary to introduce new areas of study and refine program content. Six new programs were introduced in 1972: law clerk, industrial entrepreneurship, medical unit management, personnel administration,

41

agribusiness administration, and real estate. Programs were modified and their names changed: the child care worker program became early childhood education; the psychotechnician program became the behavioural sciences technician program. The College was also granted permission to submit proposals to the Alberta Colleges Commission for diploma programs in the following areas:

- Performing arts

- Design arts with majors in graphics, interior design, industrial design, and art in advertising

- Youth development

- Leisure time management, with majors in recreation, travel and tourism, and horsemanship

- A visual major in the communication arts field

It was apparent from the start that the College occupied a very distinct post-secondary niche. The occupational potential for what Chuck Day called the "soft and social sciences" was largely untapped.[20] The challenge that faced the College, however, was to gain credibility by attracting students to its programs and having its graduates secure program-related employment. Although the College faced an uphill battle to gain acceptance from the local post-secondary community, the public's acceptance was almost immediate. The fiat given to the farmer in the movie *Field of Dreams*— "If you build it, they will come"— most certainly applied to Grant MacEwan Community College.

The Early Budgeting Process

In October 1971, when the Alberta Colleges Commission requested an annual report from each college, a financial statement qualified as an acceptable annual report.[21] The requirement for fiscal responsibility has always existed; however, reporting methods were far from the complex systems in use today. The first College budgets were experimental efforts, since there was no previous budgetary information available for consultation. For John Haar, building the College, not the budget, was the principal concern. According to Chuck Day:

> He was not interested in the budgeting process, nor did he have a particular skill in that area. In the early years, nevertheless, in order to keep "tabs" on everything, he signed every cheque![22]

A perceived lack of budgetary acumen should not imply a laissez-faire attitude. Haar was, in fact, not unlike many of his contemporaries. In Haar's words:

You have to realize most educators grew up in the generation of educational affluence. There was an aura of mystery around post-secondary education and the public would blindly hand over the money these institutions asked for.[23]

Haar certainly recognized public accountability as a justifiable and growing concern. GMCC went on record in November 1971 as supporting the development of a uniform system of accounting to be used by all colleges under the jurisdiction of the Alberta Colleges Commission. However, the major administrative effort was focused on getting the College operational. In short, College development was given a higher priority than budget planning in the early years.

Funding issues in the College's embryonic days provide a useful lesson on the expectations administrators held concerning the financing of programs. A brief was submitted by the College in September 1972 to the provincial government's task force on manpower training and re-training which illustrates these expectations. The College believed the federal *Adult and Occupational Training Act* and the provincial *Apprenticeship Act* were out of date because of their emphasis on technological rather than social or human vocations.[24] The College's position regarding this issue was so strong that the local media provided extensive radio coverage for two days, particularly on CJCA and CHED, and Edmonton CBC television coverage even included a taped interview from the College board room.[25]

The College brief indicated that the aim of manpower programs should be to meet the educational and training needs of adults, "not as a welfare program to reduce unemployment statistics."[26] The brief urged that colleges should receive the same provincial grants as school boards for general education, specialty, cultural, social, and recreational adult and continuing education courses. "Government manpower and retraining legislation should not include only narrow drill and training programs, but encourage creativity and understanding of the broader societal issues."[27]

The College's brief was a clear statement about the status of its programs and the belief that the social sciences could be a viable career area. The College felt that continuing education was particularly beleaguered due to existing government funding structures. This was a serious concern for an institution that placed a great deal of its early emphasis on these programs. The College recognized a growing attitude that "continuing education programs should pay their own way," an attitude that, according to the brief, "caused adult career, cultural, and leisure oriented programs to suffer."[28] Few could have suspected that cost-recovery programming would become an increasingly important reality for the College.

43

The Basic Philosophy of GMCC

In November 1971, the Board of Governors approved the following basic philosophy of Grant MacEwan Community College:

> The basic philosophy of Grant MacEwan Community College is to create an atmosphere in which the individual student can develop his total personality: intellectual, physical and social. This is achieved by establishing the greatest possible interplay, both formal and informal, between faculty, students, administration and the community.
>
> The College curriculum should be designed to allow the student to either generalize or specialize, to the extent he or she wishes, subject to the requirements of the particular program selected by the student. Furthermore, the College will strive to render educational services to those areas not served by existing educational institutions.
>
> It is recognized that the basic function of the College is to provide for each of its students a sound academic base of post-secondary level, specialty vocational courses with the further provision of electives to broaden the individual's understanding of self and society. In addition, the student has some freedom of choice in deciding the sequence of courses in her or his programme of studies.
>
> Finally, the curriculum should allow students maximum opportunity to prepare for integration into society, for: work and adaptation to change, re-training and re-education, service to the community, and leisure.
>
> A supplementary role of Grant MacEwan Community College is to contribute to the development of the community through the sharing of its facilities and services; and to address its resources, financial, human and physical, to leadership in assisting to resolve problems of the community in which it finds itself operating.[29]

Efforts were made to see that College policy reflected this philosophy.[30] Initiatives were taken to create a high degree of interaction, both formal and informal, between faculty, administration, students, and the community. Arrangements were made to use community resources such as the libraries of the University of Alberta and NAIT, and to participate in the community through such activities as a speaker's bureau, President's Lecture Series, adult basic education, and program advisory committees. Extensive community service courses and programs were made available and, in order to make the College easily accessible to the people of Edmonton, GMCC adhered to a multi-campus approach to development. The College was designed as a teaching institution. Emphasis was placed on program development and teaching methodologies that reflected this role. Master planning workshops and a staff development program, directed by a committee of the Academic Council and the board, were maintained. Most importantly, the idealistic goals and the novelty of the new college were supplemented by the energy and dedication of its new employees. In essence, the human element was, and remains, the central ingredient for the success of Grant MacEwan Community College.

Academic Issues Surface

Degree granting status, or the evolution of academic programming toward this end, has been debated among community colleges since their inception. The question of granting associate degrees was raised early in 1971. Section 51 of the *Universities Act* specified:

- With the exception of degrees in divinity, no person other than a university may grant or confer any academic degree.

- A likely definition for degree is: a title conferred in recognition of academic work or special distinction.

- A likely definition for academic is: pertaining to a school, college, academy, or the like or to higher learning.

Grant MacEwan Community College was steadfast in its resolve to avoid entering the debate concerning degrees and even skirted the inevitable question of university transfer, to which the other provincial community colleges gave great importance. Gordon Mowat's paper on the issue of transferability—"Statement of Policy Regarding Transferability of Students within the Alberta College System"—was put forward by the Alberta Colleges Commission at this time. However, transferability was not supported by John Haar, who had come to GMCC from the Ontario post-secondary system, which had avoided including university transfer programming in its curriculum.[31]

Early in its history, Grant MacEwan Community College had a unique opportunity to get involved with university transfer programming. In June 1971, President Haar attended a meeting with officials of College Saint-Jean, which was facing particularly hard financial times and small student enrolments, and invited them to address the GMCC board. On January 12, 1972, Father Paul Poirier, acting rector, and Father Frank McMahon, dean of College Saint-Jean, proposed a jointly established and operated organization that would be an integral part of GMCC. Its purpose would be to provide college-level courses and programs for students desirous of pursuing their studies—in whole or in part—in French and to study and/or live in a predominantly French environment. Although this proposal was not acted upon, it acknowledged GMCC's potential for university transfer programming.

The College's Board of Governors concurred with John Haar's ardent opposition to the university transfer function for the College and, for the 1970s, GMCC devoted only nominal attention to this area. Eventually, community responsiveness would require GMCC to enter the debate and by the end of the second decade of its existence, university transfer programming would be a major element in the College's course offerings.

Provincial Guidelines

On December 15, 1971, a resolution was passed at the Annual Meeting of the Alberta Association of Colleges Administration in Calgary that endorsed the commission form of governance for Alberta public and agricultural and vocational colleges, and such non-university post-secondary institutions as might be added to the college system. The Alberta Colleges Commission was charged solely with the governance of colleges such as GMCC.

In 1971 the Alberta Colleges Commission developed an educational master plan for the Alberta college system. *Master Plan Number One*, published the following year, was intended to develop alternative proposals regarding the coordination and planning of non-university post-secondary education in Alberta.[32] The original expectations that the document would serve as a blueprint for the system were not met; nevertheless, it did provide a major impetus for the immediate and long-term development of Grant MacEwan Community College.[33]

The College was generally in agreement with *Master Plan Number One*. Although it required further elaboration concerning the incorporation of other institutions such as Vermilion College into satellite campuses of GMCC, it concurred with the items in the document that gave GMCC a major role in health education, and with the proposal to transfer NAIT's business administration programs to the College. The College also agreed with the proposed incorporation of the Alberta Vocational Centre, Edmonton, into the College. Finally, GMCC reaffirmed its belief in a regional multi-campus structure for the College and the proposals of *Master Plan Number One* that called for a concerted effort in special programs and projects.

Another key document was the 1972 report from the Alberta Commission of Educational Planning, *A Future of Choices: A Choice of Futures*. Commonly referred to as the Worth Report, it offered a number of general proposals for colleges:[34]

46

(In the following section, the numbers in parentheses refer to pages in *A Future of Choices*.)

1. Agricultural and vocational colleges should become fully integrated into the public college sector. (p. 88)

2. Hospital-based schools of nursing should be phased out at the earliest possible date. (p. 88)

3. Allied health programs (e.g., courses for nursing aides, nursing orderlies, dental technicians, etc.) should be offered by colleges or technical institutes. (p. 88)

4. All colleges should continue to offer one-year programs of a vocational nature, academic upgrading, and further education opportunities. (p. 89)

5. University transfer courses must be available in those locations that do not also have universities. (p. 89)

6. The programs of colleges outside of Edmonton and Calgary require broadening to include transfer courses of a technical nature. After one year of technical studies in a college, students should complete their work by taking more sophisticated courses at one or two institutes of technology. (p. 89)

7. The existing policy that prohibits a college located in the same city as a university or technical institute, or in close proximity to another college, from offering duplicate programs warrants continuation for at least the next decade. (p. 89)

Specifically relating to Grant MacEwan Community College, the Worth report recommended the following:[35]

1. Intensification of the college's efforts in the inner-city is essential to ensure improved life-chances for the unemployed, the poor, and Native peoples. (p. 90)

2. Provisions for women to obtain marketable skills through stretched-out, part-time study programs and field placements warrant special attention.[36] (p. 90)

3. The college might also seek to develop a distinctive capability in the preparation of health care personnel, such as nurses, nursing aides, and orderlies. (p. 90)

4. The preparation of learning assistants to aid in the schooling of exceptional children in early and basic education is another possible area of specialization. (p. 90)

Another influential document prepared at this time was Reno A. Bosetti's report, *Advanced Education in the 70's*. The Alberta Colleges Commission's task was to develop a coordinated academic plan for all post-secondary institutions, including continuing education, in consultation with post-secondary education systems. This included determining workforce and social needs. Bosetti believed that education should take a humanistic approach; community colleges should strive for an open-door system which provided individualized instruction and gave credit for non-formalized education.

The work of the Alberta Colleges Commission, and the reports of Walter Worth and Reno Bosetti, provided a framework that gave some direction to the community college.

Enrolment Grows and Programming Expands

By February 9, 1972, there were 506 FTE (full-time equivalent) and 119 priority employment training program students enroled at the College. A total of 625 students were enroled in one or more credit programs and 213 in special interest courses in the continuing education division. As enrolments continued to increase, a proposal was submitted March 6, 1972, to purchase the Assumption College at 107 Avenue and 98 Street, primarily to house the continuing education division. Renovations costing more than $150,000 were made to the former Académie Assomption private school so that the following new regular daytime programs could be added: instructional assistant, urban studies, music diploma, design arts diploma, law clerk, Canadian studies diploma, adolescent development diploma, and horsemanship.

In 1972, an innovative self-study program was designed and developed by philosophy instructor Ted Kemp. The goal of this program was the pursuit of education outside the context of classes, subjects, and disciplines. It involved such diverse areas as basic mathematics, international diplomacy, and existential psychology and philosophy. The program was part of an attempt to provide people who wanted to learn on their own terms with an educational environment in which to do so. Reflecting the open ideals of the program, students paid a fee based on the extent of their use of the College.

Kemp zealously believed in the community college. Having worked for both the University of Alberta and the College, Kemp believed Grant MacEwan Community College:

> ...was not divorced from the community to the extent U of A is; our three campuses are in the community and because of this our theory about what's going on has to be rooted in the inner city. In fact, most of the programs at Grant MacEwan take the student into the community.

...[the community college concept is] a movement towards making society its own school, where education is not abstracted from life.[37]

To his colleagues and students, Kemp was a spirited and compelling personality. He represented the type of unique individual who was attracted to the community college movement, and it is unfortunate that he did not witness the dramatic changes that would befall not only GMCC, but the whole of higher education. A memorial fund established after Kemp's death in 1978 continues to provide bursaries for students in GMCC's arts and science program.

Other developments that occurred in 1972 merit recognition. Discussions were conducted at GMCC concerning the provision of educational opportunities, ranging from basic literacy to college and university courses, at the correctional institutes.[38] A Grant MacEwan Community College Scholarship Trust was approved[39] and a Canada Council Poetry Reading Series consisting of ten readers per year was initiated. It was also at this time that the first constitutions and bylaws were developed and submitted by the Students' Association[40] and the Academic Council.[41]

The Reappointment of Barry Moore

A University of Alberta United Church chaplain for five years and a staunch supporter of the New Democratic Party, Barry Moore had been appointed to chair the first GMCC Board of Governors in 1970, when the Social Credit party was in power. The issues surrounding his reappointment provided the College with its first notable public controversy. At the September 15, 1972, board meeting, Moore announced that James L. Foster, minister of advanced education, had informed him that he would not be reappointed as chair of the board. Moore indicated that he had been recommended for reappointment to Cabinet, but Cabinet did not accept the recommendation. The refusal was not based on performance. Moore expressed his dismay, but was not surprised:

...partly because of some indication of the long delay in the reappointment, partly also because of some indication on the part of the new Conservative Government of wishing to centralize the operations of institutions of higher education, in part by having as chairmen of the boards of such institutions "spokesmen" for the government.... Also, when I saw that in other appointments in the last few weeks (at the University of Alberta and at Lethbridge Community College) strong supporters of the Conservative party were chosen, I began to be less hopeful of my own reappointment.[42]

A letter dated September 5, signed by Rick Mulcaster, chair of the Students' Association and John S. (Jack) Scharf of the Faculty Association, was sent to the government expressing concern and recommending the reappointment of Moore. Five hundred students wrote individual petitions to the minister in support of Moore.[43] Phil Shragg, vice president of the Faculty Association, told the *Edmonton Journal* that Moore was passed over "because he's not of the right political persuasion." Continued Shragg, "I would base this view on the appointments made to other colleges and to the universities."[44] Former Social Credit education minister Robert Clark called for the resignation of the minister of advanced education over the issue.[45] Clark went so far as to declare he was convinced that the government should reconsider the whole concept of an advanced education department.[46]

Foster rejected allegations that political affiliation affected such appointments, saying, "I don't really care if they are card-carrying PCs, in most cases, I don't know their politics...the system would be in serious trouble if we checked political affiliation first."[47]

The support for Moore's reappointment solidified students and faculty and resulted in an emotional meeting at the College's Assumption Campus on September 27, 1972. Most of the early afternoon classes were cancelled when "students debated steps they could take to support Mr. Moore."[48] Foster commented that he appreciated the students' concern and "felt it was his responsibility to reply in person to demonstrate that someone is listening."[49]

On October 3, 1972, at the Assumption Campus, Foster announced the reappointment of Barry Moore to another term, set to expire on June 30, 1975. To the applause of the audience gathered to hear the announcement, Moore thanked the students and faculty for their strong support. Ted Kemp provided an interesting observation concerning the Moore reappointment:

> Well, after thirty years of being out in the cold power-wise, the Conservatives want to get a machine going. They want to place their party people in places of influence in community institutions. Moreover, with the abolition of the College and Universities Commission, the government will have a direct line of access to the educational institution.[50]

In Kemp's estimation, this transformed the post-secondary education system into a branch of the civil service, but this was not necessarily a bad situation, as it could make the government "more immediately responsive to the public."[51]

Moore informed the board on February 14, 1973, that he was looking for a job and that if his search took him outside Edmonton he might have to resign as chair in June of 1973. Moore eventually resigned in September and chaired his last board meeting on September 12, 1973.

Judge Edward D. Stack, who had chaired the Edmonton Separate School Board from 1960 to 1962, became the College's second chair. Stack would have a long association with the College, serving on the first Board of Governors and later on the College Foundation's Board of Directors.

Early Relationships with NAIT

The College's relationship with the Northern Alberta Institute of Technology demanded careful scrutiny in the early years. Alberta Colleges Commission guidelines for program allocation between NAIT and GMCC were proposed in March 1971. The general philosophies of the two institutions were stated to confirm NAIT's primary concern with industry and trade-oriented engineering technologies based on mathematics and the physical sciences, while for GMCC the primary concern would be with the sciences, humanities, service occupations, and business fields. "To avoid unnecessary duplication and re-deployment," the proposed guidelines stated, "it is agreed that for the time being the philosophies would not be implemented in their entirety."

In a letter dated February 27, 1973, to Dr. Henry Kolesar, chair of the Alberta Colleges Commission, Haar expressed concern that the NAIT business administration personnel did not feel particularly bound to honour this agreement. He may have been aware of a letter that the chair of the advisory committee for NAIT's teller training and general business technology department had written to the Alberta Colleges Commission a month earlier:

> It seems to me N.A.I.T. has made a name for itself and its students for which it can be proud. Why then should it give up some of its courses to Grant MacEwan College who has not established a name for itself. Moreover the expense and cost of establishing new facilities when N.A.I.T. already has them available seem to be redundant and unnecessary. "To do so would cost the tax payers more money." ... I agree that courses should not be duplicated. Then let Grant MacEwan offer new courses that may be required.[52]

The relationship between GMCC and NAIT has remained cordial over the years, but there can be no mistaking the level of competitiveness that has persisted in the program areas involving business administration, secretarial skills, and accounting.[53]

Reorganization and Refinement

At the February 14, 1973, board meeting, Haar proposed the reorganization of senior officials at GMCC, effective January 1, 1974. The new organization established a dean of academic affairs in charge of the three administrative departments. The dean, the director of student affairs, and the head of the information office were then the only positions that reported directly to the president. Haar also proposed a development officer position which would be charged with the coordination and recruitment of funds in addition to government grants.

An inter-campus system was proposed February 6, 1973, to permit greater choice of courses and/or electives in programs without assuming the cost of supplying courses on more than one campus. This, it was felt, would foster an inter-disciplinary climate between programs. Also in 1973, the board approved in principle the establishment of a western base for the Association of Canadian Community Colleges at GMCC,[54] and the College became the only post-secondary academic institution in western Canada to offer a dance program. By 1978 this program would be recognized as an important contributor to the arts community through its nationally known teachers and choreographers.[55]

Advanced Education Reorganizes

On October 16, 1972, Advanced Education had introduced plans for a departmental reorganization. The Alberta Colleges Commission announced on March 27, 1973, that it would be disbanded effective March 31, and its responsibilities transferred to the Department of Advanced Education. Although short-lived, the Alberta Colleges Commission played an extremely important role in the early development and history of Grant MacEwan Community College. The *Colleges Act* had assigned the Alberta Colleges Commission responsibilities in six major areas, and it is useful to review these responsibilities and the effect they had on Grant MacEwan Community College.

The first responsibility of the Alberta Colleges Commission was to act as an intermediary between the college system and others, including government, other institutions of higher learning, and the public.

The second responsibility of the commission was to support and participate in research and planning activities which would rationalize and enhance college operation and development in both qualitative and

Assumption Campus, formerly the Académie Assomption (front view)

quantitative terms. The commission supported more than 25 research projects and in 1972 published *Master Plan Number One*, which addressed the future of college development.

The third responsibility was to promote the college system. There was initially a great feeling for the college system as an entity, despite the unique identities each college in Alberta eventually developed. During the commission's tenure, student enrolment in college programs almost tripled in full-time equivalent (FTE) units, with an even greater proportional increase in the number of people served.

The fourth responsibility was to provide assistance in coordinating program development within colleges. Approximately 50 new programs were introduced in the colleges and program services were extended by the colleges to centres other than those in which they were located.

The fifth responsibility was to recommend and facilitate the establishment of new colleges where a need was defined. GMCC was established in 1970, and since 1971, college services have been provided in all six major population centres of the province.

Finally, the sixth responsibility of the commission was to secure both operating and capital finances from the government to support college operation and development and to distribute such funds among colleges in an equitable way. College operating support more than tripled and changes were made in base funding distribution to better accommodate the unique characteristics of each college. Most observers agreed that the Colleges Commission carried out its responsibilities successfully during its 3¹/₂ years of operation.

A Master Plan for the College

Early in 1972, the board minutes reported that 16 applications were received for the development of a College master plan. The Property-Facilities Committee conducted interviews from a short-list of three in February, and the board approved the firm of John A. MacDonald, Architect, in association with A. M. Ingleson, for the preparation of the first Grant MacEwan Community College master plan.

The initial plan received a mixed reaction. The board expressed concern about over-enthusiastic adherence to short timelines proposed by the architect. This resulted in a resubmission of the plan to the College solicitor.[56] The completed master plan contained a number of interesting points. One important recommendation was for the continuing development of a multi-campus community college. The plan also proposed leasing Assumption College and renovating existing facilities, and phasing out the Old Scona Campus. The recommendation to consider developing a permanent "core" campus was another interesting highlight of the first master plan.

President Haar made a public presentation of the master plan at the Cromdale Campus on September 25, 1973. Approximately 110 people were invited to attend the meeting, including members of the Board of Governors, senior officers, chairs, academic council members, Faculty Association executives, Students' Association executives, members of the original master planning committee, and staff members. Others attending included members of the Department of Advanced Education, MLAs, former Minister of Advanced Education Bob Clark, the mayor of Edmonton, superintendents and chairs of the Edmonton Public and Separate School boards, and representatives of the news media.

The 1973 *Master Plan Report* was prepared by the architects with considerable input from staff, faculty, and board members. The plan recommended the development of a major "core campus" for the heart of Edmonton to provide "special facilities for the total college—serving an inner-ring area along with small satellite campuses that will serve an outer-ring area within the Edmonton region." This concept was dropped from the mid-1970s until the early 1980s, when a new College president revived the idea of a city centre campus and provided the initiative that would bring forward the realization of this objective.

Continuing Growth through the Mid-1970s

In 1973 a fourth campus, Jasper Place, was opened in west Edmonton. With an enrolment of 1,500 students anticipated for the fall trimester, the College leased Central Elementary School at 100 Avenue and 156 Street from the Edmonton Public School Board. The College's multi-

Mill Woods Campus, the College's first purpose-built space

campus approach to "bring education to the community" was not viewed without some concern. Bob Christie, head of the audiovisual technician program, noted:

> One of the big disadvantages is the tremendous duplication of resources.
>
> What we are doing now is wrong; it wastes money. We should have more efficiency in the utilization of our resources and we are paying a hell of a price for being located in four different places.[57]

A northeast Edmonton campus had been proposed since GMCC's inception. It became apparent to College officials in 1975 that the originally proposed site adjacent to the Cromdale Campus would not be appropriate in either economic or physical terms. A northeast campus site remained a request in the five-year capital projections; however, an additional capital budget request was filed regarding site acquisition and planning funds for northeast and Jasper Place campuses. Two proposals were developed during the year, a Northeast Campus Proposal in November and a West Campus Proposal in December. In both cases, user committees spent considerable time addressing program needs and making recommendations regarding much-needed additional space. Unfortunately, facilities development in the early 1970s was characterized by a short-term vision, small building sites, and small amounts of government funding. This was in sharp contrast to other Alberta colleges like Mount Royal, Grande Prairie, and Red Deer, which received substantially larger capital funding support during this period.

In May of 1976, the Mill Woods Campus, the first facility specifically designed for and built by the College, accepted its first students. This facility, on 9.7 acres at 73 Street and 29 Avenue, was built at a cost of $5 million by the firm of John A. MacDonald, one of the authors of the first GMCC master plan. Mill Woods housed 165,000 square feet of classroom space, offices, recreation facilities, a cafeteria, a learning resource centre, and central storage. Over 700 full-time equivalent students were initially enroled in 14 programs.

The lease of the Old Scona Campus from the Edmonton Public School Board was relinquished in 1976.

The 1976–77 academic year did not involve any major building programs. Planning for the future continued, however, and an agreement was made with the Edmonton Public School Board for the transfer of the Jasper Place site and use of the Assumption Campus until 1980.

In 1977–78, capital funding approval was given by the Department of Advanced Education and Manpower for the building of the Jasper Place Campus. This property was obtained in exchange for the Assumption Campus property that was transferred to the Edmonton Public School Board in 1980. Jack Cooper,[58] Assumption Campus Director in 1979, submitted a nostalgic, if somewhat abridged, history of the Assumption Campus to the *Alumni Newsletter*.[59] Cooper's essay, "Assumption Campus—The Days are Numbered," remains an entertaining account of one of the most affectionately remembered College facilities:

> With a five piece brass band playing outside and the newest in hurdy-gurdies inside the tavern clattering out "Alexander's Rag Time Band"—and a host of slushy ballroom ballads, Edmonton's newest hotel opened for business.
>
> It was 1913 and the bright brick and stone accented, four storey structure was an imposing building. Its location, now addressed as 10765-98 Street, was near the small railroad station, just north of the trail that led out of the city towards the penitentiary grounds (near present stadium), and was a compromise between the rival city centres actually on Rice Street (101A Avenue) and those businesses located in the centre planned by the wishful first city fathers on Portage (now Kingsway Avenue).
>
> The longest bar in the west was located on the ground floor at the west end of the building and the main lobby of the hotel was centred on a fancy loop-shaped, tree-lined driveway on the north side.

Assumption Campus – featuring the original Grand Hotel section (right) and the chapel, now library (middle left)

Like so many who guessed wrong in where the real growth of the city would occur, the hotel fell on sad days. A succession of owners in turn came and went. Its name and status changed, too. It became an apartment hotel but never seemed to attract a very genteel clientele. Even a claim to notoriety, in the prohibition era, with a supposed underground connecting tunnel to the two small houses across from it on 97 Street whose ladies sold their favours didn't save it from a succession of bankruptcy sales.

In the 30's, the area had stabilized as a solid residential area for the workers of Edmonton and the visionary band of Catholic Sisters, Les Soeurs de l'Assomption, with the blessing, if not the backing, of the city's Separate School Board, purchased the still usable but faded "Grand Hotel" and set up a school. Over the years they consolidated their land holdings to the north of the original building and demolished the infamous houses of ill repute for the school playground.

In 1958-59 they built a modest two storey school on the 97 Street side of the property. The hotel's ground floor classrooms were converted into the refectory for the nunnery and their special pride, an ample chapel. Priests came regularly from the nearby French-speaking parish of the Immaculate Conception to conduct services.

Over the years, they had from time to time requests from anxious parents who felt their daughters needed a more structured life, or from those who lived so far away from the school that attendance as a day pupil was not possible and, in these special cases, they would board the girls so that it became in fact, little by little, a convent—a residential school.

In 1965, they added a third floor onto the school, the main part being mostly two very large, dormitory style sleeping rooms and the north wing being their library and study hall.

But as it had earlier grown, it now became less and less popular to send their daughters to a residential school. With fewer students and rising costs, the sisters finally in 1972, turned their teaching duties over to the Edmonton Separate School Board and sold the "Assomption Acadamie" to Grant MacEwan Community College.

With a few new walls on the third floor, and an LRC in the former library and study area, we were in business. The chapel became again Caesar's Territory and even, on an occasional Friday, once again a bar.

Leaving behind the glories of our first year at Cromdale and giving the "Applied Arts" (as they were called then) space to grow, the Business and Secretarial Arts departments as well as the Social Workers and other programs of the Community Services Department moved into the anglicized "Assumption Campus." As the early graduates will remember, we used to have to schedule Bob Leong's classes in the first floor classrooms so the blackboards were at an appropriate height. Clearly, many of the dear teaching sisters had favoured blackboards at a more appropriate height for their diminutive students.

As the student numbers grew, we had to move the Management Department to the old Scona Campus the following year. They moved into basement offices in "Tony's Place"—the old St. Anthony's School a block from old Scona proper. The maintenance staff of the day used their own particular native colour sense in a kaleidoscope of eleven—literally eleven— different colours of all the brightest hues. As so frequently happens with a small group who tend to be otherwise somewhat disadvantaged, the gang at Tony's Place became very close-knit and students and staff of the day will doubtless remember many escapades as we were all learning. Christmas parties of the day even featured special chorus lines.

By 1976 with the opening of Mill Woods, the Community Service programs moved south on their way to Calgary. The College Executive Officers moved into Assumption from the Canada Trust Building, following the Registrar who had moved in earlier from the old WCB Building downtown; and in May the Management Department moved back into Assumption from Tony's at Scona.

The former playroom from the neighbourhood day care centre that had been used as a practicum project for the Early Childhood Worker program, was converted to the Student Study Services drop-in centre and the coat racks were once again raised up a few feet. The LRC was moved downstairs to add space and preserve the sanity of the poor librarians who were having to tote boxes of books up and down three flights of stairs. The move also made more classrooms available on the third floor.

Today, the now "old" Assumption Campus has over 600 business students in programs that range from the original secretarial programs majoring in Administration, Accounting, Legal and Medical Secretary and of General Admin and Accounting through Clerk-Typists, Law Clerk, Property Management, Retailing, and Travel Consultants. As well, a varying number of GAS students and those in pre-college studies with Student Study Services swell our ranks. The cafeteria is still a place of meditation—if you can stand the heat (and the blue smoke by 10 a.m.) and the crowds. The LRC never seems to have much room but it is the busiest hive of activity in the place most hours of the day. Most of the old blackboards are gone, or at least raised up several feet. Classes still compete with the noise of the traffic that regularly roars down 97th; and stop dead with great regularity as the large planes roar down the glide path across Assumption to touch down at the mid-city Industrial Airport.

But the site is sold, too small and too restricted by flight paths and parking requirements to last forever. So Business is planning its next move in 1980 into the new JP Campus presently being built in the west end of the city. The instructors will never again find sinks in every office and we'll probably have less worries with the buckets under the leaks that followed every spring melt and summer shower, but we'll miss the old place.

Do you suppose, though, when we move, there'll be a band?

The "old" Jasper Place Campus, circa 1979

By 1978 the College provided educational services on four campuses to over 2,400 full-time equivalent students in credit programs, and over 10,000 students in non-credit and general interest courses. In the same year, the College opened the first equine studies program in western Canada at the Whitemud Stables.

The College was also willing to assist with the space requirements of other community groups and, at the request of the Edmonton Public Library, the board allocated space at the Mill Woods Campus for a public library during this community's early construction.

In September 1980 a new Jasper Place Campus opened, replacing the old Jasper Place and Assumption campuses. Overcrowding at the old Jasper Place Campus had forced 100 design arts students into temporary space at Westmount Junior High School. The new Jasper Place Campus, south of Stony Plain Road on 156 Street, was designed by Bittorf, Holland, Christianson Architects Ltd. as an ultra-modern, high technology structure, laid out as three separate buildings, staggered from one another and connected by skylighted concourses or gallerias. The lowest level provided spaces for laboratories, studios, racquetball courts, and offices for dance, music, theatre, and design arts programs, many of them two-story rooms with natural lighting from either outside walls or the gallerias. Secretarial sciences, business administration, merchandising, travel, and drafting programs were located on the second level. The main entrances were located on the third level, with access to the registrar's office, learning resources centre, gymnasium, and a 350 seat perform-

The "new" Jasper Place Campus, circa 1981

ance theatre. The College's central administration offices and the office of the president occupied the fourth level. Upon completion of the new facility, the campus director, George Naylor, remarked:

> For the first time, we have something that's made for us...now we're able to do something that says: "Hey, this is what your world will be like. You'll be able to do it for real now." There's an ambience here... a place where discipline pressures, pressures of craft and performance can truly be felt.[60]

Opening ceremonies for the new Jasper Place Campus in April of 1981 consisted of a week-long celebration featuring concerts, exhibitions, and displays. The apricot-coloured facility retains a unique modern look that is well-suited to the College's early philosophy and image as a practical and low-profile institution.[61]

Faculty Issues and Concerns

Faculty issues and concerns were not unlike those expressed at other colleges at this time. One of the most notable involved the first two-year faculty contract that expired on June 30, 1974. At a meeting on October 10, faculty members voted 85 to 5 against the contract offer presented by the board. Under this offer, faculty salaries fell below those at Mount Royal College in Calgary, which was considered to have comparable working conditions.[62] After nearly a year of negotiations, an agreement was reached in February 1975 that gave faculty members parity with other college instructors in the province.

In 1975, another serious concern was expressed in a report by the College's Academic Council, which stated that the holdings of the GMCC library were the least adequate of any Alberta college.[63] This report also noted that the supply of counsellors was so low that students' needs could not be adequately met.[64]

At the board meeting on May 13, 1976, after discussions with respect to instructor qualifications, a motion was passed that effective July 1, 1976, all full-time staff would be required to have their qualifications validated. This issue, along with methods of evaluation and issues involving fiscal restraint, would dominate the concerns expressed by faculty during the Haar years.

Changing Political Influence

A number of political influences steered the administrative direction for GMCC during the Haar years. Important political developments included the establishment of Advanced Education and Manpower and the following legislation passed in 1976: the *Manpower, Apprenticeship and Trades Act*; the *Student Finance Board* and *Athabasca University Acts*; and the *Colleges, Universities and Provincially Administered Institutions Act*.

Edward Stack's term of office as board chair concluded June 30, 1975, and he was succeeded by Sally E. Stewart. The minister of advanced education and manpower advised Stewart of the following in June of 1976:

- The universities will follow a slow or no growth pattern.

- The emphasis in post-secondary education will be on career training and retraining.

- Boards should establish their own priorities for growth.

- The minister personally supported lay government for provincially administered institutions and agricultural colleges.

- There will be consultation before changes to policy and legislation.

- Institutional planning should take into consideration population growth.

- A new *Colleges Act* will be introduced in the 1977 spring session.

- Long-term financial planning will be explored.

- A new science research policy will be explored.

Revisions to the *Colleges Act* in the spring of 1977 included changes in the following areas:

- Academic Councils established through negotiation were replaced by statutory councils.

- Statutory procedures were set out to improve communications between the council and the board.

- Public input in college matters was expanded through increasing representation on the board.

- College boards were required to make bylaws.

- College boards were allowed wider options in the banking of funds.

By 1976 the concept of a community college was no longer completely foreign. GMCC now filled a definite, if not prominent, role in the post-secondary arena. As Bob Leong, dean of administrative affairs, pointed out:

> We're still young and experiencing growing pains, but there is a growing acceptance of GMCC. When I first started here, people would ask me what I was doing, but when I told them, they wouldn't know what I was talking about. Now, almost every one has at least heard about the college.[65]

Nevertheless, many diverse opinions regarding the College were held at this time. "GMCC should be more responsive to adult needs," commented Russ Pacey, then department head of community and agency services of the continuing education division.[66] "In some limited areas," the LRC's Peter Brown added, "GMCC is serving the community. But we could probably do more."[67] "People still ask 'What is GMCC?' The public is still completely unaware of us," Bill Pierce, section head of student study skills, noted.[68] These comments are somewhat alarming, when one realizes the overwhelming effort that was made by the early GMCC people to reach out to the community.

Ted Kemp, one of the most vocal and charismatic of the College's first appointees, provided an explanation for GMCC's condition:

> When GMCC was invented as the first, and still the only "real" community college in Alberta, we were expected to grow, naturally. Natural growth for GMCC meant a careful adjustment of our programs to educational "market conditions" in this province.
>
> ....In rapidly changing conditions, this adjustment is extremely difficult, even for long established institutions, let alone for a new kind of college serving a new "market" with new programs. But the growth of our college, even in the relatively unfriendly atmosphere created by the present government which doesn't

seem to understand us, shows that the job has been well done. Maybe not perfectly, but perfection is difficult.[69]

As is obvious from these comments, opinions about the College remained divided. Everything, from the type of program offerings, the classification of instructors, and the cost of maintaining a multi-campus system, was subjected to debate.[70]

On July 1, 1977, Laura Scott Kilgour was named chair of the board of GMCC for a three-year term, replacing Sally Stewart. At 29, she was the youngest chair of the board of a post-secondary institution in Canada. As noted previously, the College was still in the process of defining its role and function. This process also extended to the board and a somewhat difficult appraisal ensued that initiated a serious look at the board's responsibilities.

Upon invitation by the board, in 1977 Dr. Abe Konrad of the University of Alberta circulated a questionnaire on the board's perception of its role. Members' responses were compared with those of key administrative staff, faculty, and students. Konrad analyzed the record of the board's action as contained in the minutes and conducted personal interviews with board members, administrators, and others in an effort to develop a data profile and implications. Based on his analysis of the subjective responses of interviewees, Konrad identified some commendable aspects of the board's endeavours and recommended measures to improve its effectiveness.

At the August 24, 1977, board meeting, members (Haar, Kilgour, Homann, Mulka, Kok, McLeod, and Crockett) expressed concern about Konrad's recommendations. They indicated that Konrad had not conducted follow-up interviews with board members, and they were unable to ascertain whether any students had been included in the evaluation. The board also expressed concern about criticism from the College administrators that appeared in the report. It pointed out that this group had the greatest access to the board, yet none of this criticism had been voiced before the evaluation.

Konrad stressed the importance of being aware of the perceptions held by people in the College, particularly those of senior administrators. He stressed that perceptions are a reality for the people who hold them, and hoped that his report would enable the board to work on areas that might be improved.

Haar referred to the fact that the board had established certain objectives every year and that the report did not assess whether or not they had been accomplished. Laura Kilgour pointed out that the board met at the end of each year to determine if its objectives had been met.

Doug Roche, John Haar, Laura Scott Kilgour, Tommy Banks,
1979 Convocation

Konrad said he wished he had known this, to which Kilgour replied that she thought he was the expert and she did not "dream" this area would be omitted from his evaluation.

Konrad noted that very few college boards had ever attempted a self-evaluation. He apologized to the board for areas in his report where he had been "academic," but emphasized that board members often spend too much time talking around board tables and not enough time talking to students and faculty in order to get a better understanding of what is going on in the institution. It is not clear if the self-evaluation was used for any other purposes, but in October 1980, the Executive Officers of the College reviewed the 1979–80 objectives of the Board of Governors and suggested the following:

1. The board should confine itself to policy-making and not become involved in the administrative process.

2. Ensure a continued, controlled growth pattern to meet the needs expressed by the public.

3. Pursue the acquisition of additional funds.

4. Record capital needs for physical expansion of the College in terms of program growth potential.

5. Provide leadership on the provincial scene to change the basis for funding for the colleges from programs to courses.

6. Explore ways of meeting GMCC space requirements through utilizing or developing facilities jointly with other agencies.

7. Provide additional and special services to meet College needs, e.g., special counselling for Native students.

8. Ask administration to bring forward a defined role for the College within long-range planning objectives and goals vis-á-vis the role of other institutions that are existent, or planned in this area.[71]

Programs

Extended care nursing and the first phase of the theatre program, originally suggested in the performing arts proposal of 1973–74, started in the fall of 1977. Also in 1977, the Federal Department of Indian Affairs and Northern Development sponsored, under contract with GMCC's continuing education division, in-service training for band employees of all Indian reserves in Alberta. Programs under this initiative involved band managers, social services workers, secretaries, general management leadership, and government training programs for leaders of the reserves. Native students also participated, through the continuing education division, in an alcohol and drug education program sponsored by the federal government. A life skills and job readiness program was added to the field of special education.

Two programs initiated in 1977 merit some attention: the writer-in-residence program, which was proposed in March, and the student and staff exchange program designed to promote Canadian unity. Haar proposed the latter program when speaking to the Task Force on Canadian Unity in November.[72] The task force travelled across the country to promote an exchange of ideas about Canadian unity. The fervour surrounding national unity was particularly acute at this time. Speakers included former Newfoundland premier Joey Smallwood, who told a GMCC audience at the Cromdale Campus that "the Maritime provinces would join the U.S. within twenty years" if Quebec separated.[73] Another interesting point is that greetings from Pierre Elliott Trudeau, then prime minister of Canada, appeared in the 1977 student yearbook.

The research assistant program was renamed applied research assistant to better reflect the capabilities of graduates of this program. "Literacy 77" was initiated in the summer of 1977. This program was a pilot project designed to upgrade reading and writing skills. Academic Council, in consultation with the Department of Student Study Services and various programs, examined the role of the primary English course[74] for all students in the College. Academic Council concluded that such a course was needed for all GMCC students and that more sophisticated entrance evaluation testing was required in order to determine the level of study for which students were prepared.

The role of Academic Council changed somewhat in 1977. The council now concentrated on major policy items and the large number of subcommittees formerly under the Academic Council were abolished. Academic Council brought to the board's attention its concern about the role of electives in College programs, the present College testing requirements, and a change in the grading system requested by students. President Haar noted, "some may have had greater expectations of the Council's work, it is my personal feeling that it covered a great deal of ground on some very essential academic questions."[75]

Computer technology began to have greater impact at this time. A modified computerized accounting system based on that in use at the Northern Alberta Institute of Technology was implemented in 1978. In addition, a computerized student record system was being considered.

Students

A student government was elected on October 8, 1971. Composed of two committees, one each from the Cromdale and Old Scona campuses, it was incorporated under the existing provincial legislation as a legal entity. In the years that followed, students would prove to be an important part of the decision-making process.

At its June 12, 1975, meeting, the board approved the griffin[76] as the athletic symbol of GMCC. Athletics and intercollegiate competition would slowly establish themselves at the College; however, the older-than-average student population would delay success in this area for some time. In 1980, GMCC's women's volleyball team defeated the University of Alberta team for the first time. Participation in sports and athletics still was not a priority for most students, as was evident from the absence of a men's basketball team due to a lack of players.

A policy statement developed by the board in October 1975 focused on four goals in the area of athletics and recreation: (1) to motivate students toward physical fitness; (2) to encourage involvement of the entire student population on both an intra- and extramural basis; (3) to first attend to the needs of students; and (4) to use community facilities for community programs where possible and permit use of College facilities by the community when they were not being used for College purposes.

Students produced the College's first yearbook in 1975. It was eventually titled the *Scimitar*, after the short, curved swords depicted on the MacEwan family coat of arms.

In 1977 special programs were designed and implemented for disadvantaged students, including mentally retarded adults and the "hardcore unemployed."

The original director of student services, Kay Puil, resigned her position in 1978 after seven years with the College. Puil was instrumental in developing student government, introducing recreational activities in the College, and establishing the area of counselling services.[77] The office of student services was involved in the formation of an alumni association and the publication of the College's first two alumni newsletters.

In the first five years of operation, GMCC FTE credit student enrolment increased from just over 400 to 2,600 for the 1976–77 academic year. In addition, in 1976–77, over 7,500 individuals took advantage of the College's non-credit offerings. Although high school enrolments were projected to decline in the 1980s, enrolments at GMCC were expected to remain high. The College's enrolment was not considered to depend entirely on high school enrolments, and while the College was committed to controlled growth, actual enrolment was limited by the institution's financial and physical limitations.[78]

The Image of GMCC:
The Hickling and Johnson Report

The public image of GMCC was a major concern for the young college. In its first year of operation, a perceived lack of liaison between GMCC and existing educational institutions was addressed at the November 15, 1971, board meeting.[79] By 1975, the credibility issue for Grant MacEwan Community College was reaching a critical stage. The *Edmonton Journal* noted that although the College seemed to be well-liked in the community it was not always well-respected:[80]

> One segment of the public views GMCC as a haven for bored housewives, or says that it merely offers the university curriculum at a lower level of competence.[81]

At the time, the *Edmonton Journal* reported, 22 percent of the College's graduates found government jobs, with only the medical field getting a larger percentage of graduates "due to the College's highly-regarded nursing program."[82] Although respected, even nursing education at the College did not elicit universal approval. When he discussed government plans to replace hospital nursing schools with community college courses, the director of Misericordia Hospital stated, "We have a good program and it should stand on its own merits."[83]

But the College was serving a distinct purpose in providing a second chance for its students who "came back to learning" and employers were beginning to see the value of a GMCC diploma. As the *Edmonton*

Journal pointed out, the credibility question seemed to be eroding.[84] This was a notable accomplishment for a college embarking on only its fifth year.

In 1978, the Hickling and Johnson management consulting firm was retained by the GMCC Long-Range Planning Committee to undertake a study of the perceptions of the College held by certain "interested" publics. The College was now at a critical stage in its development, and felt its hard-won public credibility and acceptance could easily be lost without a serious effort to address some issues relating to the institution's image. The report prepared by Hickling and Johnson, titled *Public Perceptions of Grant MacEwan Community College*, was completed January 5, 1979. It would usher in a new era for the College.

For three months, Hickling and Johnson conducted discussions with four focus groups representing a cross-section of individuals involved with GMCC: instructors, administrators, people associated with other educational institutions and with agencies in the private and public sectors, and employers of GMCC graduates. Group participants considered questions from two points of view: as representatives of their own organizations and as tax-paying citizens. Hickling and Johnson emphasized that they were looking for perceptions, and that the accuracy of these perceptions was a secondary consideration for the purposes of their discussions.

The generally held perceptions of GMCC that Hickling and Johnson found included the consensus that after its first seven years of existence, the College was actively competing for students with other post-secondary institutions in Alberta, specifically NAIT and the University of Alberta. This perception was the cause of a great deal of concern centred on the issue that Alberta might not need an alternative to NAIT or the university, especially one that did not subscribe to the same standards for admission, performance, and program content. Also disturbing was the perception that GMCC was a "school for the underdog," or an alternative for underprivileged, disadvantaged, or underqualified individuals. Another area of consensus was the view of GMCC as a stepping stone into university or NAIT for those individuals who would not otherwise qualify for admission. The issues of transferability, standards, entrance requirements, and job opportunities appeared to be the nexus of this perception. In short, Hickling and Johnson noted:

> The problem with being all things to all people is that the components lost credibility...many (programs other than Nursing) try to gain the credibility that the Nursing program has evolved. Thus in many respects the Nursing program at Grant MacEwan has *lost* some of its credibility in the eyes of the hiring public. It is this kind of dilemma that the Long-Range Planning Committee is undoubtedly trying to deal with.[85]

Hickling and Johnson noted that the focus group thought it incumbent on the educational institution not to flood the market with graduates if only 5 or 10 percent of those graduates were going to find employment. The participants felt that GMCC was not doing a proper job in advising students about their chances of getting a job once they finished their program.

> GMCC will have to move toward greater transferability of course credit if they are going to be perceived as a viable educational institution in terms of providing an alternative to those students who could enter U of A or NAIT if they so desired....

> The consensus was that one of the reasons for Grant MacEwan's present apparent lack of direction is that the things that Grant MacEwan is doing and saying that they are capable of doing are not in keeping with the things they said that they were going to do when they were originally established.[86]

Other perceptions reported by Hickling and Johnson involved concern over the College's "growth for growth's sake." Growth, however, had not been a significant factor since 1975.

Grant MacEwan Community College required a clearly defined identity. "MacEwan," Hickling and Johnson suggested, "must consider properly communicating just what it is they are purporting to do."[87] It was Hickling and Johnson's contention that graduates of the programs were held in very low esteem by the hiring public. "Grant MacEwan," Hickling and Johnson advised, "should have a proper public relations program which is funded in adequate amounts to tell Grant MacEwan's story and to upgrade its image in the eyes of the general public."[88]

Hickling and Johnson noted that counselling, a "vital component of the educational system," was missing at Grant MacEwan Community College.[89] There was a strong consensus that the College needed to ensure the marketability and transferability of its programs. A unit was recommended for the College that would constantly survey and sample the marketplace for public perceptions,[90] including the performance of College graduates, as well as monitoring current and future needs. Very few people used GMCC's extension services for upper management or executive seminars: "One of the major problems perceived by most respondents was that Grant MacEwan does not offer a clear-cut definition of just what Grant MacEwan does."[91]

All of the respondents to the Hickling and Johnson survey agreed that the multiplicity of campuses was detrimental to the formation of a specific identify, and that a public relations program was required to inform the general public that GMCC was indeed "one identity in four locations."[92] Hickling and Johnson recommended that GMCC formulate admission standards and courses similar to those of other educational institutions to promote the transferability of some programs.[93] Hickling and Johnson concluded:[94]

1. GMCC was not a school of underdogs. For several of its programs, the educational qualifications were the same as for other post-secondary institutions in Alberta.

2. GMCC was competing with other post-secondary institutions.

3. Although it was not true, GMCC was perceived as being in a "growth for growth's sake" mode.

4. There was an overpowering need for proper counselling services.

5. GMCC was failing miserably with its public relations and public communications responsibilities.

6. GMCC should integrate some of its programming and move toward the transferability of credit for course work in specific programs.

7. The profile of extension services programs should be improved.

8. The general public tended to be misinformed about the relative worth of GMCC academic courses, perceiving them in the same light as GMCC pottery and yoga courses.

9. While perceived as an asset, separate campuses contributed to the College's splintered identity.

10. One of the major roles for GMCC was to prepare people for jobs. It was imperative for the college, instructors, and incoming students to know the exact purpose of each program.

11. GMCC was growing less flexible, less responsive, and more political.

12. GMCC was a place were people could have a second chance, but most people seemed to feel that everyone at GMCC was there for that reason.

13. Many felt that GMCC was inferior to the University of Alberta or NAIT. This belief seemed to be based on the feeling that GMCC programs are less rigorous than those of the other institutions, and that student screening procedures were less stringent.

14. GMCC needed a more effective marketing and public relations strategy, directed to both individuals and the business community.

15. "Personal growth" areas were commendable, but perhaps should focus on concerns such as divorce, separation, alcoholism, and stress, rather than macrame or yoga.

16. Some selection standards should be established for each credit program to maintain its quality.

17. GMCC will never again be a "personal interest," quality of life, geographically oriented community college. It was described as a full-scale post-secondary institution. Therefore, its emphasis must be on the careful cultivation of credibility in the marketplace.

18. GMCC must upgrade its liaison with private sector employers. This area was vital, not only for feedback on potential job opportunities but to constantly monitor perceptions of required course content.

Students also expressed concern about the College's image by noting that "potential employers are not aware of GMCC and have no idea as to what kind of students are graduating from the College and the qualifications they have."[95]

One of the first efforts to respond to these image concerns involved the preparation of a twenty-minute slide presentation by the media production unit of the College.[96]

A Look to the Future: Long-Range Planning

In a proposed role statement for the College presented to the Academic Council in 1977, the need was expressed for educational and other related services in downtown Edmonton: "Given an appropriate site and facilities in the city centre, the College would be prepared to take an even greater leadership role in inner city education."[97] Statements such as this brought attention to the needs of the College and the community, but more was needed. Planning documents and directives for the College had been developed but it was clear that a more concrete long-range planning statement was required.

By 1977–78, GMCC set in motion plans for institutional evaluation, long-range planning, and the enhancement of the role of Academic Council. It vigorously pursued the appropriate allocation of facilities and space to meet current and long-term site requirements. Concerned because the College had initially grown so quickly and then tapered off, at its retreat on July 5 and 6, 1979, the board established a broadly based, institution-wide Long-Range Planning Committee (LRPC) as a task force of the Academic Council.

Dr. MacEwan himself, in the role of teacher, at CORE Days 1979

A number of studies were designed to obtain opinions about the College in order to define GMCC vis-à-vis other institutions. These included a public opinion survey, a survey of high school graduates, a dialogue with and subsequent presentation from the Department of Advanced Education and Manpower, and the study by Hickling and Johnson. In addition, a commissioned study looked at colleges across America and the world and also provided the Long-Range Planning Committee with its impressions of the image of community colleges.

The LRPC had a mandate to bring forward recommendations to the council for a planning policy and mission and goal statements for the College. The board committed $47,000 to the committee, which took 18 months to fulfill its tasks and complete its final report. The LRPC concentrated its efforts on establishing an updated foundation and framework within which participatory, systematic, and ongoing planning could take place, effectively and efficiently linking long-range College goals to day-to-day decision making.

The LRPC systematically studied two broad areas in considering planning requirements: first, the perceptions of the various "publics" or "communities" served by the College regarding what it is doing and what it ought to be doing; and second, developments in the community college movement, particularly in other parts of Canada and the United States. Input for the study came from a number of sources, including surveys by both GMCC and Hickling and Johnson, radio and television talk shows, written submissions by individuals or groups, and demographic data from Alberta Advanced Education and Manpower. Academic Council and the Board of Governors extensively reviewed the results of the LRPC's activity. Five areas of concern were identified from the examination of all of the LRPC's sources:

1. Role Clarification—The role of the college within the post-secondary education system; community and constituent perceptions of the college's objectives; and uncertainty of both administration and faculty of their individual roles within the institution.

2. Clientele—Demographic trends showed a significant shift in clientele from the emerging high school student between the ages of 18 and 24, to older people already in the work force who are wanting to retrain or upgrade their present skills—not necessarily on a full time basis.

3. Communication with External Community—The college identity is not clear in the community, and there is considerable variation in perceptions of the quality of college programs and service.

4. Democratic Governance and Decision Making—A system of campus governance that is genuinely responsive to the concerns of all people at the institution was thought to be a highly important goal, with a low level of institutional commitment.

5. Lack of Desirable Working Environment—There is a perceived lack of a desirable working environment within the college—the lack of an open climate that encourages innovation and mutual trust.[98]

In November 1979, Academic Council unanimously approved the Mission and Goal Statements and planning policies and recommended them to the Board of Governors for final institutional approval, which was granted on February 21, 1980. The LRPC then formulated a comprehensive and systematic set of long- and short-range planning policies based on the College's Mission and Goal Statements. The LRPC called for the systematic review of the Mission and Goal Statements at least once every five years and recommended that institutional research and community input continue to support the College's planning process. It recommended that planning should be a three-year cyclical process based on College goals, and these plans should form the basis for institutional resource allocation. The plans should be openly reviewed and approved and all College constituents should be involved in the planning process.

As a result of the LRPC activities, a research and planning position was created in 1980 within the office of the president. This position held responsibility for implementing LRPC recommendations such as developing a planning system and preparation of multi-year plans.

Stabilization

Many financial concerns were expressed in 1977 and 1978. The Department of Advanced Education and Manpower's method of financing that granted percentage increases to base-line budgets was felt to have had a significant effect on the ability of the College to provide adequate service. After a period of rapid growth, a pattern referred to as "controlled development" called for a major revision in the College's administrative thinking. Thus, student enrolment became stabilized and as many as 1,500 applicants were turned away, with the College being unable to provide additional services because of restricted funding. The Board of Governors brought this situation to the attention of the minister of advanced education, as the process of adjusting enrolments downward raised fundamental questions concerning limiting the public's right to a post-secondary education.

Financial constraints imposed by the limited annual government grant resulted in a continuation of the no-growth pattern. Continually forced to turn away applicants, the College focused on alternative ways to raise additional money. The establishment of the Grant MacEwan Community College Foundation allowed the College to underwrite projects and programs that would otherwise not be possible under the existing grant structure. On February 15, 1979, Dr. Terry Flannigan, director of student services, reported to the board that the College solicitor recommended the foundation be formed under the *Societies Act* rather than as a company. Orest Mulka, the first chair of the GMCC Foundation, requested board approval for the appointment of Flannigan as executive secretary to the GMCC Foundation, responsible for its day-to-day operation.

An important early recommendation, and one that is still not adhered to by many institutions, was that all proposals for external funding that are not covered by the mandate of the College should be filed with the foundation. This was necessary to avoid duplication of requests to any possible funding source.

During the 1979 academic year the senior administration was reorganized in order to reduce administrative costs, establish appropriate financial control, enhance planning capacity, improve and decentralize decision-making to the campuses, and return the College to a growth pattern. The 1980–81 academic year also involved new construction. The building of the new Jasper Place Campus was delayed by strikes, poor weather, and the demolition of the old facilities at the site. As a consequence, the design arts and theatre programs were moved temporarily to Victoria Composite High School, which in turn resulted in reduced enrolments in these programs due to the limited space available. The closure of the Assumption Campus eliminated the College from the downtown area, though the importance of a city centre location had been stressed in the 1977 proposed role statement.

In 1979–80 programming was introduced and extended in the areas of property and real estate management, rehabilitation services for the handicapped, occupational health nursing, and extended care nursing. No programs were deleted; however, discussions and studies were conducted that included serious consideration of possible cuts.

In 1979 the College entered into a cooperative venture with Alberta Education Communications Corporation (later to become ACCESS) and the British Columbia Institute of Technology to provide library technician courses, via the Anik B satellite, to students in Grande Prairie and Fairview. Alternative methods of delivering education posed a challenge to the College as the technology began to become available that would enable students in remote areas to obtain a GMCC education.

Concerns also were expressed about the significant increase in the number of part-time students in 1978, 1979, and 1980.

President Haar called the 1978–79 academic year one of change, with some extension of programming and a solidification of administrative operations.[99] Computerized systems for the institution's financial records were now in place and plans were underway to computerize the student record system as well.

Haar noted that the administrative structure of the College needed to be changed in order to keep pace with the changing role of the institution. At the February 11, 1980, board meeting, Haar identified the following needs:

- to continue the multi-campus concept
- to continue the trimester system
- to recognize the reduction from four to three major campuses
- to provide satellite campuses if and when needed
- to reduce senior administration costs
- to clarify the roles of central services and the individual campuses
- to clarify the roles of various sub-bodies, e.g., Academic Council
- to provide for the return to a growth pattern

76

Signing of the Faculty Agreement, December 1979

• to rationalize the roles of the board and Academic Council

Haar also noted the need to delegate authority for decision making and controls to the campuses. Instead of a director of each campus, he recommended that coordinators be responsible for the major programs.

By 1980, the College had established programs and now needed to move to a developmental stage that would allow it to fill a distinct place in the post-secondary educational community. Internal concerns were abundant: a GMCC employee information survey reported in June 1980 revealed dissatisfaction related to working conditions, financial restraints, organizational structure, and communications deficiencies.

The Need to Grow

In July 1980, the Board of Governors approved a major reorganization of the operational and administrative structure of the College. Under the new structure the continuing education department was decentralized to become a part of the individual campus structures. Each continuing education unit was headed by a coordinator reporting to the relevant campus director. At each campus, a curriculum committee was to work closely with the dean of instruction (formerly the dean of academic affairs) and Academic Council in the consideration of academic matters. Each campus was responsible for its own technical services such as scheduling and timetable development. The personnel and financial offices, purchasing department, and computer services remained centralized. In addition to campus directors, coordinators of the learning resources centre, academic services, instructional development, and program development and evaluation reported to the dean of instruction. The director of student services became the director of college and student services and assumed the responsibility for the information office (formerly reporting to the president). The position of coordinator of research and planning (part-time) was created and reported to the president. The dean of administrative affairs was responsible for the director of plant and development and the coordinators of finance, personnel, and systems and computers.

The reduction of administrative costs also was discussed in July 1980. It was important for the College to return to a growth pattern and adopt a budgeting plan that would complement the newly approved organizational structure. Under the current allocation system, the College was continually in the unfavourable position of not knowing what funds would be received from the government, and it was necessary for the administration to estimate what the anticipated revenue would be from year to year. A "zero base" budgeting system was proposed, patterned largely after a similar program then used by the Edmonton Public School Board, in which the various divisions of the College were required to outline how they would operate. The advantage of the system was that it would encourage planning for the future and provide incentives for staff involvement. Even if their requests were refused, staff had the benefit of knowing that they had recorded their concerns for future reference.

There was a consensus that the three-year budget cycle suggested by Haar was more favourable than a yearly format; however, accurate information was not always available for the purpose of planning. The board, at that time, considered the budget its number one priority.[100]

In July 1980, Hay Associates prepared a report entitled *Development of Compensation Standards*, by A . C. King and R. E. Sanderson.[101] The report examined positions in the College and the existing salary levels and position content relationships for those positions, and compared them with those of other employers in both the public and private sectors, with particular reference to western Canada. Salary recommendations were made which reflected the evaluative content of the positions which were compatible with policies of the College. The report recommended principles for administering salaries in ranges, and the methodology for periodically updating the ranges.[102]

In November 1980 discussion took place regarding the ministerial statement on the Advanced Education Endowment fund, which was delivered by the Honourable James D. Horsman on May 14, 1980. It was confirmed that the government would match the principal value of capital gifts designated and approved for use on capital programs, such as the construction and acquisition of equipment, as well as the interest earned on revenues from endowment gifts for operational purposes which relate to the teaching, research, and community services functions of the institution.

The new decade was viewed cautiously but with optimism. The serious concerns about the College's image were being discussed and employers were becoming more aware of its graduates. It was understood that there was still much to be done, but there was little doubt that Grant MacEwan Community College had become a major part of the educational system.

Haar Resigns

The 1980–81 academic year was the tenth anniversary of classes at Grant MacEwan Community College and, for John Haar, the conclusion of almost a decade of service to the institution. New programs were added that included fibre arts, dance teacher training, insurance administration, microcomputer management, volunteer management, and Native communications. The Jasper Place Campus housed students in design and performing arts and business programs for the 1980 fall term. Built to accommodate 1,400 students, the completed facility was already filled to capacity. During this year, the College joined the Yellowhead Region Education Consortium—a group of institutions formed to provide post-secondary educational opportunities for residents of the communities between Edmonton and the Rocky Mountains. Outreach activities continued to be offered through the Alberta Educational Communications Authority (ACCESS) in the library technician and equine programs for students in Alberta, the Northwest Territories, and British Columbia.

On February 16, 1981, John Haar resigned as president of Grant MacEwan Community College. In a prepared press release he stated that he had given the College as much as he could in the past ten years:

> The college foundation has been put down. We have recruited some very good staff and recorded growth patterns. That has provided me with a good degree of satisfaction.[103]

Haar felt the multi-campus College was on the threshold of new potentials in growth and should look to new ways to deliver education and continue to grow. He noted that it was a "good time to change institutions and change personalities." Haar said that he had been thinking about retiring "for a couple of years."[104]

Haar hoped the College would continue to respond to the needs of special groups in the community, including Natives and the disabled, and that the government would provide the College with adequate funding for continued growth. He believed the College had not met its potential because of budgetary restrictions. "I would have felt happier," Haar commented, "if we had more operating funds to render more service to more people."[105]

Haar was given an educational leave effective December 31, 1981. He intended to take a series of courses in Canadian studies at institutions in British Columbia, Saskatchewan, and Ontario. The new president, Gerald Kelly, approved a plan for him to return to the College in September 1982 to assume an instructional position in Canadian Studies. Board of Governors Chair D. Robert McLeod noted the board was "particularly pleased Mr. Haar wishes to remain at the College to teach in this important area in which he has great interest and knowledge."[106]

On May 20, 1982, only one year after his retirement, John Haar died suddenly at the age of 62. He was survived by his wife Pauline and four daughters. During his ten years as president, the College grew from two small makeshift campuses with 410 students in 16 programs to three campuses with 2,417 full-time equivalent students enroled in 26 diploma and 17 certificate programs. His successor, Dr. Kelly, called Haar's philosophy of a community college flexible and responsive, "...a post-secondary education that was accessible to the common man."[107]

Accessibility characterized his personality and his vision for the College. Chuck Day recalled that Haar was an approachable man of considerable presence:

> Although lacking in formal education, he was a visionary and instilled loyalty. People would go the extra mile for him. He had a very commanding presence physically, and he was an eloquent speaker. This, coupled with the fine oratorical style of Barry Moore, was very useful for the College in the early years. There was a great spirit of camaraderie in the early years. Often, maybe most of the time, we didn't know what we were doing, but it was filled with excitement and a willingness to work hard for what we believed in.[108]

His humanitarian approach was not without austerity. Bert Giles, who served on the College's Board of Governors as faculty representative, recalled that very few people called him John. "You would often feel he was your biggest adversary," Giles recalled, "but he was always there to support you."[109] Expanding on the personality of Mr. Haar, Day noted:

We had a lot of parties...of course the staff was small so we could do that kind of thing. John may have appeared gruff to an outsider but to an insider he was an extremely sensitive man.[110]

Bert Giles's remembrances offer an interesting glimpse of John Haar's personality:

Haar usually opened meetings with the remark, "Why are we here?" He detached himself from the discussion process by addressing meetings through a series of "This is what the President wants" statements. His belief was that no one can really fail; there were only varying degrees of success.[111]

Under John Haar, Grant MacEwan Community College went from a concept to a functioning reality. What had once been an idealistic vision was now fully operational. Taking a vision and making it happen is no small achievement, and for this accomplishment John Haar will remain a dominant figure in the history of GMCC.

After Haar's retirement, a ceremony was held on November 13, 1981, at which the Jasper Place Campus performing arts theatre was named in his honour and Gerald Kelly was inaugurated as the new president of the College. The theatre and the John L. Haar Memorial Scholarship Fund, established after Haar's death, remain as lasting tributes to the first president of Grant MacEwan Community College, but his vision of a institution that was truly a "community" college with the "city as its campus" remains his most enduring legacy.

---

[1] Barry Moore, quoted in *College Comment*, vol. 1, no. 1 (1971).

[2] GMCC Board Meeting Minutes, November 26, 1970.

[3] John Haar, *Perspectives*, January 22, 1976, p. 4.

[4] T. C. Day, personal interview, February 19, 1993.

[5] Ibid.

[6] Programs included: child care worker, fashion sales technology, library technician, secretarial science, medical equipment technology, behavioural science technician, general arts and science diploma, social care worker, journalism, advertising, public relations, audio-visual technician, police science, business administration, nursing, and recreation leadership.

[7] Many people deserve recognition for their involvement in the early history of the College. Some of the early College appointments included, in no particular order, the following:

Sheila Campbell, Paul Otke, Rita Peirog, T. Charles Day, Clark R. Tingley, Donna Mitchell, Alan Clarke, R. H. S. Hardy, Jack Allan, Ted Kemp, Robert Leong, Jack Cooper, Wayne Cunningham, C. Stewart Robertson, L. E. Wells, A. McLeod, Allen Watson, B. J. Haughey, George Porter, Leonard Rust, John Hart, Eric Robinson,

Sister Therese Castonguay, Charles Boylan, Robert Eggers, Lili Kopala, Jack Scharf, Philip Shragge, Samuel Yakimishyn, Donald Burfoot, Rose Woodhams, Wesley Alexander, Andi Pallas, Bert Giles, Constance Land, Alberta Kosowan, Derek McCune, Susan Hutchison, D. McDonald, Deanna Piwowar, Vijay Gupta, Caterina Loverso, Christiana Bell, Shirley DeBow, Lucille Rudiak, William Besse, Rhoda Ann Cucheran, Eric Tripp, Mary Kachmar, Peter Brown, Wendy Muscroft, Bud McNairn, Bert Beckman, Joy Shaw, and Shirley Kniazky.

[8] Bert Giles, personal interview, May 11, 1993.

[9] Wilbur J. Collin, "The Role and Mission of Grant MacEwan Community College," unpublished paper, GMCC Community Relations files, March 7, 1982.

[10] T. C. Day, personal interview, February 19, 1993.

[11] GMCC Board Meeting Minutes, February 19, 1971.

[12] Letter from R. E. Rees to the College, GMCC Archives.

[13] T. C. Day, personal interview, February 19, 1993.

[14] Ibid.

[15] Nursing Advisory Committee Annual Report, 1973, p. B–1.

[16] A program for such purposes was understood to be a 15–18 credit program of courses.

[17] T. C. Day, personal interview, February 19, 1993.

[18] "A New Kind of College for A New Kind of World," promotional brochure, 1971. GMCC Archives.

[19] John Haar, *Grant MacEwan Community College Student Handbook*, 1971, p. 2.

[20] T. C. Day, personal interview, April 19, 1993.

[21] GMCC Board Meeting Minutes, November 15, 1971.

[22] T. C. Day, personal interview, February 19, 1993.

[23] John Haar, *Perspectives*, January 22, 1976, p. 4.

[24] *Edmonton Journal*, September 8, 1972, p. 53.

[25] With Eric Robertson and Bob Leong.

[26] *The Albertan*, September 9, 1972.

[27] *Edmonton Journal*, September 8, 1972, p. 53.

[28] *The Albertan*, September 9, 1972.

[29] GMCC Board Meeting Minutes, November 10, 1971.

[30] The College's philosophy was reviewed five years later. Clark Tingley, the chair of the academic planning committee of the Academic Council, suggested there was "a continuing danger in the College becoming elitist, with stiffer requirements to weed out certain people." Committee member Millard Evans added, "the college may not serve all the clientele it set out to serve originally, according to the original philosophy. It seems people most likely to succeed are often picked to enter programs." (The previous comments and a revised philosophy were published in the March 25, 1976, edition of the student newspaper.)

[31] The Ontario college system's avoidance of, or reluctance to include, university transfer programming in its curriculum is still a topic of debate. Many believe a lack of university transfer programming has had an adverse effect on the Ontario college system.

[32] Reno A. Bosetti, *System Integration—Coordination—Growth, The Alberta System of Post-Secondary Non-University Education: Master Plan Number One* (Edmonton, AB: Alberta Colleges Commission, 1972).

[33] See Grant MacEwan Community College, *Response to "Master Plan Number One" on Post-Secondary Non-University Education* (Edmonton, AB: Author, February 8, 1973). This response represents, in many ways, the first formal presentation by GMCC concerning its future plans and status within the college system.

[34] Taken from an unpublished position paper prepared by Desmond E. Berghofer, "Worth Commission Proposals Relating to Program Development in Higher and Further Education," July 1972.

[35] Alberta Commission of Educational Planning, *A Future of Choices: A Choice of Futures* (Edmonton, AB: The Queen's Printer, 1972).

[36] John Haar noted this point should also include the needs of men. From the personal files of J. Haar, GMCC Archives.

[37] Ted Kemp, *Gateway*, September 26, 1972.

[38] GMCC Board Meeting Minutes, May 10, 1972.

[39] GMCC Board Meeting Minutes. March 8, 1972.

[40] Submitted March 29, 1972, to the Management Committee.

[41] GMCC Board Meeting Minutes. March 28, 1972.

[42] GMCC Board Meeting Minutes, September 15, 1972.

[43] *Edmonton Journal*, September 21, 1972, p. 67.

[44] *Edmonton Journal*, September 19, 1972, p. 1.

[45] *Red Deer Advocate*, September 21, 1972.

[46] *Edmonton Journal*, September 20, 1972, p. 77. Clark also expressed concern that there was an "over-emphasis" on the University of Alberta by citing that the deputy minister of advanced education, Walter Worth, was a former U of A vice-president, and the chair of the U of A's new board of governors, Fred Jenner, was the father of Peter Jenner, Foster's executive assistant.

[47] *Edmonton Journal*, September 20, 1972, p. 77.

[48] *Edmonton Journal*, September 21, 1972, p. 67.

[49] *Edmonton Journal*, September 26, 1972, p. 81.

[50] *Gateway*, September 26, 1972.

[51] Ibid.

[52] Letter from J. A. Bain to Alberta Colleges Commission, January 31, 1973.

[53] J. P. Cooper, in a memorandum to G. O. Kelly dated September 23, 1981, noted that competition in these areas existed "from 1971 onward."

[54] February 14, 1973.

[55] *Edmonton Journal*, August 26, 1978.

[56] GMCC Board Meeting Minutes, April 12, 1972.

[57] *Perspectives*, December 13, 1974, p. 3.

[58] Cooper, who eventually became dean of administrative affairs in April 1980, had been with the College since 1971. He was also chair of the Business Administration Department and director of the Business Division.

[59] *Alumni Newsletter*, vol. 1, no. 2, pp. 1–2.

[60] *Edmonton Journal*, April 21, 1981, p. E9.

[61] The colour was chosen for durability on the porcelain enamel painting surface. Porcelain panels were used extensively by the construction industry at this time and examples abound throughout Edmonton, notably the University of Alberta "Butterdome" and Edmonton Public Schools Centre for Education. During a personal interview on April 12, 1993, Andi Pallas, GMCC facilities director, attributed the extensive use of this material to the architectural influence of Toronto's Eaton Centre.

[62] In 1974, 95 percent of the 110 full-time faculty members held university degrees.

[63] Library acquisitions, under tough provincial spending guidelines, were kept to a minimum. GMCC had an average of only 9.1 volumes per student compared to the provincial average of 36.2. Department of Advanced Education guidelines recommended 50 volumes per full-time student. This would have cost close to 900,000 1975 dollars.

[64] The ratio of counsellors to students was 1:700. This was double the provincial average for post-secondary institutions. At GMCC, three counsellors divided their time among 2,200 students on four campuses.

[65] Bob Leong, *Perspectives*, February 5, 1976, p. 3

[66] Russ Pacey, *Perspectives*, October 7, 1976, p. 3.

[67] Peter Brown, *Perspectives*, October 7, 1976, p. 3.

[68] Bill Pierce, *Perspectives*, October 7, 1976, p. 3.

[69] Ted Kemp, *Perspectives*, March 25, 1976, p. 2.

[70] *Perspectives*, March 18, 1976, p. 1.

[71] GMCC Board Meeting Minutes, October 16, 1980.

[72] The task force was co-chaired by Jean-Luc Pepin and John Robarts.

[73] *Perspectives*, April 5, 1978, p. 1.

[74] Communications, EN 100.3.

[75] John Haar, *GMCC Annual Report*, 1976–77, p. 3.

[76] The griffin is on the MacEwan family coat of arms. It is a mythical creature described in Roman legend as having the body of a lion and the head, wings, and talons of an eagle. Because of its legendary and zealous protection of its golden nest, the griffin is recognized as a symbol for vigilance and the guardian of valuables.

[77] Terry Flannigan became interim director of student affairs.

[78] Proposed Role Statement for GMCC, September 1977.

[79] It was pointed out to Bev Facey, superintendent of the County of Strathcona Public School Board, and Harold MacNeil, superintendent of the Edmonton Separate School System, that the College had indeed sought liaison with these bodies and had two meetings with representatives of these groups. Haar stated that he had personally met with Dean Coutts, dean of the Faculty of Education at the University of Alberta, and had attended a meeting chaired by MacNeil. Haar further stated that the Student Affairs Department had contacted and visited every high school in the Public and Separate School systems in Edmonton.

[80] *Edmonton Journal*, June 28, 1975.

[81] Ibid.

[82] Ibid.

[83] Charles Gravett, quoted in the *Edmonton Journal*, May 23, 1975.

[84] Ibid.

[85] Hickling and Johnson Management Consultants, *Public Perceptions of Grant MacEwan Community College*, 1979, p. 6.

[86] Ibid., pp. 8–10.

[87] Ibid., p. 10.

[88] Ibid., p. 13.

[89] Ibid., p. 14.

[90] Ibid., p. 17.

[91] Ibid., p. 19.

[92] Ibid., p. 20.

[93] Ibid., p. 23.

[94] Ibid., pp. 25–28.

[95] GMCC Board Meeting Minutes, February 21, 1980.

[96] May 1980.

[97] The proposed role statement made in 1977 to Academic Council was not officially endorsed.

[98] Grant MacEwan Community College Long-Range Planning Committee, *Final Report* (Edmonton, AB: Author, 1980), Appendix B.

[99] John Haar, *GMCC Annual Report*, 1979–80, p. 3

[100] GMCC Board Meeting Minutes, July 4, 1980.

[101] Hay Associates, *Development of Compensation Standards* (Edmonton, AB: Author, 1980).

[102] Sixty-two positions were evaluated, ranging from president to program assistants. A "compa-ratio" or index of the relationship between the salaries being paid and the midpoints of the current salary structure was calculated by dividing the

total salaries by the total midpoints of the jobs. It was recommended to bring the current compa-ratio to 98 percent. This represented a 10.8 percent increase in payroll. It was noted that while internal inequities existed, compensation at GMCC was, generally, externally competitive. The board approved the implementation of the Hay system.

[103] John Haar, press release, February 16, 1981, in GMCC archives.

[104] Ibid.

[105] Ibid.

[106] *Edmonton Journal*, April 1, 1981.

[107] Gerald O. Kelly, quoted in the 1982 GMCC *Yearbook*, p. 3.

[108] T. C. Day, personal interview, February 19, 1993.

[109] Bert Giles, personal interview, May 11, 1993.

[110] T. C. Day, personal interview, February 19, 1993.

[111] Bert Giles, personal interview, May 11, 1993.

Chapter Four

The Kelly Years

With the retirement of John Haar, Grant MacEwan Community College began a new era. The excitement of building a college had subsided, although the enthusiasm about working for an institution barely ten years old was hardly dampened. There existed, however, a new realism. It was as if the honeymoon period had ended. Money was now tighter, expectations were higher, and the issue of credibility was of paramount importance. Many, both inside and outside of the College, were unsure of its direction or the place GMCC would eventually establish in the post-secondary milieu.

Generally, in the period from 1975 to 1980, most Alberta colleges experienced growth in both enrolment and facilities; however, Grant MacEwan Community College did not. While it is true that GMCC facilities were built, their construction addressed existing, rather than long-term, needs. Enrolment patterns for GMCC had reached a plateau, and the overall lack of growth was considered a serious concern by the College's Board of Governors, one that a new president would have to address.

The College required a new president with the administrative ability to confront the immense challenges facing the institution, in particular, the increasing pressure from the community for access to Grant MacEwan Community College programs and the development of facilities to meet this demand.

A presidential search was initiated on February 19, 1981. The Board of Governors contracted The Caldwell Partners executive recruitment firm to handle the initial advertising, searching, and selection of a short

Willliam (Bill) Lord
Board of Governors Chairman 1981-83

list of candidates. The board was to control the process and final decision. Eventually, six of the 60 applicants were interviewed.

William R. (Bill) Lord was appointed chair of the Board of Governors on July 16, 1981, for the period from July 16, 1981, to September 1983. Among his first responsibilities as chair was the important task of hiring the new president.

The board confirmed the appointment of Dr. Gerald O. (Gerry) Kelly as GMCC's second president effective September 1, 1981. Early in its history, it was determined that the College must be innovative, forward-looking, and willing to accept progressive change. Thus, an individual who possessed energy, vision, and a solid academic background was sought to lead the College. While it could be said that John Haar was the right fit for the role of college builder, Gerry Kelly was certainly the right fit to lead the College into its next decade. Kelly was a firm believer in the community college philosophy espoused by Haar, but also brought a professional depth of educational and managerial training to his position. The August 21, 1981, board meeting saw Kelly as the incoming president and on August 31, 1981, he assumed full leadership.

At the time of his appointment, Kelly, at the age of 40, was the youngest president of a post-secondary institution in Alberta. He had had six years of teaching experience at the elementary, high school, and college levels, and an additional 11 years of college administrative experience. Despite his youth, Kelly was well prepared for his new assignment and well acquainted with the community college concept.

Prior to his Grant MacEwan Community College appointment, Kelly had been academic dean at Red Deer College since 1973, and had taught part-time at the University of Alberta from 1972 to 1979. He was director of student services, counsellor, and animateur at Dawson College in Montreal from 1969 to 1971. He had also taught science, geography, and physical education at Montreal's Lower Canada College from 1964 to 1969. In addition, he held a postgraduate fellowship at the University of Alberta from 1971 to 1973, and was among ten Canadian educators chosen by the Association of Canadian Community Colleges

(ACCC) to tour British colleges in 1976. From 1979 to 1980, Kelly worked as a visiting tutor for the British Further Education Staff College in Bristol, England, an experience that would have a considerable impact on his vision of the community college. This was augmented by a six-month appointment as Executive in Residence at the world renowned International Management Institute (IMI) in Geneva, Switzerland. In June 1994 he was awarded an honorary doctor of laws degree (L.L.D.) from McGill University for his work in Canadian college education.

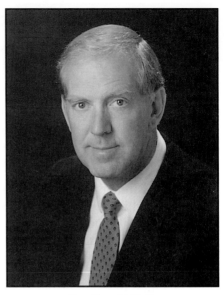

Dr. Gerald Kelly
GMCC President, 1981-present

As the holder of three earned degrees from McGill University (a B.Ed. in physical education, M.Ed. in counselling, and M.A. in education) and a Ph.D. in educational administration from the University of Alberta, Kelly was eminently qualified to bridge the gap between academe and the community. As a professional educator and manager of education, he brought new skills to the president's office that were augmented by his educational qualifications and personal administrative experience in two of the three vice-presidential areas of the College—student services and academics.

Robert McLeod, past chair of the Board of Governors, believed Kelly understood the needs of Alberta's community colleges: "We feel confident that Dr. Kelly is the man to lead our College into the 1980s and that he will be able to direct the College in meeting the community's ever changing needs."[1] Kelly saw the assessment of GMCC's expansion needs as the major challenge for the College in the 1980s, and hoped several campuses would be built around the city in the next ten years.[2]

The new president was a high profile and extremely energetic leader. He had been captain of the McGill University basketball team and was avid about fitness, which would enable him to cope with the stress of the president's job. Early in his GMCC career, he enjoyed daily lunch hour jogs and jokingly noted that he knew every dog within 15 blocks of the new Jasper Place Campus.[3] His sporting exploits carried over to the golf links and on one occasion he had the distinction of scoring a hole-in-one! To his satisfaction, he did it while playing with GMCC Board Chair Bill Lord and vice-presidents Chuck Day and Terry Flannigan at the Derrick Golf Club.

Board Objectives and Administrative Changes

With Kelly's leadership, the board approved four major objectives. The first objective was to address the stagnation of the College's enrolment that existed between 1975 and 1980. In short, the new president needed to ensure that the College was responsive to the community. It is important to point out that College growth was not the goal of this objective; rather, it was to improve the organizational and administrative systems of the College which were inhibiting its ability to respond to the growing community need for college education.

The second objective was to improve the governance of the institution and build a sound relationship between Academic Council, administration, and the student body.[4] The board itself was heavily involved in the administrative affairs of the College, and in September 1981, Academic Council had been "on strike" for several months over perceived board interference. In addition, in the past, senior administrators had not been included in much of the decision-making at the presidential level. In response, Kelly set up an Executive Officers Committee for senior administrators. This objective was in complete harmony with Kelly's preparation for his role as president. His studies in higher education management culminated with his doctoral work on "participatory college governance."[5] According to Kelly, "Learning to work with each other through collaborative working relationships is an education in itself! We can set a tone for the entire College, including the teacher-student relationship, by encouraging people to get involved in matters of importance to them."[6] Kelly would meet this objective by working with the faculty member on the Board of Governors, Dr. Peter Furstenau, to clarify the relationship between Academic Council and the board. In Kelly's words, "Administratively we embarked on a highly participative approach to management for all senior administrators, planning that this would filter down to all levels in the College."[7] This approach symbolizes the administrative focus of the Kelly years and was to be reflected in a later Task Force on College Governance at GMCC.

The third objective of the board was to enhance the image of GMCC in the community; as the primary spokesperson and promoter of the College, its new president was encouraged to become a public figure.[8] At the August 25, 1983, Board of Governors meeting, Kelly reported on the activities he was called upon to perform as College president. He added that he was but one of many people in the College who took part in such community-based activities and stated that such participation is inherent in the concept of the community college. Kelly later established a College "facts and figures" card that was distributed to all employees, who were encouraged to become public relations ambassadors for the College in promoting the need for new facilities.

Enhancing the College's credibility with the community was a critical concern for Kelly. His first goal in developing a public relations profile "was to make sure that the local high schools, students and administrators, knew more about Grant MacEwan Community College."[9]

The fourth board objective approved with the new president concerned the problem of space and inadequate College facilities. By the 1981–82 academic year, the College offered over 28 two-year and 15 one-year programs. After a five-year period of no growth, questions arose concerning the direction the College should take. Under review were the multi-campus concept and the efficiency and effectiveness of the institution. The possibility of one central campus and the use of existing facilities were reviewed in order to determine how the College might provide greater service to the Edmonton community. An emphasis on technological training was reflected by government funding grants that had resulted in expanded facilities and programs for many Alberta colleges. Kelly argued that community services and business related programs were now due for expanded funding as well.

John Ramsey
GMCC Foundation Chairman, 1979-89
Board of Governors Chairman, 1989-95

The College had recently graduated a record number of students. Ninety percent of the students responding to a GMCC graduate survey indicated that they found employment in areas directly related to their Grant MacEwan Community College training. Continuing education now focused on outreach, and significant increases in the number of part-time students were experienced in several programs as a result of this new thrust.

Economic restraint became a reality in 1981–82; several programs were evaluated and some were reduced or terminated.[10] Two major market surveys were conducted in behavioural sciences and equine studies as the viability of these programs became questionable. Fiscal restraint also led to administrative cuts and a complete review of College policies concerning personnel, finance, and budgeting procedures. It was not without difficulty that the administration and Board of Governors produced a balanced operating budget that allowed for a small increase in enrolment.

During the 1981–82 academic year, the Grant MacEwan Community College Foundation, led by its executive director, Terry Flannigan, with support from Foundation Chair John Ramsey and President Kelly, raised approximately $500,000, including matching funds from the Advanced Education Endowment Fund.

As revealed by the Hickling and Johnson report, an additional prime objective for the College was to enhance its image,[11] which was described in the *Edmonton Journal* as being "all over the map."[12] In addressing the public's perception of the College, Kelly recalled the impact of the 1979 Hickling and Johnson survey:

> The central conclusion of this study was that the College was still new and the public tended to try to define it as part of something else, in other words, the tendency was to look at the College and say: What part of the university is the College, or what part of the technical institute role does the College perform? The College was not yet ready to consider that the community college has its own distinct identity and is not simply a vestige of already existing institutions. In addition to that, our multi-campus operation led to a greater dilution of identity, the diversity of our programs, over 40 of them, seemed to be confusing to the public, and finally the multitude of general interest courses that the College was offering seemed to also interfere with establishing an identity for the College.[13]

Since defining the identity of Grant MacEwan Community College became a key element during its second decade, public relations and information assumed a much higher profile. Follow-up surveys to alumni and the refinement of the College Foundation played a large part in this objective. The Kelly administration "put the name of the College in neon lights on the exterior walls of its campuses around the city."[14] In 1983, Kelly confidently remarked:

> The public's perception of the College is turning around. More people seem to be aware of our academic programs; it is our estimate that there is an enhanced academic image of the College in the community.[15]

In a memorandum dated February 18, 1982, administrative changes were proposed to provide a better balance in the workload among senior instructional officers. A "flat" structure was intended to improve communications and responsiveness, and the College's program priorities were adjusted to prepare for future growth and extended programs to meet the needs of part-time learners. The changes became effective July 1, 1982.

In April 1981, the Executive Officers Committee had established three criteria for examining the discontinuation of the behavioural science program:

1. Success of the graduates in finding employment;

2. Results of a market survey conducted by the Program and Development and Evaluation Department of the College; and

3. Documented support for the program by the Psychologists Association of Alberta.

This event merits some attention, as similar guidelines would form the basis for future decisions about program termination.

The equine program, a special interest of the former president, was discontinued on June 30, 1982. A number of reasons for eliminating the program were offered, but the predominant one was that the program did not fit the College's mandate. The cost of continuing equine studies as a diploma program was high. During times of financial constraint, it was exceedingly difficult to defend the allocation of funds for equine activities at the expense of business and human services programming priorities. Funds were transferred to Business and Community Services programs, resulting in a fivefold increase in students over those in the equine program. Chuck Day noted that the equine program had prepared graduates for a select industry that did not pay salaries commensurate with the training involved. The program was transferred to Lakeland College in Vermilion. A controversy arose about the bidding procedure for the sale of the horses.[16] This affair was, according to Kelly, symbolic of many loose administrative procedures at the College which needed tightening,[17] and resulted in an evaluation of the guidelines for the sale of College property.

In 1980 the board had approved a policy that aligned continuing education more directly with the academic units of the College. Board Chair D. R. McLeod stated that administrative reorganization was done:

…in order to reduce administrative costs, to establish appropriate financial controls, to enhance its planning capacity, to return to a growth pattern for the College, to decentralize the continuing education operations and to hasten academic decision-making through the delegation of this process to the campuses.[18]

It was generally agreed that the image of the College could be improved by abandoning "kite-flying and log-cabin-building" courses and concentrating on the extension of credit programs. "There was a feeling that continuing education required focusing," Kelly explained.[19] Because continuing education programs had to operate on a cost recovery basis, they placed a heavy emphasis on advertising; hence, to a great

Barry Moore, Gerald Kelly, and Bill Lord at Convocation, 1981

extent, the public's perception of Grant MacEwan Community College programs was shaped by this area. The elimination of the position of the coordinator of continuing education was necessary, according to Kelly, in order to refocus continuing education. Such hard decisions, of course, had an effect on staffing and it was not without some concern that a new structure was put in place. Academic Vice-President Chuck Day emphasized that the College would continue to offer general interest courses, but not as a primary focus.[20] "When Grant MacEwan Community College found it had an identity problem,"[21] remarked the *Edmonton Journal*, "the college did something about it." Kelly recalled:

> The administrative organization of the College was at loose ends. Streamlining and improved managerial organization were required to enable the College to be effective.[22]

Under the new arrangement, coordinators of continuing education reported to the directors of individual campuses, as did the coordinators of academic programs.[23] At each campus, a curriculum committee worked with the dean of instruction and Academic Council regarding academic matters. Services such as scheduling and time-tabling became the responsibility of each campus. The coordinators of learning resource

94

centres, academic services, instructional development, and a newly created position, evaluation, reported to the dean of instruction (formerly the dean of academic affairs). The director of student services became the director of College and Student Services and assumed responsibility for the information office, which formerly reported to the president. The dean of administrative affairs was responsible for the director of plant and development and the coordinators of finance, personnel, and systems and computers.

Intensified Demands for Programs and Facilities

In 1982 Kelly initiated the "Fall Welcome," which became an annual event, serving as a social "mixer" and informing all College staff about future plans and challenges. Another feature during the Kelly administration was an emphasis on long-range planning. Due to increased marketing efforts from all parts of the College, student demand for programs reached an all-time high, and created an unprecedented pressure on the College to provide educational opportunities. The challenge, however, was amplified by a decline in government funding levels and facilities that were woefully inadequate.

After a period of little or no growth, the College's second decade began with talk of expansion. By 1982, Grant MacEwan Community College had become Alberta's second largest college. At a private session of the board on May 20–27, 1982, it was pointed out that the College had existed for ten years as small decentralized campuses. Although advocating the retention of the Mill Woods and Jasper Place campuses, upon reviewing the pros and cons of this experience, the executive officers of the College decided the small campus concept was no longer viable. In addition, the Department of Advanced Education agreed with GMCC that multi-campus development was considerably more expensive than one large campus.

In August 1982, President Kelly corresponded with Dr. Henry Kolesar, deputy minister of Advanced Education and Manpower, expressing the need for additional space.[24] He reviewed the College's plans for site development in northeast Edmonton and stressed the importance of replacing the Cromdale Campus. Printed materials were prepared and distributed that described the necessity for expansion in order to meet the needs of the community.

In 1982, non-academic staff requested incorporation under the *Societies Act* as the "Grant MacEwan Community College Non-Academic Staff Association," or NASA.[25] On January 20, 1983, NASA was officially recognized. As the agent representing the interests of support and supervisory staff, NASA was subject to the following terms:

1. The Association, as a condition of initial and continued recognition, obtaining and maintaining a membership of not less than 51 percent of the staff members in the college eligible for such membership. Membership may be audited by the Board periodically.

2. Membership in the Association shall be on a voluntary basis, shall be limited to members designated by the college as support and supervisory staff, and shall exclude the administrative assistant and secretary of the President, Deans, and Coordinator of Human Resources, and such other positions as the Board may from time to time declare excluded.

3. Terms and conditions of employment negotiated by the Association on behalf of its members shall apply to all support and supervisory (non-academic) staff.

4. Recognition of the GMCC NASA will not impinge upon the rights and responsibilities, as currently defined, of the non-academic staff board member. Subsequent board members are to be recommended by the Association through due process.

5. The current board policies governing terms and conditions of employment for support staff...supervisory staff...will remain unchanged and have full force and effect until such time as the board and association negotiate, and accept, new terms and conditions, provided that negotiations for the development of such terms and conditions be entered into....[26]

In 1982 the board reviewed two documents, the "Planning Model" and "Institutional Development Plan,"[27] and agreed that they would be forwarded to Academic Council for consideration and later to the board for approval. The board expected that the Institutional Development Plan, as updated on a regular basis, would "become the 'bible' of the College."[28]

A donation of 18,000 records from Dr. Dick Rice, President and General Manager of Sunwapta Radio Broadcasting Company Ltd., was another noteworthy 1982 event. Valued at $70,000, the collection contained popular, jazz, and classical music. The excellent condition and rarity of the recordings made the collection a valuable public resource.

During the 1982–83 academic year, Grant MacEwan Community College continued to cope with increased student demand for programs.[29] The College now offered over 40 programs on its three main campuses, and the demand for programs was never higher. Credit enrolment now topped 3,000 full-time equivalent students (over 5,000 individuals), while another 9,000 participated in program related non-credit activity. This was all happening in a college with facilities

*Terry Flannigan, Chuck Day, Gerry Kelly, and Jack Cooper at an
early Grant MacEwan Foundation fundraising event*

designed to house about 2,800 full-time equivalent students.[30] This made
the construction of a new campus in northeast Edmonton, as recommended in the College's five-year development plan, a high priority.[31]

To accommodate increased student numbers, additional government funding for the lease of space was requested as an interim measure.
Program review and serious budget discussions resulted in what was
referred to as the "rationalization" of the College's program offerings.
Once again, the result was that some programs were eliminated, and their
funding was redistributed to programs deemed as having greater student
and employer demand. Business Division and outreach courses for part-
time learners in Community Services were among the programs that
were expanded at this time. College facilities were utilized more than
ever before, with many programs offered on weekends and evenings.

Computer-managed learning and a new student information and
record system were introduced in 1982–83. Reflecting the economic
downturn and restricted budgets, recruitment of new College employees
declined. The Non-Academic Staff Association and the Board of Governors negotiated the first NASA collective agreement, and over 80
percent of non-academic staff participated in one or more staff development courses or workshops during the year.[32] Policies regarding recruitment, section and program heads, employment, and administrative
development were revised and updated. Energy consumption costs were
a concern, and a central microprocessor linked to room monitors that
controlled heating and air conditioning was installed. Unfortunately, a
10 percent drop in consumption was offset by increased utility rates.

Planning for a northeast campus continued, while additional space was leased next to the Jasper Place Campus and at four other locations. Part-time enrolments continued to grow, and resulted in a decision to administer outreach offerings through program or instructional divisions. The increase in part-time students placed additional strain on the College's service units. Five programs and four projects underwent extensive evaluations. Proposals for new programs for academic development and interpreters for the deaf were submitted, along with a resubmission of a proposal for the ongoing funding of theatre arts, theatre production, and arts administration. Assessment materials implemented in the fall of 1983 for faculty evaluation and development continued to be reviewed and refined.

The increase in activity and enrolment forced College and Student Services to extend itself almost beyond capacity, resulting in extended evening hours and multi-campus services. Although the computerized student information system allowed faster processing of applications and registrations, the record level of full-time student enrolments contributed to mounting pressures. Faced with a 65 percent increase in counselling demand, College and Student Services still managed a number of notable achievements at this time, including the introduction of special counselling for disabled students, an increase in the number of student workshops, events for international students, and counselling for outreach and summer students. Participation in recreation and athletics was at an all-time high.

Largely as a result of the emphasis President Kelly placed on how the College image was communicated to the Edmonton community, there was a great increase in the quality and amount of College advertising, including media campaigns and major displays at exhibitions, career fairs, and trade shows. He believed recognition by the community and government would help GMCC to gain the support and funding needed to build a new campus. *MacEwan Today*, a bi-weekly employee newspaper, began production in 1983, and the Community Relations Department received communications awards in recognition of its outstanding work from the International Association of Business Communicators (IABC) and the Association of Canadian College and University Information Bureaus.

Internal College communications, however, remained a persistent problem. In a study conducted in 1982 as a graduate student in educational administration, Julie Lazaruk, section head of the nursing program, found that a major concern for students was "the need for improvement in communication between programs, campuses and administration."[33]

Managing Continuing Growth

Kelly believed that his role as college president was first and foremost as an educator sensitive to the teaching and learning process. Nevertheless, he recognized that a president must have the skills of a general manager as well. His administrative style was illustrated by a paper he presented at the Association of Canadian Community Colleges conference in Montreal in July 1983 as part of a panel discussion on the roles of presidents and boards of governors:

> Gone are the days when the new president could simply emerge from the teaching ranks—be good at public relations with the Board—and leave the overall management of the institution to fate or an illusion that it runs itself.

> ...on top of this (managerial skills and talents required of college presidents) a new and interesting role for many Canadian college presidents is that of fund-raising!

> The Board of Governors, the majority of whom are lay community members, are entrusted by the provincial governments to develop policy and monitor the overall direction of the college.

> The roles of the president as an agent of the board and the board itself are quite interdependent, but in order to be effective, there are key distinctions which must be made—particularly the distinction between development of policy (board's role) and implementation of policy (management's role).[34]

Exceeding expectations, enrolment in 1983–84 increased 18 percent and was now listed at 3,600 full-time equivalent students. This represented a 50 percent increase in enrolment over the previous three years. Budgetary increases for the College, however, were marginal during this period of enrolment growth. Student demand for programs continued to rise and additional space was leased to create additional classrooms. Rooms in a pool hall neighbouring the Jasper Place Campus provided some relief to the pressures of overcrowding! The College continued to make an extensive effort to acquire more space. A campus in northeast Edmonton to replace the Cromdale facility remained a high priority, and steps were initiated to lease space in the downtown core as an interim measure and to provide a downtown presence for the College's Business Division. This measure was intended as a vital strategic first step toward the realization of a proposed new campus for the downtown core.

In off-campus activity, the Yellowhead and Pembina Educational Consortia continued to provide educational services to as many as 20 different communities outside of Edmonton. The College also graduated its first outreach students in general business administration in Hinton, in correctional services at Blue Quills, and in the teacher assistant program in Grouard. Faculty and staff continued to participate in development programs and the library introduced a computerized system.

But financial restraint remained a reality. Increased student enrolment put an additional burden on already overcrowded facilities and demand for additional services grew. The solution to these problems was an interim one at best, and new facilities were badly needed.

College and Student Services remained under pressure. The number of applications continued to rise and the demand for extended services was unrelenting. Recognizing the importance of fund-raising to the future of the College, the administrative structure of College and Student Services was revamped to allow staff to devote more time to duties related to the GMCC Foundation. This resulted in an acting director of student services being appointed.

The College experienced a 25 percent increase in intramural participation and students won medals in volleyball and basketball in Alberta Colleges Athletics Conference (ACAC) competitions.[35] The College hosted ACAC golf, bowling, and badminton tournaments.

The Community Relations Department continued to produce work of high quality. The "Grant MacEwan Works" and "Downtown Bound" public relations campaigns stood the test of comparison with similar materials produced anywhere, and the department received awards from the Alberta Print '84 Graphic Artists Exhibition for symbols for Continuing and Consumer Education.

Peter Kossowan was appointed as the new board chair on September 15, 1983. Outgoing chair Bill Lord predicted even tighter budgetary constraints which might force a restructuring of education at all levels. He reminded the board that "student concerns must be paramount—without them, there would be no need for a Board of Governors."[36] His major disappointment was that a northwest campus was no nearer to fruition.

> The concept of the College is growing; people now know it exists and what it does. It has a history of good people and known achievers. The Board's challenge now is to take the College from adolescence into adulthood, thereby enhancing its contribution to the community.[37]

According to Gerry Kelly, the opportunity to be creative is one of the most enjoyable aspects of the duties associated with the office of a college president.[38] During the years of his service to Grant MacEwan Community College, President Kelly would be instrumental in a number of lesser, yet nonetheless noteworthy, accomplishments. In 1983, an idea of his resulted in a new benefit offered by Student Study Services—the Grammar Hotline. Its function was to provide answers to questions concerning grammar usage, ranging from the simple to the complex. The Hotline, located at the Jasper Place Campus, was well received; soon the outside community began placing calls to the College in order to "fine-tune" sentence structure, vocabulary, and spelling. In the years to come, Kelly would also be instrumental in establishing an instructional development fund supported by surplus monies and fostering board support for university transfer programs and faculty sabbaticals.

Meeting the Challenge—The Mid-80s

Grant MacEwan Community College was clearly responsive to the community in the mid-1980s. Responsiveness, however, involved meeting serious challenges. The main challenge for 1984–85 was to cope with high student demand, overcrowded facilities, and continued funding problems.

In 1984–85, the College accommodated 3,700 full-time equivalent students in facilities designed for 2,800. In total, over 14,400 people registered for College credit and non-credit courses. The number of applicants greatly exceeded the space available, forcing the College to apply quotas to all programs. However, the success of College graduates was undeniable; 84 percent of them were employed within six months of graduation and another 8 percent went on for further education. Major revisions were implemented in the Audiovisual Technician, Correctional Services, and Occupational Health Nursing programs in order to provide a level of training that would meet community needs. Proposals for new programs in business administration, visual arts, and university transfer were presented to the Department of Advanced Education. The Grant MacEwan Community College Foundation was increasing in importance, having set a goal of raising $6 million over the course of a five-year fund-raising plan.

A budget surplus in 1984–85 was attributed to improved budgeting practices and financial monitoring systems, coupled with unexpended funds allocated for a major facility lease. The surplus allowed the College administration to fund projects in instructional development, international education, faculty development, and future capital facilities replacement.

Performing and Visual Arts students gained recognition throughout the province and across Canada. Two stage bands from the music program area went to Quebec City for the national finals. Theatre productions were successful at the local Fringe Festival and on tour, while the dance programs were allocated an entire evening of performance at the TriBach Festival in Edmonton.

University Transfer

Chuck Day recalled the establishment of university transfer courses as one of the major developments at GMCC during his time at the College.[39] During the 1970s, the College had opposed a formal university transfer program but did request credit recognition for some courses taken in diploma programs. The individual course transfer system was brought up as early as 1971, when the College established its first transferability committee.

In April 1973, when GMCC submitted a brief to the Task Force on Entrance Requirements to the University of Alberta, the frustration in dealing with this issue was obvious. After Chuck Day and Bob Leong met in May with university representatives to discuss the course transferability issue, it was recommended that:

> ...the Board record with the Minister of Advanced Education and the President of the University of Alberta that if the quality of teaching of the graduates of the University of Alberta hired by Grant MacEwan Community College is inadequate to meet transferability requirements, this college will have to review its policy of hiring graduates from the University of Alberta.[40]

The Task Force was clear in its assessment of the "gulf" between the university and colleges, and in its view that relationships between the university and colleges and institutes required review and improvement. In 1975, Day cited admission and advanced credit (advanced standing), as the two primary aspects concerning transferability.[41]

The University of Alberta's influence, once dominant in transfer relationships, had diminished since the establishment of the University of Calgary and its negotiation of independent transfer arrangements with Mount Royal College.[42] In general, the University of Alberta was reluctant to pay attention to the Task Force recommendations. It was only when Minister of Advanced Education Jim Foster initiated the steps toward creating general transfer policies and guidelines that a province-wide transfer system began to take shape. Meetings with Alberta's four universities and six colleges led to the formation of the Alberta Council on Admissions and Transfer (ACAT) in 1974.[43] For GMCC, initial agreements with the University of Alberta were reached through a slow and tedious process. As Day noted:

> It was obvious that the University had not resolved the basic question—who has the authority to speak for the University in matters related to transferability?[44]

Board Chairman Peter Kossowan and Gerald Kelly with Culture Minister
Horst Schmidt and Dr. MacEwan

The Alberta Council on Admissions and Transfer set about preparing a formalized set of policies and procedures pertaining to admissions and advanced credit assessment that have undergone constant refinement to the present day. It may be perceived as a far from perfect arrangement, but it was far superior to the arrangements existing in other provinces.

During his first three years of the presidency, Kelly gradually convinced the GMCC board that full university transfer programs would enhance the College's overall mandate. The College and the University of Alberta were close to an agreement about transfers in 1984, but the university still expressed serious reservations over the College's admission policy and mandate.[45] Recently appointed University of Alberta President Myer Horowitz, cited by Kelly as a strong advocate for a community college role in transfer programming,[46] offered his personal opinion that the university should advocate university transfer programs.

By March 15, 1984, an initiative to establish university transfer programming was taken in the form of a recommendation to file a letter of intent for university transfer parallel programming with the Department of Advanced Education. On May 17, 1984, President Kelly advised the board that the Department of Advanced Education had indicated that the University of Alberta might not be able to enrol all qualified students, and had asked how quickly Grant MacEwan Community College could move to accommodate them.

Information was submitted to the deputy minister and final approval was required through the board and Academic Council if directed to move by the minister. At its retreat on November 21 and 22, 1986, the board unanimously reaffirmed its commitment and support for the further development of university transfer programming. To this end, the board directed the introduction of a first-year university transfer program in commerce, within the limits of approved resources. Further, the board was to work with administration to obtain government approval for university transfer programming in other areas as soon as possible.

The university transfer function provided GMCC with a level of independence and, in a sense, further established the institution's credibility. President Kelly remarked:

> ...there has been a need in the Edmonton community for students to be able to attend a smaller institution, to be in classrooms that are student-centred, with teachers whose primary responsibility is teaching.

> The Council on Admissions and Transfer was set up in the mid 1970s with the support of then Advanced Education Deputy Minister, Wally Worth, followed by Henry Kolesar. Jim Foster, Minister of Advanced Education, at the time, lent political clout to the process by threatening to legislate transfer, if need be. Colleges offer university transfer programming as a result of Alberta government approval to offer transfer. That approval does not come from the University of Alberta, although success of transfer is contingent upon consultation with the university. Transfer relationships between colleges and universities are governed by the rules and regulations set out in the transfer guide. Colleges offer programs because they have government approval, not because a particular university says so.[47]

A proposal developed by Peter Furstenau, Allen Watson, and Harry Davis that outlined three options as to how GMCC could respond to community demand for university transfer programming was presented to Deputy Minister of Advanced Education Lynne Duncan in a letter dated January 13, 1988. University transfer programming was to encompass a blend of arts, science, and commerce. In February 1988 the Department of Advanced Education announced the minister's approval for the College to provide university transfer programming comparable to that offered by any other community college in the province. Over 40 new courses were developed and 11 new instructional staff were hired in response to this development.

The City Centre Concept, 1980 to 1990: Promoting a Dream

Nothing happens unless first a dream. Carl Sandburg

As might be expected for a youthful college, the planning and development of new facilities has been a continuing and pervasive theme. As previously mentioned, the need for a major "core campus" facility was expressed as early as 1969.[48] The idea of a core facility was again raised in the 1970s; however, plans were never pursued to the point of acquiring the necessary financial resources and a suitable building site.[49] Under John Haar, the College decided to develop small multi-campus facilities around the city. Unfortunately, these facilities were inefficient and expensive to operate.

In August 1981 the board moved to make representations to the minister of advanced education to consider expanding GMCC to include a small northeast campus. The appointment of Gerry Kelly as president gave a great deal of momentum to the idea of expansion. Kelly led efforts to change the 1981 board policy[50] that favoured small campuses throughout the city. The issue was how to gain the government's political and financial support for a major campus, most likely located in the downtown area.

By the 1981–82 academic year, Kelly concluded:

> ...the policy of small campuses was dangerously detrimental to GMCC's future and would continue to make us facilities poor. Shortly after arriving at the College, I realized an inordinate amount of administrators' time was spent dealing with space and facilities problems. The provincial politics of campus construction meant that GMCC was continually being short-changed by its own small campus policy. For example, Red Deer College, with far less enrolments than GMCC, built a theatre in 1982 which was almost the equivalent cost of the entire Jasper Place Campus built in 1980. Mount Royal College in Calgary, with enrolments similar to GMCC's, received funds to expand an already beautiful and expensive campus three times the total amount spent in the history of all GMCC facilities—a total of $60 million. One of the ongoing political arguments used in Calgary was that GMCC in Edmonton had also just built a whole new campus—no mention was made that the cost was only $13 million....[51]

During the 1980s, the Board of Governors' commitment to expansion, encouraged by the College's administration, cannot be overlooked. Devotion to this cause is evident throughout the board minutes of the time. By October 1981, the board was prepared to lobby MLAs and city officials in its effort to promote a new campus. Despite the provincial government's reluctance to fund the construction of a new core campus, the board's proposal gained a favourable response from the City of Edmonton.

The board originally looked at replacing the Cromdale facility.[52] A northeast campus planning committee was formed in 1982 and funding requests for such a campus were included in the College's five-year capital plans. The president, city alderman June Cavanaugh, and some board members held several town hall meetings in northeast Edmonton. The northeast location did not generate the required political support from Edmonton MLAs, but lobbying from the board continued. Kelly became increasingly aware of the need to approach the issue of facilities development from a new angle:

> In 1982–83, it became obvious that despite spending countless hours trying to rally the community of northeast Edmonton that the provincial government and our own Department of Advanced Education were just not interested in funding a new campus in that area.
>
> GMCC needed to find a better location and tie it in with another politically supportable objective, if possible.[53]

Some assiduous political wrangling was required to push forward the concept of a campus for the downtown core. President Kelly's plans for a downtown campus encompassed a much broader scope than was envisioned by earlier designs. The Board of Governors was at this time highly political, and not all members received Kelly's suggestions regarding campus development favourably.[54] Kelly astutely tied his proposals to previous ideas. Referring to the strategy and tactics behind this decision, Kelly recalled:

> One way for me to overcome the board's resistance was to fall back to early 1970s plans—more like discussion papers on facilities development that made some mention of a campus close to the downtown area. Besides that I noted the College had started with a six-room administrative office in the heart of downtown. I explained to the board that this idea of a city centre campus wasn't just a figment of my "liberal" mind—rather it was, in a sense, a return to our original plans and roots. The board cautiously agreed to allow me to pursue a presentation to the Mayor's Task Force along with the current board chairman.[55]

In addition to convincing the board, Kelly still faced the challenge of gaining support for a downtown campus from the media, the MLAs, city council, the entire business community, and the federal government.

The apprehension of the GMCC Board of Governors was hardly disguised. At least one board member wanted any new campus to be located in their own suburban constituency. Others were somewhat overwhelmed when Kelly had architect Dennis Christianson prepare and present a fully developed campus model at the May 4, 1984, board meeting. Christianson's 15-minute presentation included a film showing various examples of Scandinavian architecture and a table model representing his perception of a downtown campus that incorporated "images" developed from previously built educational facilities. The model sat outside Kelly's office for several months before it mysteriously disappeared.

By mid-1984, the board was prepared to give serious consideration to a city centre location for a major campus.[56] The board approved the College administration's proposal to develop the concept of a central campus which would include educational, cultural, recreational, and residential facilities. A site was desirable that would accommodate a long-term vision of campus growth (50–100 years). The initial design was to accommodate 4,500 students, with the capability to expand to 15,000 students within twenty years.

On May 17, 1984, the president accompanied by the board chair made a presentation to the "Mayor's Task Force on the Heart of the City." Mayor Laurence Decore appointed local lawyer Joe Shoctor to head the task force which was to examine the topic of downtown revitalization. Having attended a downtown university campus, McGill University, Kelly remembered how that institution served as a catalyst for vibrant life in downtown Montreal.[57] Struck with the idea that a GMCC campus might possibly tie in with the politics of revitalization, he met with Shoctor and explained the idea of a downtown campus, likely located on the current CN railyards. Coincidentally, Shoctor's wife was a McGill University graduate, and "Joe," Kelly noted, "immediately became excited about the idea."[58]

On June 23, 1984, support for the idea on the board was gaining momentum and the following lobby plan was developed regarding the proposed city centre campus:

1. The City Centre Approval Committee will consider the hiring of an outside consultant to firm up a game plan for approval.

2. Arrangements will be made for a reception in September with Board members and aldermen.

3. All MLA's who did not attend the reception held June 18th are to be sent copies of the "Downtown Bound" brochure and related information.

4. Each Board member agreed to lobby with at least one City

Council member. A listing of specific contacts will be mailed to aldermen prior to their being contacted.[59]

The College received very favourable attention from the "Mayor's Task Force on the Heart of the City." Kelly noted on October 29, 1984, that the board had moved away from the policy of small decentralized campuses and endorsed the concept of a central campus with some satellite campuses. During a meeting with the minister of advanced education, he asked for support from the ministry as well.

Although attention had already been drawn to the CN location politically, a more objective analysis was needed. The architectural firm MacKenzie Spencer Associates Ltd. was asked to identify alternative sites in the city centre area and to analyze the pros and cons of each.

On October 29, 1984, Minister of Advanced Education Dick Johnson, not an enthusiastic supporter, responded to intensive lobbying by the board, stating that the GMCC board must decide whether it wanted to continue providing regional multi-campus education or consolidate its operation.[60]

The seven years between the meeting with the Mayor's Task Force and the beginning of construction on the City Centre Campus in 1991 were dominated by the desire to keep the College responsive to enrolment demand while maintaining support for the downtown campus. A great deal of behind-the-scenes lobbying with significant opinion leaders in the business community and the three levels of government was imperative. Kelly was a master at this process. A case in point occurred in 1984 when an article written by William Thorsell appeared in the *Edmonton Journal*:

> If downtown Edmonton needs help from many sources, other players can also benefit from downtown Edmonton.
>
> Grant MacEwan Community College, for example, is not yet what it could be, and the prospect of a downtown campus makes considerable sense. MacEwan's Jasper Place campus is already over capacity, Mill Woods is too small and isolated to serve city-wide needs, and the rather tacky Cromdale campus was meant to be temporary.
>
> MacEwan now has 3,400 full-time students in facilities designed for 2,700, and projects 6,400 students by 1989. There are 9,000 people taking credit courses, another 11,000 in non-credit activities. The college administration would very much like a central campus to accommodate immediate needs and growth of adult education.

Aerial view of the CN railyards, showing their proximity to existing downtown development (1989)

The province could address two problems at once by building MacEwan's main campus on CN railyards just north of 104th Avenue. Mary LeMessurier is MLA for the area and appears supportive of the idea. What the rest of the Edmonton caucus thinks is anybody's guess—if they think of good things like this at all.

Better than a traditional campus, we might conceive a MacEwan "network" through more varied urban redevelopment. Whatever, the prospect of 10,000 students of all ages converging on downtown night and day must have Joe Shoctor smiling.

Joe, meet Mary.[61]

Thorsell was certainly well informed. Indeed, the impetus for his knowledgeable commentary can be traced to Kelly, who wrote to Thorsell after hearing his presentation to the Rotary Club on downtown revitalization three months earlier:

> ...I began to wonder what role Grant MacEwan Community College, in attempting to be the community's college, might play in this development.
>
> For example, might a large college campus which includes a concert hall, other community facilities and attracts thousands of adults to the downtown area during evenings and weekends be a key piece in the downtown development puzzle?[62]

Cultivating support for the City Centre Campus included many activities and involved many people. A number of significant events contributed to making the downtown campus a reality. Bettie Hewes, an alderman at the time, was appointed chair of the board of CN. After Kelly visited her twice in her Montreal office in 1984, Hewes expressed support for the idea. Kelly supported the appointments of new members of the GMCC Board of Governors who were politically influential and enthusiastic about the proposed City Centre Campus. They included John Steffensen, Fred Singer, and Rick Angus (who engineered access to Premier Don Getty's office) and Ralph Young, who chaired the Facilities Planning Committee and provided lobbying leadership for the campus with City Council and the government.[63]

The importance of civic acceptance for Grant MacEwan Community College was never more evident than during this period. Kelly was the principal source of information about the College's facilities concerns. When Olive Elliot, of the *Edmonton Journal*, commented on GMCC's facilities problems in 1987, few people realized that the information in her article was supplied by Kelly.

Following five years of what Gerry Kelly called "intensive planning, lobbying, scheming, and dreaming,"[64] the City Centre Campus was announced on April 28, 1988. Premier Don Getty committed $100 million for the City Centre Campus—an amount that represented the largest single capital project in the history of the Department of Advanced Education. The new campus was to contain 775,000 square feet of space and would accommodate 4,500 full-time equivalent students. This would eventually enable the combined campuses of GMCC to serve up to 10,000 students. The campus would be designed as a comprehensive, full-service facility, including instructional, social, recreational, cultural, meeting, and conference facilities for community use.

Dr. Kelly summarizes the events that lead to this most noteworthy announcement:

...the growth of Grant MacEwan can be viewed in three phases. From its opening in 1971 until 1976, the College grew dramatically, from around 400 to 2,500 full time equivalent (FTE) enrolments. Over the next five years, enrolments remained basically stable, largely as the result of limited facilities to accommodate further growth. Since 1981, the College has again experienced significant and steady growth, in response to ever increasing community demand for post-secondary education. Despite an enrolment increase of nearly 85 percent since 1980–81, demand for College programs continues to exceed capacity by more than five to one.

This high demand can be explained in large part by the College's emphasis on high quality education, and the level of success enjoyed by our graduates.[65]

Kelly noted that the enrolment trends and programming demands of the previous six to seven years indicated the need for the construction of a new purpose-built facility to house at least 4,000 FTE students. The combined purpose-built campuses, including Mill Woods and Jasper Place, would place the capacity of GMCC at around 6,500 FTE, a figure that would be reached, it was predicted, by the mid-1990s. The new facility and future role the College would play within the community were significant. As Kelly emphasized:

...it should be clear why, at the end of the 1987–88 year, Grant MacEwan Community College was viewing its future development with considerable optimism. Planning had begun on the most significant capital project in its history—a main campus which will provide the College with the capacity to meet more effectively than ever the needs of its community for educational services....it is the human activity of teaching and learning that is the College's reason for existence—the new campus development will simply provide Grant MacEwan with more effective tools for achieving its purpose.[66]

Opening of the new facility was set to coincide with the end of the College's lease of the Seventh Street Plaza facility. The $100 million approval included $65–70 million for campus construction, $6–7 million for architectural planning and management fees, $10–12 million for furnishings and equipment, and $7–10 million for utilities and site preparation involving landscaping, roadways, parking, and so on. The cost of land acquisition was not included. Approval of the Canadian National land acquisition for the City Centre Campus was noted at the October 20, 1988, board meeting. As could be expected, the construction of the City Centre Campus began to take priority in most of the board's affairs.[67]

The foregoing should not imply that everything was now in place for the new campus. Kelly recalled:

> Even after the campus was approved in 1988, it was still touch and go politically—it was delayed once. Several new Board members lead by Chair John Ramsey, Vi Becker, Phyllis Anderson, and Werner Jappsen re-intensified the efforts with Government.[68]

Nevertheless, a major downtown campus for Grant MacEwan Community College was wholeheartedly supported by the Downtown Development Corporation, the Downtown Business Association, and the Chamber of Commerce—again supplied with an abundance of information by the president.

Another key development in the City Centre Campus story is worthy of mention. The auspicious hiring of a new vice-president, administration, provided the College with an individual qualified to bring everything together. On Barry Snowden's appointment in 1985, Kelly reminisced:

> Another fortuitous circumstance lead to the hiring of Barry Snowden, whom I met at a house party. I knew Barry had been involved in building Lethbridge University and was responsible for the development of Athabasca University. Barry was captivated by the novel, and perhaps crazy, idea that we would convince CN to give up its cross-Canada rail connection in downtown Edmonton and build on it one of the biggest one-time college campuses in the world. His experience, savvy at dealing with Advanced Education, and knowledge of educational facilities made him the right man in the right place at a time when we had to make sure it was going to be right with our sponsor—the Government of Alberta.

> As vice president, Barry was instrumental not only in planning for the City Centre Campus but also in helping to ensure that the College's financial affairs were kept in good order. This was one of our keys to stabilizing the growth mode of the College, assuring that our program expansions were always on solid financial footing. If the College had overexposed itself during the tumultuous growth in the '80s, it is unlikely we would ever have had the confidence of the Department of Advanced Education to build a new campus.[69]

Snowden relished the challenge of building a new campus, although he was not without doubts about its feasibility. "When I was told by Gerry Kelly of the plans to move the railyards for the City Centre Campus, I thought it was a crazy idea," said Snowden, "but, just in case it could be done, I wanted to be a part of it."[70]

During the next few years, political commitments for the initial approval of the campus in 1988 wavered back and forth. In the 1988 provincial election, the City of Edmonton had elected a large number of Liberal MLAs, and the College lost many of its Conservative supporters in government. Meanwhile, it was important for the College to demonstrate the need for expanded space by continuing to grow even though grants were severely curtailed at this time. The College did this, according to Kelly, "through budget efficiencies resulting from excellent work done by our vice presidents, deans, and program chairs."[71]

Barry Snowden
GMCC Vice President, Administration

Looking back, Kelly described some interesting activities after the 26 acre site for the new campus was purchased from CN on October 5, 1989.

> We couldn't let people think this project was on hold, which it was! In fact, active political forces were looking for the opportunity to kill it. Fortunately, we had an equally active board and Premier Don Getty on our side. Activity on the site was needed! Fifty foot letters urged "Go Oilers Go" during the 1989 Stanley Cup playoffs. Three months later, an exact scale chalked outline of the City Centre Campus appeared on the site. Of course, it was noticed by the downtown business community from their high-rise office windows, as well as by MLAs who regularly flew over the site to land at Edmonton's municipal airport.[72]

The College breathed a sigh of relief when it learned that Premier Getty had insisted that initial campus development funds be included in the government's 1989 budget.

The Edmonton Downtown Development Corporation, of which Kelly was a founding member, reaffirmed support for the City Centre Campus in a letter to Premier Getty on November 15, 1990. It was predicted that this campus would generate more than 800 jobs during its three-year construction period, bring 8 to 10 thousand students into the downtown core daily, add an estimated $7 million in retail sales and create up to 100 new jobs in the retail sector, serve business and community agencies through more than 1,000 field placements, and provide cultural and recreational facilities for the community.

Chalked outline of buildings on the site of the future City Centre Campus

During the winter of 1990, the College was permitted to utilize some of the existing funding to site service the City Centre Campus location. The city hooked up water and sewage and thirty-foot-deep ditches were excavated. Kelly and Snowden decided to leave piles of earth on the site to give the appearance that campus work was underway. Finally, construction on the City Centre Campus started in June 1991. The incredible amount of work done by all people associated with the College was to be recognized, and future College students would have a facility comparable to that enjoyed by their counterparts elsewhere in Alberta.

The timing was right for Grant MacEwan Community College. Through the College's marketing efforts, community demand for College programs was very high during the 1980s, and without this interest it is likely the City Centre Campus would have remained only a concept. But the City Centre Campus became a reality through an approach taken by the Kelly administration that emphasized "partnership" in the planning and development of the institution. Community needs converged with a plan and a vision, and once a suitable location was made available through the efforts of the College's administration, the plan became congruent with the need for downtown revitalization. Added to this was the fortunate circumstance that construction costs were within realistic expectations. For the driving force behind the City Centre Campus, Gerry Kelly, the new facility was:

> ...the work of hundreds of College employees, students,
> community leaders, particularly our board, that helped MacEwan
> to become a dynamic, responsive, and growth-oriented college in

114

the '80s. Although it is an absolute thrill and privilege for me to see the notion of the campus, fuelled by a burning sense of mission, become a reality, the City Centre Campus is largely testimony to the success of all who participated in "growing" the College.[73]

New Structures and Programs: 1984 to 1988

Although College administrators and the Board of Governors devoted much of their time and energy during the 1980s to securing approval and funding for the new central campus, staff and student concerns remained priorities. On September 20, 1984, a new administrative structure was announced: the dean of administrative affairs became vice-president, administration; the dean of instruction became vice-president, academic; and the dean of College and Student Services became vice-president, College and Student Services.

Also in 1984, Kelly presented to the Board a proposal to proclaim one day in February as "Grant MacEwan Day" at the College in honour of Dr. MacEwan. It was wholeheartedly endorsed, and Grant MacEwan Day has been observed ever since. Grant MacEwan has used this day to visit the College and tour its various campuses. His bus trips to Edmonton from his Calgary home and overnight stays at the downtown YMCA have become part of the MacEwan legend, and his personal visits have made MacEwan Day an eagerly anticipated event. Since 1986, another annual feature of MacEwan Day has been the presentation of the MacEwan Medallion to an outstanding College employee.[74]

The College's mission, multi-campus perspectives, long-range facilities plans, and the concept of university transfer were discussed at a retreat on November 16 and 17, 1984. In conducting a self-evaluation exercise for board members at this retreat, Dr. Abe Konrad had been asked to focus less on evaluation and more on role development. The evaluation was designed, first, to examine the role perceptions of board members and other college constituency members; second, to evaluate the actual performance of the board; and third, to clarify the results of the evaluation. It appears that, unlike his earlier attempt at this task, Konrad's 1984 board evaluation effort went smoothly.

By the 1985–86 academic year, College enrolment had reached nearly 4,000 full-time equivalent students in credit programs. This was an increase of more than 6 percent from the previous year. In total, Grant MacEwan Community College now had over 14,000 people enrolled in credit and non-credit courses. The greatest indicator of its success was that nearly 80 percent of graduates found employment in their respective areas of study within six months of graduation, and another 11 percent went on for further study. Operating expenditures, however, grew only 3 percent during 1985–86, and as a result only modest increases were made to the numbers of staff and faculty.

The shortage of classroom space continued to be a problem. On January 16, 1986, the Board of Governors authorized the engagement of Resource Management Consultants to undertake a master planning study. Following the completion of this study, the minister of advanced education granted permission to the College to lease 15,000 square metres, on an interim basis, in Edmonton's downtown core. The Seventh Street Plaza Campus was the result of many political manoeuvres between the administration, the deputy minister, and an unconvinced ministry. It served, however, to establish a "beachhead" and demonstrate the viability of a GMCC presence in the city centre. After this new facility was obtained, some programs were relocated and the most extensive renovations in the College's history were undertaken. Twenty-eight programs, college administrative offices, and over 2,000 students and staff were affected by this development.

The Cromdale Campus became a community education and outreach centre concentrating on continuing education programs and services, including English as a second language and consumer education. Long-term planning was given priority and a facilities master plan project, supported by the Department of Advanced Education, was initiated though a market assessment study and review of the College's facilities master plan.

By this time, the establishment of a major new campus was an extremely high priority. Financial initiatives were now set in place that relied less and less on direct funding from the government. Cost-recovery outreach programming, for example, accounted for approximately 20 percent of College revenues and the GMCC Foundation continued to strive toward meeting the $6 million dollar objective of its fund-raising campaign initiated in 1984–85.

College and Student Services was streamlined in an attempt to offer better services to full- and part-time students. Information centres were established at each campus to be responsible for registration, records information, awards, student finance, and scheduling, and were open for extended hours. Athletics, recreation, and intramurals continued to be successful programs and the women's basketball team finished in first place in its ACAC regular season.

The Community Relations Department maintained a vigorous approach to public relations through various themes such as "Right in Your Own Backyard," the 1984–85 slogan which emphasized the accessibility of the College to the community.

Although alumni were nominally recognized in the early years of the College, it was not until 1985–86 that an Alumni Association was established in its present form. A seven-member executive included a part-time alumni officer who operated out of the Community Relations Department. One of the first goals set by the Alumni Association was to raise $70,000 for the Student Activities/Alumni Centre planned for the proposed City Centre Campus. Community college alumni generally recognize individual programs more than the institution itself, a point John Haar emphasized in 1977, when he observed, "Most college students do not enter a college, they enter a program."[75] The development of new and impressive facilities could provide a challenge to this assumption.

Seventh Street Plaza Campus, 1986

The 1986–87 academic year was the College's 15th anniversary. Forty credit programs were now offered and over 19,000 full- and part-time, credit and non-credit students were served. Full-time equivalent students now numbered 4,300, an increase of 8.8 percent from the previous year. Non-credit enrolment increased nearly 60 percent to over 11,000 people. Even more dramatic was the fact that 89 percent of the College's 1986 graduates who entered the workforce were finding employment within six months of graduation. The downside to this success was that increased popularity led to increased demand for limited space. The College received over 6,000 applications for less than 2,000 first-year program places.

The Business Division was now housed in the Seventh Street Plaza Campus. This location allowed many students to gain practical experience in downtown businesses through field placements, and to have valuable interactions with business and government professionals hired as part-time instructors. In addition, advisory committee membership was greatly enhanced through the use of the business community as an "extended classroom."

Planning was now a solid part of the College agenda. A market assessment study, a review of the College's facilities master plan, and an updated Institutional Development Plan that integrated program, service, and facilities development were undertaken at this time. This planning culminated in the Board of Governors' endorsement of the concept of a main campus, plus satellites, as the future model for development. A target date of 1992 was set for the opening of the City Centre Campus, as this date coincided with the expiration of the lease agreement for the Seventh Street Plaza Campus.

In 1986–87 a new certificate program was developed in International Business. In addition, curriculum materials were designed for university transfer courses in arts and commerce, and course materials were revised for independent learning and distance delivery in the Occupational Health Nursing, Rehabilitation Practitioner, and Voluntary Sector Management programs. An office for multicultural and Native programming was established to coordinate relevant instructional and student services.

A government-sponsored *Equity Study into Post-Secondary Operating Grants in Alberta* indicated that costs per student remained relatively stable at this time. As a reflection of the increasing importance of fund-raising, Dr. Terry Flannigan was promoted by the president to assume full-time responsibility for the GMCC Foundation. A significant donation from Dr. Charles Allard led to the establishment of an endowed chair; the Allard Chair in Business enabled experts from outside the College to participate in the Business Division for an academic year. The GMCC Foundation was fortunate in its early history to have matching funds from the Alberta Advanced Education Endowment and Incentive Fund, established by the Department of Advanced Education to encourage private sector contributions to Alberta post-secondary institutions.

The additional space available in the Seventh Street Plaza Campus allowed enrolment in the Business Division to increase over 13 percent. Nevertheless, it was the Community Education Division, housed on the Cromdale Campus, that experienced the most growth. With an increase of nearly 20 percent, outreach programs accounted for approximately one-third of the College's total FTE. New programs developed at this time included Security and various majors in Voluntary Sector Management. University transfer programming in arts and commerce continued to expand. A co-op accounting program was also introduced at this time. The Insurance Administration, Microcomputer Management, and Teacher Aide Programs were evaluated.

Alberta post-secondary institutions now exchanged expertise and GMCC conducted curriculum development workshops at Lakeland College, Red Deer College, and Olds College, along with workshops in

Edmonton on faculty and program evaluation. This was in addition to a number of program-related workshops and conferences, the most notable of which were the Teacher Aide Conference and Family Violence Conference that attracted a total of over 2,000 participants.

By now, fiscal restraint was a fact of life. It seemed that each year involved greater adjustments to support increased enrolment demands and to provide better services with limited resources. Limitations on operating and capital grants required the adjustment of financial planning and budgeting methods. As a result, a multi-year financial planning strategy was introduced that extended opportunities to a maximum number of potential students while maintaining appropriate levels of quality. Two-year agreements were reached with faculty and non-academic staff and a new faculty sabbatical program successfully completed its first year of operation.

One of the major concerns in 1986–87 involved computer technology. New technology soon became old technology, and constant revision and modification were required in order to keep up-to-date. Microcomputers were now an integral part of classroom instruction and commonplace in the administrative area. In order to respond to the need for training and support, the Systems and Computers Department was established. Among other things, the department recommended the acquisition of appropriate hardware.

The College continued to provide services and support to the Yellowhead and Pembina Regional Educational Consortia. College and Student Services, after the separation of the GMCC Foundation from the division, was renamed Student Services and Community Relations. The division also assumed the responsibility for the coordination of the College's international education activities, and formed an International Education Office. Athletics, intramurals, and recreation remained popular and the College soccer team won the ACAC championship and hosted the National College Championships.

Community Relations continued to focus on themes, and its six-month public awareness campaign "GMCC Enterprise" was considered a prime reason for the successful relocation of the Business Division to the Seventh Street Plaza Campus. Community Relations used a proactive approach in response to a marketing plan developed and implemented at this time that reinforced the College's motto—"Lifelong learning, responsive to the community."

The Alumni Association was becoming a more viable entity. As mentioned previously, working with and identifying alumni is difficult for community colleges. The identification and location of over 70 percent of the College's graduates and the number of fund-raising

*Advanced Education Minister Dave Russell and President Kelly
at kickoff of "GMCC Enterprise" Campaign*

activities held in support of the planned Student Activities/Alumni Centre are clear indications of the outstanding work that was being done in this area.

Among other prominent developments at the College in 1988, the Ukrainian Resource Development Centre[76] and the Senior Studies Institute were established, and in October the Students' Association began publishing its *Intercamp* bulletin.

College enrolments continued to grow. For the 1987–88 academic year, almost 17,000 people enrolled in credit programs and another 25,000 in non-credit offerings, an increase of over 10 percent from the previous year. The extent of the College's outreach activities was truly remarkable. Fourteen major conferences were coordinated by the Conference Management Centre and credit programs were offered at Blue Quills Native Education Centre, Muskwachees Cultural College, and Yukon College, and through the College's continued involvement with the Yellowhead and Pembina Educational Consortia. The Nurse Credentialling Program was brokered through agencies in New Brunswick and Prince Edward Island, and planned for in Nova Scotia and Newfoundland. On the advice of College staff, this program was even adopted at Curtin University in Perth, Australia.

Evaluations of the Travel Consultant, Audiovisual Communications, and Visual Communications programs and specific areas of the Accounting Co-op, Interpreter Training, and Secretarial Studies programs were completed. Program and faculty evaluations were now systematic processes. Parallel evaluative methods were developed and pilot tested for program and section heads, and similar systems began to be developed for deans and directors. Overall, reduction of the base operating grant and capital grants continued. The registrar's office began to employ new projection mechanisms for improving the College's enrolment management procedures.

International education was given considerable attention within the Student Services Department, and projects were initiated in seven different countries in Asia, Africa, and South America.

The men's basketball team won the ACAC gold medal and a bronze medal in the Canadian Championships, and one student, Aine Humble, won the national championship gold medal in the Canadian Colleges Women's Singles Badminton Championships.

Community Relations received first place recognition among colleges and universities for the production of a College video, and an award for promotional material designed for the GMCC Foundation's "Profiles of Success" campaign. Through the use of desktop publishing hardware and software, the department now produced a large amount of its material "in house."

On June 16, 1988, the board adopted a Memorandum of Understanding which set out the financial and administrative relationships between the College and the GMCC Foundation.

Changing to Meet College and Community Needs: 1988 and 1989

The term "governance" refers to the structures and processes of decision making which, in turn, engender a certain kind of organizational climate or working environment.[77] In the realm of higher education, this process involves a number of groups or individuals in a variety of areas. For Grant MacEwan Community College, the key element of the concept of governance was that it provided an opportunity for staff, students, and faculty to play a greater role in deciding their educational future. In August 1988, Kelly reported to the board on what he referred to as a refocusing on the human side of college development: Grant MacEwan, he said, is in the "people improvement business." There should be no reason why GMCC should not aspire to be a world-class organization in which students and staff would experience the highest quality of working and learning environment available anywhere. All we had to do was commit the same energy to this cause as we did to the City Centre

Campus. He expanded on his ideas for an approach to management and teaching which emphasized greater delegation of responsibility and the empowerment of people throughout the organization.

Kelly established the President's Task Force on College Governance in 1989.[78] This committee sought input from across GMCC on how the institution might organize itself to enhance employee and student satisfaction, to make better decisions and resolve problems more effectively in response to the challenges facing the College in the coming decade. Committee membership included representatives of students, faculty, support staff, administration, and the Board of Governors. Kelly noted that the committee was established in response to a priority objective proposed to the board at its 1988–89 retreat.[79] Addressing the issue of college educational governance would allow Kelly to fulfil what he called his life's work as an educator and college administrator.[80]

The 28-member Task Force on College Governance compiled a set of recommendations and strategies in support of the key principle entitled "Empowerment of Learners." Kelly's goal was to set the stage for an organizational process that empowered each individual within the College to respond to both professional and community needs.[81] In 1990 the effects of this process, in Kelly's estimation, were already being felt:

> The impact of this focus was visible during the year, as a more open process on next year's budget was held, and the Board of Governors made a conscious effort to place every possible item on the public agenda. A belief that we can make our College organization as good as we want it to be underlies the spirit of the task force.[82]

By the 1988–89 academic year, the College had reached a high level of sophistication and the increases in applicants and enrolments attested to its success. There was little doubt that the institution had changed so much from its early days that it would be hard to recognize it as the same place. However, many members of the GMCC community were concerned about the consequences of the introduction of the university transfer program. Some senior instructional staff expressed apprehension that transfer programming would create a dichotomy between instructional divisions and that salary grids based on academic achievements might not give full recognition for years of practical hands-on experience. Overall, there was real concern that the sense of community that bound the early GMCC staff together in a close-knit family unit was now seriously threatened and had in fact eroded dramatically in the past several years. It may have been that this was merely the price of progress, for it was unrealistic to think that GMCC could possibly stay in any kind of "holding" pattern.

In 1975, John Haar commented that the College was "growing by leaps and bounds, but we'll never get too big. That's the way we want it."[83] We can only speculate about what Haar meant by "too big," but by the late 1980s it was clear that GMCC, with increased maturity and public recognition as a significant post-secondary institution, demanded growth. The community was changing and, true to the mission of the College, GMCC was responsive to the community.

College enrolment grew to over 20,000 full-time, part-time, and non-credit students (4,800 FTE credit) in the 1988–89 academic year. This 7.7 percent increase was coupled by an increase of 10 percent in the number of people enrolled in credit outreach programs and an increase of 26 percent in non-credit programming. The College was now 800 FTE students over its designed capacity. Entrepreneurial outreach activity now provided 25 percent of the College's operating revenues, which made GMCC the Alberta college least dependent on government operating grants.

Planning the new downtown campus was exciting and was accomplished while still attending to the myriad of day-to-day college operations. A design philosophy paper, "MacEwan 2000: Forms for Thought" (Appendix L), was drafted by the president with input from across the College community in order to ensure that the philosophy and aims of the College were reflected in the new campus.

The Academic Services Instructional Unit was renamed the Arts and Science Division as a reflection of recently introduced university transfer programming. Additional instructional staff were hired and further expansion of this area was planned.[84] The dean of the Business Division, Dr. Paul Byrne, resigned to become vice-president, academic, at Mohawk College in Ontario, and his position was filled by Tom Collier. Curriculum changes were made in the Advertising and Public Relations Program, and a second year was added to the University Transfer Program in Commerce. The title of the Library Technician Program was changed to Library and Information Management and a certificate program was added to the Management Studies Program to go along with the existing diploma program.

The Business Outreach Department offered a Canada-wide Post Supervisory Certificate Project in cooperation with Humber College, and sponsored the Third Annual Women in Business conference with the Federal Business Development Bank.

The Community Education Division received final approval for a certificate program in interpreter training and experienced overall enrolment increases in both credit and non-credit programs.

City Centre Campus under construction with Edmonton downtown skyline in view

Community Services conducted two major conferences that attracted a very favourable response,[85] and plans were initiated for a conference in senior studies to be held in the fall of 1989. The Senior Studies Institute began offering courses and the Board of Governors approved in principle the concept of developing a family institute. The Extended Care Nursing Program became the Gerontological Nursing Program and the Nurse Credentialling Program was expanded to all four Atlantic Provinces and brokered through nine Alberta colleges and at Arctic and Yukon colleges.

The name of the Performing and Visual Arts Division was changed to the Performing, Visual, and Communication Arts Division. Under a contract with the Alberta Museums Association, a museum management certificate was offered. A stage band was established, played almost daily during the summer, and won the gold medal at the spring Regional Stage Band Festival for Alberta. One of the division's students, Angus Cockney, received a unique distinction when cited for his participation in a team walk to the North Pole!

Student Services and Community Relations added the areas of systems and computers and the reporting lines for human resources to the office of the president. This allowed the vice-president, administration, to devote more time to campus planning and project management. Systems and Computers completed a major long-term plan for the use of information technology entitled "College Information Resource Planning Process."

A new student orientation program was introduced through the combined efforts of the Registrar's Office, Community Relations, and the Students' Association. The program allowed over 700 students to preview and get a head start on the academic year. A successful educational advisor project piloted by the counselling department provided basic program and course information to prospective students.

Community Relations reported that its *MacEwan Today* publication was enjoyed and read by 82 percent of the College staff who responded to a survey. *MacEwan Tomorrow* was developed in an effort to keep everyone posted about the development of the City Centre Campus.

The College badminton team won three national gold medals and GMCC hosted the 1989 national men's and women's volleyball championships. In addition, plans were put in place to develop a College-wide health and wellness program.

During its tenth year of operation, the GMCC Foundation was ranked in the top five college foundations in North America and had raised a total of approximately $14 million since its inception.

On October 19, 1989, John Ramsey was appointed chair of the Board of Governors. Ramsey's association with the GMCC Foundation Board and involvement with numerous Edmonton activities made him one of the most dynamic chairs in the College's history. His skills in the business community were a considerable asset to the College, especially in light of the College's future:

> In a sense, the College, with a multi-million dollar budget, is "big business" and must incorporate procedures which reflect a high standard of corporate practice.[86]

Entrepreneurship and Continued Growth: the 1990s

Entering a new decade, and in the midst of planning the most ambitious undertaking in its history, the College devoted the 1989–90 academic year to continued expansion to accommodate student demand. Enrolment once again was up 7 percent from the previous year, to over 5,100 full-time equivalent students. The University Transfer Program now made the College a viable alternative for many students beginning their university level studies. More than 300 business and community representatives were serving on advisory committees that ensured that the College's programs were current and met changing needs. Students came from every strata of the community, with 57 percent now being 25 years of age or over. The number of graduates finding employment within six months of graduation remained at a very respectable 93 percent.

The first year of physical education was added to the highly successful University Transfer Program; the number of applicants to this program increased 54 percent over the previous year. An accredited accounting certificate, diploma, and post-diploma certificate were now offered and a program was started in Hong Kong in cooperation with Hong Kong Polytechnic. Students in the Advertising and Public Relations Program won the Canadian Student Advertising Competition in May 1990 for their Red Cross campaign.

The College's new entrepreneurial thrust blossomed. The Management Studies Program contracted with the Alberta Tourism Education Council (ATEC) to develop a Leisure Facility and Golf Management Program, coordinated a "Partners in Education" agreement with Holy Cross Elementary School, offered first and second years of its program at Blue Quills and the Yellowhead Educational Consortium, and involved program staff in international education projects in Uganda and Hong Kong. The successful Travel Consultant Program increased the amount of computer training offered students to reflect the increased use of technology in the travel industry.

The Community Education Division expanded programming in a number of areas, including English as a Second Language, which grew by 50 percent. In addition, workshops such as "Lifeskills for Caregivers" and the community enrichment project "Life Skills and Living Skills" developed for the Canadian Paraplegic Association were extremely successful. Community Education Division projects also involved settlement worker in-service training, heritage language instructor training, and education for abusive men.

The Community Services Division was most notable for its longstanding programs in social work and correctional services, but the development of the Institute of the Family and Senior Studies Institute added a new dimension to this division. In recognition of a donation of $250,000 from the Minerva Foundation, the Senior Studies Institute was renamed the Minerva Senior Studies Institute.

The Health Sciences Division gave considerable attention to the planning of a collaborative nursing education curriculum that allowed students either to complete a diploma in nursing through the College or to complete a nursing degree at the University of Alberta. The nurse diploma and nurse credentialling programs received highly commendable evaluations from a committee appointed by the Alberta Association of Registered Nurses. The division's involvement with international education contributed to a large increase in the number of foreign nurses taking courses in order to meet North American standards. The division finalized plans to send two instructors to teach a course in Hong Kong, and assistance was provided to enable the University of Central Queensland to adapt the nurse credentialling program to Australian needs.

By 1990 the Performing, Visual, and Communication Arts Division boasted the largest and most comprehensive arts programming of any post-secondary institution in Canada. Transfer arrangements for the music program were negotiated with McGill University and the visual arts programs reached agreements with the universities of Alberta, Calgary, and Lethbridge; York University; and Emily Carr College in Vancouver.

The "Learning—Life Enrichment and the Older Adult" conference attracted 600 participants in October. In November the International Education Office hosted a team of administrators from the China Enterprise Management Training Centre.

An Academic Policies Committee was formed in November 1990 to review all of the College's academic policies.

Student Services and Community Relations experienced a record level of activity in all areas. The Counselling Department, for example, conducted over 10,000 consultations. The Health and Wellness Department was now a reality and produced a newsletter and promoted activities related to personal health.

The Athletics and Recreation Department was involved in planning the recreation centre for the new City Centre Campus. Intramural participation increased and the badminton team won another national gold medal. A new academic monitoring program required student athletes to maintain good standing in their academic programs. With 20 athletes receiving ACAC academic awards for maintaining a grade-point average of 3.5 or better out of 4.0, the program was an obvious success. High school liaison staff visits to a record 182 schools complemented a successful poster campaign declaring "You're Different, So Are We."

The GMCC Foundation completed its "Profiles of Success" fundraising campaign, grappled with a million dollar sweepstakes lottery, and hosted the successful Mad Hatter's Ball for the fifth time. Dianne Allen, the former chair of the College's Arts Administration Program, succeeded Executive Director Terry Flannigan, who retired early in 1990.

Applications from foreign students were up 100 percent over the previous year, as the registrar's office handled a 20 percent overall increase in applications.

The Alberta Management Development Institute (AMDI) was initiated by GMCC's vice-president, John Cruickshank, in cooperation with several other Alberta Colleges and held its first conference June 3–8, 1990, at the Rafter Six Guest Ranch. AMDI was intended as a professional development experience for managers similar to that offered by British Columbia's Pacific Management Development Institute (PMDI).

"Building Your Future" was selected as the theme for the College's twentieth anniversary year, 1990–91. For Kelly, the year marked ten years in the office of president, an accomplishment rarely achieved in community college circles. The energy Kelly brought to the position remained and, if anything, increased as the prospect of the new City Centre Campus became closer to reality. Without Kelly and, as he would

President Kelly receiving a ten-year service plaque from Board Chairman John Ramsey

argue, a very competent supporting cast of College employees, Grant MacEwan Community College might have been assigned a lesser role in the shadow of established post-secondary institutions such as the University of Alberta and the Northern Alberta Institute of Technology. GMCC was small enough that it received somewhat benign and, in the early days at least, patronizing attention. By 1991, GMCC had not only arrived, but in many ways was more than an equal partner in the educational community. By fulfilling its mission of lifelong learning and responsiveness to the community, GMCC was capable of meeting the educational needs of more people than any post-secondary institution in the area.

A total of 24,932 credit and non-credit students were enrolled at the College in 1990–91. This represented a relatively small increase of 2 percent from the previous year, limited only by space restrictions.

The College's programs continued to receive high praise. Travel Consultant Program faculty member Paul Ancel was named Educator of the Year for Canada by Agent Canada and instructional assistant Lil

Bennett was named Woman of the Year by Professional Women in Travel in Northern Alberta. English as a Second Language experienced its largest enrolment to date and a pilot project for francophone bursary students from Quebec was conducted. The Heritage Language Instructor Training project continued to offer the only community-based program in Canada for the training of heritage language instructors.

The collaborative model in nursing education received government approval and the Health Sciences Division continued to gain recognition as a leader in nursing education in Alberta and internationally.

The University Transfer Program, particularly in arts and science, attracted a growing number of applicants that greatly exceeded the number of spaces available. A total of 107 students, an increase of 35 percent over the previous year, were enrolled in first- and second-year classes.

The Minerva Senior Studies Institute was a remarkable success. Course offerings were expanded and over 2,800 registrants took advantage of programming in this area. The Institute of the Family was not at the same stage of development as its senior studies counterpart; nevertheless, workshops, seminars, and family day activities were initiated, including a three-phase "Conference on the Family" that was the first major event developed by the institute.

Outreach programming in community services extended as far as Yukon College, and a Teacher Assistant Conference that attracted 1,850 delegates was a notable achievement.

The Performing, Visual, and Communication Arts Program, long respected locally, grew in stature nationally. Graduates were now employed in such respectable artistic venues as the Citadel Theatre, the Stratford Festival, and La Groupe de la Place Royale, one of Canada's premier modern dance companies. Music students in the Stage Band, Dixieland Band, and Trombone Band won gold medals at the Musicfest competition in Vancouver, and performed at the International Association of Jazz Educators in Washington, D.C. The division's faculty also received acclaim. Paul Saturley, from the Native Communications Program, received the Ilford Award for outstanding achievement in photography, and an art video written and directed by Cherie Moses, with technical production by Coleen Finlayson, was added to the permanent collection of the National Gallery in Ottawa.

A survey in February 1991 indicated that the College needed a new logo. The proposed logo would represent the third such effort in the College's history. Implementation of the logo was scheduled for September 1, 1991, but was not formally approved until June 18, 1992. Even then, after a lengthy debate process, there were one opposing vote and

City Centre Campus under construction, 1991

one abstention. For those unfamiliar with college boards, it must seem odd to devote this amount of time to an issue such as the merits of an innovative symbol. Nevertheless, the development of the logo reflected GMCC's strong commitment to maintaining a vigorous and healthy public image.

The success of the College's athletic teams continued. The men's basketball and badminton teams won ACAC gold medals, the men's volleyball and curling teams won silver, and the canoeing team won bronze. Student Wang Wen won an unprecedented third national gold medal in men's singles badminton.

In June 1991 GMCC established a "Green Group" to examine how the College could best respond to environmental issues.

On October 24, 1991, the GMCC Foundation identified three goals for the coming year: first, to determine how the foundation's board functioned; second, to develop a fund-raising master plan; and third, to

continue to grow as a team. The GMCC Foundation established the Cornerstone Club in recognition and appreciation of more than 3,000 hours of service to the foundation contributed by 125 volunteer supporters. The foundation also held its first Tournament of Aces golf fundraising event. More than 180 golfers participated in this activity cosponsored by the Northern Alberta Food Brokers Association and Labatt's Alberta Brewery Limited.

By 1991 GMCC had established an excellent data base of indicators of College success, including program evaluations, from which to draw pertinent data regarding its performance. Administrative Affairs reported that the College budget was balanced and that it held healthy reserves and fund balance positions. Budget planning in the 1990s raised the possibility of abolishing positions and terminating programs. The College was forced to make difficult curricular changes,[87] and the fact that this was accomplished with a minimum of hardship can be attributed to the collaborative efforts of administration, faculty, and support staff at GMCC.

The City Centre Campus Nears Completion

By the 1991–92 academic year, construction of the City Centre Campus was almost finished. The facility was referred to as a "taxpayer's dream."[88] The fiscal plan for the new campus was a striking example of progress despite tough economic conditions. Designed by architects Barry Johns, Laura O'Neill, and John Webster, the campus emphasized practicality, flexibility, and accessibility, in accordance with the design philosophy expressed in "MacEwan 2000: Forms for Thought," a discussion paper written by President Kelly in November 1988 (see Appendix L). Distinctive towers housed stairways and elevators, and a privately operated health and sports medicine clinic, drug store, and cafeteria were included in the design. Impressive features of the new campus were a Learning Resource Centre that incorporated state-of-the-art electronics and traditional library features, and the largest single-level parkade in western Canada. The new facility will accommodate approximately 9,000 credit students and 18,000 people enrolled in special interest and credit-related courses. With an estimated 8,000 to 10,000 students and staff attracted to the downtown core daily, and over 1,000 living in the area, the City Centre Campus will most definitely "humanize the downtown."[89]

The entire project was completed $6 million under budget and six months ahead of schedule. Barry Snowden provides a perspective of the long-range cost for the facility:

> The cost of the City Centre Campus (or its equivalent) is less than 10 percent of the operating costs for the students that it will serve over its lifetime.
>
> Taking the long-range view, the "capital funding issue" may be a relatively small component of the overall funding challenge. That is, an amount equivalent to 10 percent of the operating budget, appropriated to a "sinking fund" annually would provide capital facilities in perpetuity.[90]

For many programs, the move to the new facility meant saying goodbye to familiar structures and systems. The Cromdale Campus, long targeted for elimination, would no longer function as a GMCC building. For all of its deficiencies, the Cromdale Campus exemplified what the College stood for and, in a sense, represented the last vestige of the College's "storefront" era. Cromdale's first building superintendent, Olga Eliuk, remembered the opening of the converted supermarket:

> We toured the premises...areas that were somewhat complete, which were a few classrooms and offices...if you can imagine one person trying to make headway in this mess, to prepare this building for operation by September 21st.[91]

The concerns about opening a new facility are magnified but remain the same. One consolation that is granted with the absence of an equine studies program is that custodial staff will not face Olga's Herculean task of dealing with horses in the classrooms.[92] The pride developed at the Cromdale facility through roughing it in relatively Spartan surroundings will be hard to emulate.

The hopes and aspirations of GMCC have remained, but the expectations are dramatically different. The new campus is ready, as the 1985 request for campus planning funds stated, to "serve the community now through the 21st century." Classes in the new facility began in the fall of 1993.

President Kelly viewed the new campus as an example of the collaborative governance model he strongly believed was the key to GMCC's future. The principles and recommendations of the Task Force on College Governance, Kelly noted, "led to evaluation and changes from the classroom to the boardroom."[93]

While it is true that the impressive physical presence of the City Centre Campus will be seen by some as his most tangible legacy, for Kelly, implementing collaborative governance and being known primarily as an educator are more important than building facilities:

During my tenure as president I suspect my name will be associated with the development of new buildings. That's fine, because the college community desperately needs them and our faculty and students deserve them. Amid all of the flurry of facilities planning, and construction, we need to remember that it's not the facility, but what goes on inside it that counts as the measure of success for a community college.

I believe it is crucial that a president be first and foremost an educator. I must tell you that I didn't decide to become a teacher thirty years ago to put up buildings. I would be pleased if I was known for doing the right thing as an educator, supporting student learning and professional development, international education, promoting transfer programming and so on. Hopefully, the pioneer work we are doing on collaborative governance to promote a quality learning and working environment at GMCC will, over time, be seen as the most valuable seed I have sown and my most important contribution. I would also be very pleased if I were considered at the end of my days as a good teacher by students and colleagues; that's what really counts in a college. As a president, one can easily be distanced from these important matters. I now believe I can be of greatest service to GMCC by lending more visible support to them.[94]

Decreased funding and increased student demand for programs remained a serious concern for the College. Budgetary planning for the 1992–93 academic year addressed a projected shortfall of $1 million. This resulted in a continuing reduction of expenditures and the need to generate additional revenues. College administrators had been dealing with fiscal restraint for so long that cutting back became an annual challenge, one that GMCC seems quite capable of handling.

In the 1990s, it is rare to find educational administrators in the post-secondary system who have the luxury of discussing issues such as programming and methods of instruction from a purely philosophical context. Visionary zeal and enthusiastic ardor still exist in the excitement associated with GMCC's new purpose-built campus; however, enthusiasm has been tempered by decreases to base funding budgets, lack of job security, and the increasing demands for greater service and production with increasingly diminished resources. It is within this scenario that administrators must now lead their institutions and instructional staff must educate their students. President Kelly acknowledged this reality in his President's Report for 1991–92:

> The demand for career-related and retraining programs continues to escalate for Alberta colleges and technical institutes. In 1991, Grant MacEwan Community College rejected more than 6,000 individuals because enrolment capacity set by funding limitations had been reached. Alberta Career Development and Employment estimates that by the year 2001, 50 per cent of new jobs will require a diploma or certificate from a college or institute, and 15 per cent will require a university degree. How can that demand be met? Government funding for post-secondary education needs to reflect this new reality and be apportioned to the areas of greatest need. While maintaining its educational vision, Grant MacEwan itself must become increasingly cost-effective and entrepreneurial. We need to seek new avenues to generate revenue which will allow student access and create job stability. And, greater effort must be placed on a sharing of funding costs between colleges, their clients, government, and industry.[95]

The future for GMCC is as an institution that bridges the educational needs of industry, employers, and students. Lifelong learning is a worldwide movement which both reflects and contributes to social transformation.[96] Education must be viewed as a continuum of lifelong learning experiences from the start of formal schooling until death.[97] After all, it was Aristotle who claimed education was the best provision for old age![98]

At the time of the opening of the City Centre Campus, Grant MacEwan Community College offered 50 diploma and certificate programs in arts and science, business, community services, community education, health sciences, and performing and visual communications. University transfer is now an integral component of the institution, with programs offered in arts, science, commerce, nursing, and first-year physical education. Over 300 business and community representatives serve on program advisory committees.

The Board of Governors approved in principle a major fund-raising campaign to be conducted by the GMCC Foundation in conjunction with the College.[99] Fund-raising has been encouraged since the early days of the community college movement; however, the urgency of this activity has never been felt more strongly. On the brighter side, college administrators have begun to view self-funded or entrepreneurial activity and, to a lesser degree, fund-raising, as a way to ensure continued creativity and lessen dependence on outside forces in directing their institution's destiny.

GMCC graduates continue to be recognized by the service, business, and arts communities. Despite an increasingly tough economic climate, as of 1991, 90 percent of responding graduates surveyed were still finding employment within six months of graduation.

In 1992 program areas were marked by continuing success and noteworthy achievements. University transfer was growing to the point that some in the College envisioned the possibility of degree-granting status for the institution at some point in the future.[100] Programs that involved cooperative learning, such as the newly introduced cooperative Accounting and Hearing Aid Practitioner programs[101] were becoming a viable way of meeting the educational needs of the community.

Confluence magazine, launched in 1990 as a "flowing together of voices and images," featured the best writing and visuals produced by GMCC students. The 1991–92 edition received a literary magazine award from the Community College Humanities Association based in Philadelphia.

Nursing at GMCC had always held a position of respect, which was enhanced by the refinement of the collaborative model of nursing education in Edmonton and the development of programs such as the Gerontological Nursing Certificate Program.

Secretarial Studies was now called Office Administration and Secretarial Studies. Students travelled from as far as Singapore to meet the requirements for an International Business course, and the highly respected Travel Consultant Program was considered a leader by the travel industry.

In Management Studies, a self-funded two-year Golf Operations Management diploma program was developed, the first program of its kind in Canada. A program was also offered for individuals seeking certification with the Canadian Professional Golfers Association (CPGA). Accounting programs were a strong component of the Business Division and continue to receive increasing numbers of applicants each year.

Performing, Visual, and Communication Arts maintained its position as the most comprehensive and largest program area of its kind in any Canadian post-secondary institution. Instructor Brian Webb of the dance faculty received the first grant awarded in Western Canada for interdisciplinary work and performance art.

With the retirement of Dr. Paul Otke, plans were made to restructure the administrative reporting lines for Community Education. The division, which contained many of the College's most recognizable programs in the early days, responded to the community in ways that set the stage for long-term programming. Modifications to the Child and Youth Care and Early Childhood Development programs kept pace with community needs. The Teacher Assistant Conference, now in its seventeenth year, attracted over 2,000 delegates from Alberta, the Yukon, Manitoba, and the Northwest Territories. The Social Work Program addressed cross-cultural needs along with concern for international and environmental issues.

Community Education filled a unique role in the College's educational programming. The English as a Second Language Program was growing, Interpreter Training was highly sought, and the Consumer Education Program was in its fifteenth year. Training programs for aboriginal women and courses to assist inmates in making a successful transition from prison to society illustrate the scope of this division.

For Student Services and Community Relations, supporting the learning process was an increasingly difficult task. The counselling area was now serving over 13,000 people and over 200 special needs students were assisted through special services for the disabled. Although the International Education Centre was viewed as a necessary part of the College which provided a global perspective for its educational mission, cost-recovery funding put additional pressure on this area.

Health and wellness programming was established among the College community by this time and with the opening of the new campus would be offered to an expanded clientele, including the corporate community. In athletics, student Mark Lee's performance allowed the College to claim its fourth national championship in men's singles badminton.

Certain processes are in place, such as institutional research and planning, information systems, and personnel and program evaluation, that attempt to keep the institution responsive to internal and external needs. Grant MacEwan Community College now features a central purpose-built facility that will accommodate 9,000 students in credit courses and 18,000 in career-related courses. In addition, the College reaches out to the community through its facilities in Mill Woods and Jasper Place and its flexible programming.

Finally, the development of the City Centre Campus dominates the Kelly years outlined in this document. For Kelly, however, as noted in several of his speeches during the 1980s, facilities are not as important as what goes on inside them. The true challenge is to make student-centred learning a reality by aligning the entire College organization behind the quality principles of college governance.[102] Currently, work is underway with a Curriculum 2000 Task Force which will guide the College into the future. The Grant MacEwan Community College story is just beginning.

[1] GMCC Press Release, June 25, 1981.

[2] *Edmonton Journal*, November 14, 1981.

[3] *Edmonton Journal*, September 29, 1981.

[4] GMCC Board Meeting Minutes, September 17, 1981.

[5] Gerald Kelly, "Application of Participative Management to College Governance" (Ph.D. diss., University of Alberta, 1973).

[6] Gerald Kelly, personal interview, July 6, 1993.

[7] Ibid.

[8] Board Retreat Notes, September 12, 1981.

[9] Gerald Kelly, personal interview, May 12, 1993.

[10] Funding allocations were redistributed to other programs.

[11] Board Meeting, August 19, 1982. (Effectively marketing the image of the College and utilizing the public relations office to its maximum potential were raised as important issues at the October 14, 1982, board retreat.)

[12] *Edmonton Journal*, March 28, 1982.

[13] Gerald Kelly, "Public Perceptions of a College," President's Speeches, GMCC Office of the President, June 1983.

[14] Ibid.

[15] Gerald Kelly, President's Speeches, GMCC Office of the President, June 24, 1993.

[16] See *Edmonton Journal*, August 25, 27, 1982; and *Alberta Report*, September 13, 1982.

[17] Gerald Kelly, President's Speeches, GMCC Office of the President, June 24, 1993.

[18] GMCC Press Release, July 25, 1980.

[19] *Edmonton Journal*, March 28, 1982.

[20] *Edmonton Journal*, August 30, 1982.

[21] Ibid.

[22] Gerald Kelly, personal interview, May 12, 1993.

[23] These later became divisional deans.

[24] Gerald Kelly, correspondence to Henry Kolesar, August 11, 1982.

[25] GMCC Board Meeting Minutes, Volume 14: 1982–1984, September 16, 1982, and October 21, 1982.

[26] GMCC Board Meeting Minutes, Volume 14: 1982–1984.

[27] GMCC Board Meeting Minutes, October 15, 1982.

[28] GMCC Board Retreat, October 15, 1982.

[29] Gerald Kelly, *GMCC Annual Report*, 1982–83, p. 1.

[30] Ibid.

[31] The proposed campus was intended to replace the Cromdale facility in use since 1971, which was clearly inadequate.

[32] *GMCC Annual Report*, 1982–83, p. 3.

[33] *MacEwan Journalist*, February 9, 1983.

[34] Gerald Kelly, "Role of Presidents/Role of Board of Governors," panel discussion, ACCC Conference, Montreal, July 23, 1983.

[35] The Alberta Colleges Athletics Conference is arguably the premier college-level athletic conference in Canada. Representatives from the ACAC have consistently achieved a high level of performance at the national level and winning a conference title is, without question, an indication that the team or individual is among the nation's best in that activity.

[36] GMCC Board Meeting Minutes, October 20, 1983.

[37] GMCC Board Retreat, November 18, 1983.

[38] Gerald Kelly, "Role of Presidents."

[39] T. C. Day, personal interview, March 4, 1993.

[40] GMCC Board Meeting Minutes, Volume Five: 1972–1973.

[41] T. C. Day, "Transferability and Grant MacEwan Community College: 1971–1975," unpublished paper, November 1975, p. 1.

[42] John D. Dennison and Paul Gallagher, *Canada's Community Colleges* (Vancouver: University of British Columbia Press, 1986), p. 21.

[43] While vice-president, academic, at Red Deer College, Gerry Kelly, a founding ACAT member, working with the registrar at the University of Alberta, drafted the first transfer guidelines used in the province in 1975. He noted that Minister of Advanced Education Jim Foster was made particularly aware of the transfer problem

from his vantage point as the local Red Deer MLA.

[44] T. C. Day, "Transferability," p. 5.

[45] *GMCC Journalist*, March 7, 1984, p. 1.

[46] Gerald Kelly, personal interview, August 27, 1993. Kelly and Horowitz held a long-standing personal and professional friendship. Horowitz was one of Kelly's professors during his first year as an undergraduate student at McGill University.

[47] Gerald Kelly, President's Speeches, GMCC Office of the President, 1987.

[48] Edmonton Planning Committee to the Board of Post-Secondary Education, *The Edmonton College*, 1969, p. v.

[49] Obviously, new building had continued for GMCC; the satellite campuses at Mill Woods (1976) and Jasper Place (1980) were greatly needed additions. However, these facilities were small by college standards and constructed at relatively low cost; they did little to address an ongoing space shortage.

[50] Board Policy E3010, 1981.

[51] Gerald Kelly, personal interview, July 6, 1993.

[52] The replacement campus was proposed for an area west of the Manning Freeway at 137 Avenue and 50 Street.

[53] Gerald Kelly, personal interview, July 6, 1993.

[54] Kelly observed that some Board members even believed that he was "a closet Liberal" trying to get Laurence Decore, then mayor of Edmonton, elected provincial premier. Kelly also recalled that an *Edmonton Sun* article (March 25, 1990) declared he was really a Progressive Conservative "hack" trying to get Terry Cavanaugh re-elected as mayor. He insists that all college presidents can best serve their institutions by being apolitical. Ibid.

[55] Ibid.

[56] A satellite city centre location was first considered in a 1973 proposal for the development of a small campus about ten blocks from the present City Centre Campus location.

[57] The front "gates" of the new City Centre Campus, either by coincidence or design, bear a remarkable resemblance to McGill's Roddick Gates.

[58] Gerald Kelly, personal interview, July 6, 1993.

[59] GMCC Board Meeting Minutes, Volume 15: 1984–1987.

[60] Ibid.

[61] William Thorsell, *Edmonton Journal*, May 17, 1984.

[62] Gerry Kelly, personal correspondence to William Thorsell, January 27, 1984.

[63] Kelly noted that the whole board acted as a team in promoting the City Centre Campus. Board members included Peter Kossowan, Linda Wood, Pat Moffat, Bev Mahood, Rose Marie Nicas, Rick Angus, John Steffensen, Ralph Young, Fred Singer, Werner Jappsen, Dave Milner, and John McGee.

[64] Gerald Kelly, personal interview, July 6, 1993.

[65] Gerald Kelly, *GMCC Annual Report*, 1987–88.

[66] Ibid.

[67] The acquisition of CN land involved a wide range of proponents, including Laurence Decore, Jim Edwards, Don Mazankowski, Lillian Staroszik, Ross Walker, Les Young, Dave Russell, and Lynne Duncan, working with College officials.

[68] Gerald Kelly, personal interview, July 6, 1993. New board members included Scott Rutherford, Jack Phelan, Mike Jenner, Betty Andrews, and Pat Bentley.

[69] Ibid.

[70] Barry Snowden, personal interview, July 21, 1993.

[71] Gerald Kelly, personal interview, July 6, 1993.

[72] Ibid.

[73] Ibid.

[74] Recipients of the MacEwan Medallion have included: T. C. Day, vice-president, academic (1986); Bruce Vincent, coordinator, Operations, Facilities (1987); Dorothy Gray, instructor, Student Study Services (1988); Terry Flannigan, vice-president, GMCC Foundation (1989); Doug Smith, coordinator, Social Work Outreach–Blue Quills (1990); Judy Koch, instructor, Legal Assistant Program, and coordinator, Faculty Development (1991); Sharon Schnell, manager, Business Department (1992); Allen McQueen, chair, Accounting (1993); Eva Roche, instructor, Early Childhood Development (1994); and Andi Pallas, director, Facilities Division (1995).

[75] John Haar, *Perspectives*, February 17, 1977, p. 8.

[76] April 21, 1988.

[77] Carnegie Commission on Higher Education, *Report on the Governance of Higher Education* (New York: McGraw-Hill, 1973).

[78] GMCC Board Meeting Minutes, September 21, 1989.

[79] Objective III: College Climate Development—to continue to develop and implement mechanisms to facilitate appropriate involvement and input in decision-making by all College employees.

[80] Gerald Kelly, personal interview, May 12, 1993.

[81] Gerald Kelly, *GMCC Annual Report*, 1990–91, p. 3.

[82] Ibid.

[83] John Haar, *GMCC Calendar*, 1975–76.

[84] Twelve probationary or full-time term instructors were hired and five additional instructors were added during the summer.

[85] Eighteen hundred people attended the Native Education Conference and approximately 1,300 participated in the Teacher Aide Conference.

[86] Gerald Kelly, Collected Speeches, GMCC Office of the President, June, 1989.

[87] GMCC Board Meeting Minutes, December 19, 1991.

[88] *Edmonton Sun*, April 26, 1993, p. 6.

[89] *Edmonton Journal*, August 1, 1992, p. A8.

[90] Barry L. Snowden, presentation, March 20, 1992.

[91] Olga Eliuk, personal correspondence dated July 1986, GMCC Archives.

[92] "It would take quite a few paragraphs to explain the frustrations and tense moments the presence of a horse in the classroom presented," wrote Olga Eliuk in 1986. The Care of the Hoof classes offered in room 117 became infamous. Dianne Hunt, in an unpublished paper from the GMCC Archives, remembered the vision of Olga "at the back of the building chipping away at frozen horse droppings with an ice pick."

[93] Gerald Kelly, *GMCC Annual Report*, 1991–92, p. 3.

[94] Gerald Kelly, "Moving Into the '90s," President's Fall Welcome, September 7, 1989.

[95] Gerald Kelly, President's Report for 1991–92, GMCC Office of the President, 1992.

[96] Marcie Boucouvalas, "Social Transformation, Lifelong Learning, and the Fourth Force—Transpersonal Psychology," *Lifelong Learning*, March 1983, p. 6.

[97] Samuel Brodbelt, "Education as Growth: Life-Long Learning," *Clearing House*, October 1983, p. 72.

[98] Aristotle, in *Bartlett's Familiar Quotations* (London: MacMillan Press, Ltd., 1980), p. 87.

[99] GMCC Board Meeting Minutes, April 16, 1992.

[100] The question of degree-granting status is a debatable point. For some, the process is seen as an inevitable outcome of student demand. A few colleges now grant degrees, either independently or in cooperation with an existing degree-granting institution such as Athabasca University. The College is now turning away 6,000 applicants and the present board, aware that diploma graduates are finding jobs, has no desire to make GMCC a degree-granting institution.

[101] The Hearing Aid Practitioner Program is offered in cooperation with the Alberta Hearing Aid Practitioners Association.

[102] See Appendix K: College Governance Principles.

Chapter Five

The Future

A few years after Grant MacEwan Community College was established, Milton R. Fenske, director of administrative services for the Alberta Colleges Commission, pointed out that although historical studies provide information about the past that is useful in determining our relationship to where we have been and where we are now, they rarely provide suitable future directions.[1] It is fitting, therefore, to conclude this historical reflection by briefly identifying areas that loom as particular challenges for Grant MacEwan Community College. Meeting these challenges will undoubtedly provide the blueprint for the future direction of the College.

It is safe to assume that the egalitarian belief in educational opportunity and responsiveness to diverse needs and abilities is found in no greater measure among post-secondary institutions than in the community college. The future of Grant MacEwan Community College, therefore, will no doubt reflect the future of the community in which it is located—the city of Edmonton and its surrounding area—and the College and its community will face many of the same challenges.

A major challenge for Grant MacEwan Community College is to ensure that the institution remains responsive to what Chuck Day called the key to our educational future: the ability to synthesize and process knowledge. Designing programs and courses that will meet this challenge is a key element in the GMCC story, as indicated in the role statement proposed for the College in 1977:

> The College will continue to place a great emphasis on the
> development of innovative instructional methodologies and
> delivery systems. In this regard, increasing emphasis will be placed

Douglass Clock viewed through the front gates

on off-campus delivery systems utilizing other institutions as brokers. It is anticipated that this will mean greater involvement in the development of multi-media materials. An integral part of this approach will be the development of an instructional design capability and a movement to competency-based curricula.[2]

Upon his return from a tour of British colleges in 1983, President Kelly indicated that British institutions were under considerable financial strain.[3] British colleges had implemented early retirement schemes, reduced programs, and merged several institutions. "In 20 to 30 years," Kelly stated, "it may be inevitable that we (Grant MacEwan Community College) will be amalgamated with the non-university post-secondary educational facilities in Edmonton, such as Alberta Vocational Centre and NAIT."[4] So far, Kelly's prediction has not been fulfilled; however, the pressures that faced the British colleges are now realities for their Canadian counterparts.

Ten-year goals set by the Board of Governors in 1990 identify the need for accommodating increasing demand by raising alternative revenues. College administrators are now expected to increase revenues. For GMCC, they will come from three sources: tuition fees, user charges, and outreach programming. Chuck Day says we are experiencing a loosening of government control:

More funding from the user, whether student, faculty, or staff, will be required. This will come from areas such as programs being offered through a student-pay basis, and increased expectations for funding to come from the ancillary service areas such as parking, rentals, and so on. Self-funded programming will become a larger part of the curricular offerings and might exceed regular based program funding.[5]

The reduction of expenditures will continue into the foreseeable future. Duplication of services will face continued scrutiny and colleges will look to their foundations and development offices for more financial assistance. For Grant MacEwan Community College, and post-secondary education in general, budgetary concerns will continue to contribute a great deal to the anxiety, but also to the exciting opportunities concerning the direction the colleges will take. According to Gerry Kelly:

Colleges like GMCC will have to become increasingly entrepreneurial to raise revenues, but also to demonstrate to the public that we can operate as efficiently as any business while providing quality experiences for the public's dollar. We must also realize whether we like it or not that we will be in direct competition with private educational interests for student customers. Whether it be in educational quality or in efficient business practice, MacEwan can excel either way.

This is not a storm to be weathered, but a transition to a new way of doing business. Through the motivation and creativity of our College staff, we will respond to the challenge and prosper.[6]

The College has always faced challenges, and funding can be seen as just another hurdle. The solution to this concern rests with the community; financial support, therefore, must be gained by convincing constituent populations that supporting the community college is, in reality, supporting themselves.

As Stephen Hume reminds us:

...we know that 65 per cent of the new jobs to be created will demand between 12 and 17 years of education, we put up with a system in which 30 per cent of young Canadians fail to even finish high school.

The current trend is for 100,000 dropouts per year. That means a million undereducated Canadian workers by decade's end.

...You don't need high school math to calculate lost tax revenue, diminished retail spending power, dwindling investment capital and greater social spending....[7]

"It's the job of the community college," a professor of higher education once declared, "to make tax-payers out of tax-eaters."[8] Tough questions are being asked about educational quality and the ability to do a job beyond graduation. For both students and the College, excellence in education is tantamount to the opportunity for every member of society to reach his or her potential.

A significant number of people not only need but demand an alternative to universities or technical institutes. For many of these people the community college provides that alternative. "If GMCC became

Prospective students

something else...such as a degree-granting college," explained administrative vice-president Barry Snowden, "another institution would arise that would take its place to fill the educational void created by its absence."[9]

A spirit of optimism pervades Grant MacEwan Community College, even in the face of the most daunting challenges. Under Gerry Kelly, the College board has adopted a plan for the future. "2020 Vision"[10] proposes entrepreneurial alternatives to government funding, greater integration of technology applied to learning, a high-performance organization founded on the principles of collaborative governance, an entrepreneurial culture which will allow the College to be responsive to student access demands, and four new campuses built in each corner of Edmonton.

A study released in Gothenburg, Sweden, by the Organization for Economic Co-operation and Development found that, "the single characteristic that best describes Edmontonians' attitudes to learning is *enthusiasm*."[11] This study included Edmonton among those communities that have "taken advantage of a shared sense of purpose among residents and community organizations."[12] The same sense of purpose has characterized Grant MacEwan Community College. In 1977, Kay Puil, the College's first director of Student Services, remarked:

...there's no such thing as a typical GMCC student. That's what makes life so exciting for instructors. Both instructors and students learn from each other and there is nothing more exciting than learning or a new idea.[13]

As the College readies itself to enter the mid-90s, a new senior administration—vice presidents Bob Cowan, Sherry Rainsforth, Harry Davis, and Jim Henderson—now works with Gerry Kelly. While the majority of staff who have contributed to the College's development in the past two decades are still with GMCC, a transition to new staff is underway. A system of collaborative decision making throughout the College attempts to involve College members in problem solving, and a task force for GMCC curriculum into the 2000s charts a course for the College's successful future.

It is this synergy that has enabled Grant MacEwan Community College to incorporate an enthusiasm for learning that is a source of pride for not only Edmonton, but all of Canadian higher education.

---

[1] Milton R. Fenske, *Report to the Alberta Colleges Commission* (Edmonton, AB: Alberta Colleges Commission, 1972).

[2] Proposed Role Statement for Grant MacEwan Community College, September 1977.

[3] *Box 1796*, vol. 3, no. 3, 1983, p. 3.

[4] Ibid.

[5] T. C. Day, personal interview, April 19, 1993.

[6] Gerald Kelly, personal interview, April 26, 1995.

[7] *Edmonton Journal*, September 3, 1992.

[8] C. Carpenter, lecture on community college education, Oregon State University, Corvallis, Oregon, fall 1986.

[9] Barry Snowden, personal interview, July 21, 1993.

[10] See Appendix M, 2020 Vision.

[11] *Edmonton Journal*, July 12, 1992.

[12] Ibid.

[13] Kay Puil, *Perspectives*, March 17, 1977, p. 11.

Gerald Kelly with GMCC Student Association Executive, 1984-85
Front Row: *Shauna Liber, Wennette Schultz, April Johnson, Gerry Kelly*
Second Row: *Heather MacKenzie, Natasha Alexander, Mike Sokolvik, Jennifer Graham,*
                Terry Rhode, Melanie Owen
Back Row: *Sean Connolly, Greg Dexter*

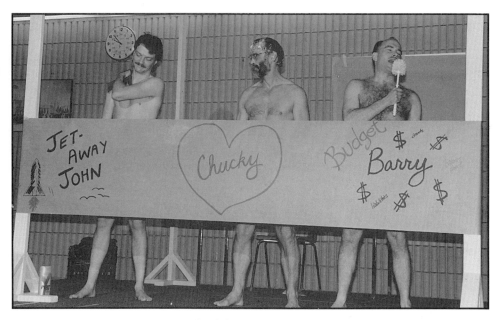

Staff Skit Night 1991
Randy Jenne, Tony Fell and Doug Ringrose being showered with attention

20-year Long Service Award recipients, 1993

top row (L to R):   *Vi Becker, Ron Rowswell,Gord Nicholson, Karl Homann, Barry Olsen, Brian Zwicker, Gerry Kelly*

bottom row (L to R): Eva Roche, John Jaglal, Julie Lazaruk, Charlene Tarver, Pat Wilson

Board of Governors, 1995

top row(L to R):   *Margo March (board sec.), Ted Bosse, Pat Bentley, Dale Dowell, Mary Cameron, Brian Zwicker, Brian Brix, Greg Dexter, Brian Reid*

bottom row(L to R): Phyllis Anderson, Gerry Kelly, John Ramsey, Grant MacEwan, Vi Becker

Early Morning at Facilities

top row(L to R):   *Bob Cowan, Dan Whelton, Chris Krozser, Andi Pallas, Tony Pogue,*
                                 Donald Young, Bruce McIntosh
bottom row(L to R): *Ron Pretzlaff, Deanna Kenwell, Bruce Vincent, Leah Covey,*
                                 Pat Pelech, Frank Salopek

Registrar Cathryn Heslep & Jack Phelan at Faculty Development Orientation

Grant MacEwan speaking to a group of listeners 90 years his junior

*Grant MacEwan
golf tournament
participants:
Gene Riel, Andy Blake
Joanne Kemp, Frank Salopek*

Bibliography

Books and Articles

Association of Canadian Community Colleges. "Grant MacEwan Community College." *College Canada* 2, 1977.

Atherton, Peter J. *Financing Junior Colleges in Alberta: A Study Prepared for the Board of Post-Secondary Education for the Province of Alberta*. Edmonton, AB: Department of Educational Administration, University of Alberta, 1969.

Berghofer, Desmond, and Alan Vladicka. *Access to Opportunity 1905–1980: The Development of Post-Secondary Education in Alberta*. Edmonton, AB: Alberta Advanced Education and Manpower, 1980.

Boucouvalas, Marcie. "Social Transformation, Lifelong Learning, and the Fourth Force—Transpersonal Psychology." *Lifelong Learning*, March 1983.

Brodbelt, Samuel. "Education as Growth: Life-Long Learning." *Clearing House*, October 1983.

Brubacher, John S., and Willis Rudy. *Higher Education in Transition: A History of American Colleges and Universities, 1636–1976*. New York: Harper & Row, 1976.

Campbell, Gordon. "Community Colleges in Canada." *CAUT Bulletin* 23, no. 3 (1974): 8–12.

Carr, Edward Hallett. *What Is History?* New York: Vintage Books, 1961.

Celowitz, Arnold Charles. "Training Needs for College Student Personnel Professionals in Western Canada." *Journal of the Association of Canadian Community Colleges* 3, no. 1 (1979): 109–120.

Clark, John C., and Darius R. Young. "Alberta Community Colleges: Ten Years in Review." *Canadian Vocational Journal* 19, no. 3 (1983): 8–11.

Cohen, Arthur M., and Florence B. Brawer. *The American Community College.* San Francisco: Jossey-Bass, 1982.

"Colleges Growing Faster than Universities in Alberta." *Canadian University and College* 6 (1971): 5.

Dennison, John D. "Goals of Community Colleges in Canada: A 1987 Perspective." *Canadian Journal of Higher Education* 18 (1): 49–63.

Dennison, John D., and John S. Levin. *Canada's Community Colleges in the Nineteen Eighties: Responsiveness and Renewal.* Toronto: Association of Canadian Community Colleges, 1989.

Dennison, John D., and Paul Gallagher. *Canada's Community Colleges.* Vancouver: University of British Columbia Press, 1986.

Devereux, M. S. *One in Every Five—A Survey of Adult Education in Canada.* Ottawa: Supply and Services Canada, 1984.

Eells, W. C. *The Junior College.* Boston: Houghton Mifflin, 1931.

Eells, W. C. *Present Status of Junior College Terminal Education.* Washington, D.C.: American Association of Junior Colleges, 1941.

Eells, W. C. *Why Junior College Terminal Education?* Washington, D.C.: American Association of Junior Colleges, 1941.

Ferrier, William W. *Ninety Years of Education in California: 1846 to 1936.* Irvine, CA: Reprint Service, 1992. (Reprint of 1937 material)

Fisher, Grant. *The Community College.* Calgary: University of Calgary, 1967.

Gallagher, Paul. *Community Colleges in Canada: A Current Profile.* Toronto: Association of Canadian Community Colleges, 1987.

Ingram, E. J., J. Kelsey, Abram G. Konrad, and James M. Small. *Towards an Interprovincial Community College: Post-Secondary Education in East Central Alberta and West Central Saskatchewan.* Edmonton, AB: Department of Educational Administration, University of Alberta, 1966.

Johns, Walter H. *A History of the University of Alberta: 1908–1969.* Edmonton, AB: University of Alberta Press, 1981.

Johnston, E. F. "Community College Environment—Neglected Research in Canada." *Canadian Counsellor* 6, no. 2 (1972): 100–111.

Konrad, Abram G., ed. *Clientele and Community: The Student in the Canadian Community College*. Edmonton, AB: University of Alberta, 1974.

Lasch, Christopher. *The Culture of Narcissism*. New York: Warner Books, 1979.

Loken, Guldbrand. *An Analysis of the Junior College in Alberta: Progress, Program and Prospect*. Edmonton, AB: University of Alberta Printing Services, 1966.

Long, John C. *An Historical Study of the Establishment of College Systems in Ontario and Alberta in the 1960's*. Research Studies in Post-Secondary Education, no. 20. Edmonton, AB: Alberta Colleges Commission, 1972.

McCartan, Anne-Marie. "The Community College Mission." *Journal of Higher Education* 54, no. 6 (1983): 666–692.

McIntosh, R. G., ed. *The Community College in Canada: Present Status, Future Prospects*. Edmonton, AB: University of Alberta, Department of Educational Administration, 1971.

Messer, T. "Alberta Study Seeks to Measure Colleges against Community Needs." *Canadian University and College* 6 (January-February 1971): 8.

Michener, James A. *Journey: A Quest for Canadian Gold*. Toronto: McClelland and Stewart, 1988.

Palinchak, Robert S. *The Evolution of the Community College*. Metuchen, NJ: Scarecrow Press, 1973.

Prokopec, D. "The Community College: Historical Roots and Purposes." *Canadian Vocational Journal* 15, no. 1 (1979): 12–15.

Ray, Douglas, et al. *Values, Life-Long Education, and an Aging Canadian Population*. London: Third Eye Publications, 1983.

Ross, Murray G. *The University: The Anatomy of Academe*. Toronto: McGraw-Hill, 1976.

Ryan, Doris W. "The Community College: Some Philosophical Issues." *Yearbook of the Association of Canadian Community Colleges*. Edmonton, AB: University of Alberta, 1974.

Seredick, M., et al. "Collective Bargaining in Alberta Colleges." *CAUT Bulletin* 23 (December 1974): 17–20.

Sheffield, E., D. D. Campbell, J. Holmes, B. B. Kymlicka, and J. H. Whitelaw. *Systems of Higher Education: Canada*. New York: International Council for Educational Development, 1978.

Skolnik, Michael L. *Diversity in Canadian Higher Education*. Toronto: Ontario Institute for Studies in Education, 1983.

Small, James M. *College Coordination in Alberta: System Development and Appraisal*. Research Studies in Post-Secondary Education, No. 18. Edmonton, AB: Alberta Colleges Commission, 1972.

Sorenson, Nathalie. *General Education in Canada's Community Colleges and Institutes*. Toronto: Association of Canadian Community Colleges, 1984.

Tolley, G. "Community Colleges in Canada: Report of a Visit...March 1978." Sheffield: Sheffield City Polytechnic, 1979.

Watson, Cicily. *New College Systems in Canada*. Paris: Organization for Economic Cooperation and Development, 1973.

Well, C. V. "Alberta Colleges: A Product of Their Times." *College Canada* 2, no. 7 (1977).

Who's Who in America, 1990–91. Chicago: Marquis Who's Who, 1991.

Wootton, George C. "How to Build a College: Some Guidelines for Physical Planners." *Canadian University and College* (November/December 1981): 40–44.

Worth, Walter H. "From Autonomy to System: A Provincial Perspective." *Library Association of Alberta Bulletin* 5, no. 2 (April 1974): 56–65.

Theses and Dissertations

Barrington, Gail Vallance. "The Impact of Environmental Forces on Alberta Community Colleges 1980–1990." Ph.D. diss., University of Alberta, 1981.

Bryce, R. C. "The Technical and Vocational Training Assistance Act of 1960–67: An Historical Survey and Documentary Analysis." Ph.D. diss., University of Alberta, 1970.

Campbell, Gordon. "History of the Alberta Community College System: 1957–1969." Ph.D. diss., University of Calgary, 1972. Microfilm.

Clarke, John C. "Alberta Community Colleges: Ten Years in Review." M.Ed. thesis, University of Alberta, 1983.

Cornish, D. J. "A Comparison of Student and Faculty Perception of Their College Environment." M.Ed. thesis, University of Alberta, 1971.

Farquhar, Hugh E. "The Role of the College System of Higher Education in Alberta." Ph.D. diss., University of Alberta, 1967.

Kelly, Gerald O. "Application of Participative Management to College Governance." Ph.D. diss., University of Alberta, 1973.

Markle, Alexander G. "Genesis of the Lethbridge Public Junior College." M.Ed. thesis, University of Alberta, 1965.

Newberry, J. J. "A Comparative Analysis of the Organizational Structures of Selected Post-Secondary Educational Institutions." Ph.D. diss., University of Alberta, 1971.

Pearce, Sandra Dale. "Citizen Participation in the Community College." M.A. thesis, University of Alberta, 1972.

Reports and Monographs

Alberta Colleges Commission. Annual Reports, 1969–70 to 1972–73.

Alberta Colleges Commission. *College Comment: Alberta Colleges Commission Newsletter*. Various issues.

Alberta Colleges Commission. Survey Committee on Higher Education in Alberta. *An Interim Report, 1961; Second Interim Report, 1963; Third Interim Report, 1965; Fourth Interim Report, 1966*. Edmonton, AB: Author.

Alberta Commission of Educational Planning. W. H. Worth, Commissioner. *A Future of Choices: A Choice of Futures*. Edmonton, AB: The Queen's Printer, 1972.

Alberta Council on Admissions and Transfer. Annual Reports, 1975–76 to 1990–91.

Alberta Department of Advanced Education. Annual Reports, 1972 to 1975–76.

Alberta Department of Education. *Vision for the Nineties*. Edmonton, AB: Alberta Department of Education, September 1991.

Alberta Government White Paper: Post-Secondary Education until 1972. Edmonton, AB: Government of Alberta, 1972.

Alberta Universities Commission. Annual Reports, 1966–67 to 1972–73.

Berghofer, Desmond E. "Worth Commission Proposals Relating to Program Development in Higher and Further Education." July 1972. Unpublished paper.

Bosetti, Reno A. *Advanced Education in the 70s*. Edmonton, AB: Alberta Colleges Commission, 1972.

Bosetti, Reno A. *System Integration—Coordination—Growth, The Alberta System of Post-Secondary Non-University Education: Master Plan Number One*. Edmonton, AB: Alberta Colleges Commission, 1972.

Carnegie Commission on Higher Education. *Report on the Governance of Higher Education*. New York: McGraw-Hill, 1973.

Clark, R. C. *Post-Secondary Education until 1972: An Alberta Policy Statement by the Honourable Robert Clark, Minister of Education*. Edmonton, AB: Government of Alberta, January 1970.

Collin, Wilbur J. "The Role and Mission of Grant MacEwan Community College." Unpublished paper, Grant MacEwan Community College public relations files, March 7, 1982.

Day, T. C. "Transferability and Grant MacEwan Community College: 1971–1975." Unpublished paper, Grant MacEwan Community College Archives, November 1975.

Edmonton Planning Committee to the Board of Post-Secondary Education. *The Edmonton College: Report of the Planning Committee to the Board of Post-Secondary Education*. Edmonton, AB: Author, April 1969.

Fenske, Milton R. "Present Status and Future Prospects of the Community College in Alberta." Paper delivered to the Conference on Community Colleges, Banff, 1970.

Fenske, Milton R. *Report to the Alberta Colleges Commission*. Edmonton, AB: Alberta Colleges Commission, 1972.

Grant MacEwan Community College. *Response to "Master Plan Number One" on Post-Secondary Non-University Education*. Edmonton, AB: Author, February 8, 1973.

Hay Associates. *Development of Compensation Standards*. Edmonton, AB: Author, 1980.

Hickling and Johnson Management Consultants. *Public Perceptions of Grant MacEwan Community College*. Edmonton, AB: Author, 1979.

Kelly, Gerald O. "Role of Presidents/Role of Board of Governors." Panel discussion, Association of Canadian Community Colleges, Conference, Montreal, July 23, 1983.

Kolesar, Henry. *Post-Secondary Education in Alberta: Toward the Development of a System.* Edmonton, AB: Provincial Board of Post-Secondary Education, 1968. Mimeographed.

Mackenzie Spencer Associates Limited. *Exploratory Study of Site Alternatives for a City Centre Campus for Grant MacEwan Community College.* Edmonton, AB: Author, October 1984.

Martorana, S. V. *A Community College Plan for Lethbridge, Alberta.* Lethbridge: Lethbridge Collegiate Institute, 1951.

Report of the Committee of Inquiry into Non-Canadian Influence in Alberta Post-Secondary Education. Edmonton, AB: Minister of Advanced Education, 1972.

Report of the Fact Finding Committee on Post-Secondary and Continuing Education in Alberta. Conference on Post-Secondary and Continuing Education. Edmonton, AB, 1966.

Report of the Public Expenditure and Revenue Study Committee. Edmonton, AB: The Queen's Printer, 1966.

Report of the Royal Commission on Education in Alberta. Edmonton, AB: The Queen's Printer, 1959.

Seger, J. E., and G. L. Mowat, eds. *The Junior College: Banff Regional Conference of School Administrators, 1966.* Edmonton, AB: Department of Educational Administration, Faculty of Education, University of Alberta, 1966.

Sheehan, Bernard S. A *Financial Plan for Alberta Colleges and Universities: Recommendations and Research Results.* Calgary: Financial Plan Project for Colleges and Universities, 1977.

Snowden, Barry L. "Grant MacEwan Community College City Centre Campus." Edmonton. Presentation. March 20, 1992.

Stewart, Andrew. *Special Study on Junior Colleges.* Edmonton, AB: Government of Alberta, 1965.

Stewart, P. G. "Grant MacEwan Community College: The Period Prior to April, 1970." Unpublished paper, Grant MacEwan Community College Archives, 1970.

Survey Committee on Higher Education in Alberta.

Thieman, Francis C., and Gordon L. Mowat, eds. Report of the Hearing by the Canadian Commission for the Community College. Edmonton, AB: Department of Educational Administration, University of Alberta, 1969.

Grant MacEwan Community College Source Materials

Albatross, December 4, 1972.

Alumni Newsletter 1, no. 2: 1–2.

Annual Reports, 1976–77 to 1992–93.

Box 1796, various issues.

Calendars, 1971–72 to 1992–93.

Eliuk, Olga. Personal correspondence, July 1986. Grant MacEwan Community College Archives.

GMCC Student Handbook, 1971.

GMCC Student Yearbooks, 1974 to 1992.

GMCC Board Minutes, 1971 to 1993.

Intercamp, 1979 to 1993.

Journalist, various issues.

Kelly, Gerald O. President's Speeches, 1981–1993.

Long-Range Planning Committee Final Report, 1980.

MacEwan, J. W. Grant. Quotations. Grant MacEwan Community College Archives, various dates.

MacEwan Journal, December 4, 1972, to December 12, 1980.

MacEwan Today, various issues.

MacEwan Tomorrow, various issues.

Master Plan Report, July 30, 1972.

Moore, Barry. Grant MacEwan Community College 10th Anniversary Convocation Address, November 13, 1981.

Northeast Campus Proposal, November 26, 1975.

Perspectives, various issues.

Press Releases.

Program Advisory Committee Reports.

Request for Campus Planning Funds: Serving the Community Now Through the 21st Century, February 21, 1985.

Task Force on College Governance: Statement of Principles and Recommendations, June 1991.

West Campus User Committee Proposal, December 1, 1975.

Personal Interviews

Couture, Sue, May 31, 1993.

Day, T. C. (Chuck), February 19, March 4, April 16, April 19, 1993.

Giles, Bert, May 11, 1993.

Gray, Dorothy, April 12, 1993.

Kelly, Gerald O., May 12, July 6, 1993; April 26, 1995.

Lloyd, Patricia, April 23, 1993.

MacNeil, Harold, March 1, March 10, 1993.

Otke, Paul, March 12, 1993.

Pallas, Andi, April 12, 1993.

Schnell, Sharon, February 10, 1993.

Snowden, Barry, April 2, July 21, 1993.

Newspapers

Alberta Report, September 13, 1982.

Calgary Albertan, September 9, 1992.

Edmonton Journal, 1969 to 1993.

Edmonton Sun, April 26, 1993.

Gateway, University of Alberta, September 26, 1972.

Red Deer Advocate, September 21, 1972.

Statutes

Province of Alberta

Act to Amend the Students Assistance Act, 1971.

Act to Provide for the Establishment of Public Junior Colleges, 1958

Agricultural and Vocational Colleges Act, 1967.

Colleges Act, 1969.

Colleges Amendment Act, 1973.

Department of Advanced Education Act, 1972.

Department of Advanced Education Amendment Act, 1973.

Department of Advanced Education Amendment Act, 1977.

Public Junior Colleges Act, 1958.

School Act, 1931.

School Act, 1952.

Students Finance Act, 1976.

Universities Act, 1966.

Universities Amendment Act, 1973.

Universities Amendment Act, 1980.

University Act, 1906.

University Act, 1910.

University Act, 1942.

University and College Assistance Act, 1964.

Canada

Adult Occupational Training Act, 1967.

Federal-Provincial Fiscal Arrangements Act, 1967.

Technical and Vocational Training Assistance Act, 1960.

Technical Education Act, 1919.

Unemployment and Agricultural Assistance Act, 1937.

Vocational Training Coordination Act, 1942.

Youth Training Act, 1939.

Appendix A

John Walter Grant MacEwan

REVIRESCO—The MacEwan Clan Motto

to grow green again

to grow strong again

to be rejuvenated

to revive

to flourish

No history of Grant MacEwan Community College would be complete without reference to Dr. Grant MacEwan. The College's history reveals that the use of Dr. MacEwan's name has recognized the eminence of one of western Canada's most beloved personalities. "When I am with Dr. MacEwan," present College President Gerry Kelly remarked, "there is the feeling that I am in the presence of greatness."[1]

It would be futile to attempt to capture in the short space of a book's appendix the many details and accomplishments of this uncommon man. A respectable biographical treatment of his life demands the singular attention of an author. It is with considerable humility, therefore, that the following details regarding Dr. MacEwan's life are presented; anyone who desires to learn more about this unique individual is encouraged to read Dr. MacEwan's writing and explore the literature devoted to his life's story.

Dr. MacEwan stressed, no matter what your field is, "you must know your history."[2] The history surrounding Dr. MacEwan's life is enormous and, from just touching briefly on his accomplishments, it is clear that he is a treasured human resource. Dr. MacEwan was born in Brandon, Manitoba, on August 12, 1902. In the course of his ninety-plus years he has been an educator, politician, humanitarian, environmentalist, historian, and prolific author. After attending schools in Brandon and Melfort, Saskatchewan, he pursued studies at Ontario Agricultural College and Iowa State College, graduating in 1926 and 1928, respectively. He held positions at the University of Saskatchewan (professor of animal husbandry and department head, 1928–1946) and the University of Manitoba (dean of agriculture, 1946–1951).

His first venture into politics was an unsuccessful attempt to gain election as a Liberal candidate in a 1951 federal by-election in Brandon. The loss was a great disappointment for MacEwan; however, his subsequent move to Calgary proved to be a fortunate occurrence for MacEwan and the province of Alberta.

MacEwan moved to Alberta to reside on land he owned there and to assume the life of a writer and farmer. He would find, however, that his political career would delay this dual occupation. His prodigious writing accomplishments would eventually inc lude four texts on the subject of agriculture and over forty books on historical topics primarily concerned with western Canada.

MacEwan's political career flourished in Alberta. He was elected as an alderman for the city of Calgary in 1953, 1955, 1957 and 1959. Recalling his success in Calgary civic politics—he was never defeated—MacEwan remembered his first thoughts about entering another election campaign:

> I was only here one year and I was asked to become a candidate for Calgary city council. A committee approached me but I told them I wouldn't be elected because nobody knew me. A friend on the committee said, "you better run. If they knew you they wouldn't elect you."[3]

MacEwan expanded his political fortunes to the office of mayor of Calgary from 1963 to 1966. His political career also saw him elected as an MLA in 1955. In addition, he was leader of the Alberta Liberal party from 1958 to 1960. Dr. MacEwan was lieutenant governor of Alberta from 1965 to 1974.

Dr. MacEwan's association with Grant MacEwan Community College has provided a rare opportunities for a public post-secondary institution. Not only do the virtues associated with Dr. MacEwan's philosophy provide a noble goal for the College, but the association with a living legend has created a sense of kinship for the College that would have been extremely difficult without his affiliation. Dr. MacEwan's thoughts about the community college concept were mixed at first, "When the idea was first broached I had reservations. I asked myself, how practical is this? "[4]

Practicality and responsiveness are MacEwan trademarks, both for the man and the College. When he visited the College in 1985, MacEwan praised the staff and students of the Cromdale Campus for its success and humble origins as a grocery store:

I salute Cromdale. I knew it wasn't the most contemporary institution, but by thunder, the people here should hold their heads high. This campus stands as a monument to resourcefulness and if I were a Cromdale student, I would swell with pride.[5]

Dr. MacEwan made a strong effort to involve himself with the College. He called the College "one of the outstanding examples of community spirit in Canada."[6] While he was lieutenant governor and living in Edmonton, Dr. MacEwan recalled:

I did not miss an invitation. I always gave the first lecture in the horsemanship course and I did it religiously. I enjoyed the students and the staff, I thought they were great ladies and gentlemen. My heart will always be with them.[7]

The College has housed a Grant MacEwan room since October 6, 1976.[8] MacEwan remarked that he and his wife could not think of a finer place than the College to keep his memorabilia.[9] The City Centre Campus will accommodate this collection in the future.

Since February 1986 a day has been set aside to honour an employee of the College deemed worthy of recognition for his or her outstanding contribution to the College. A medallion is presented to commemorate this distinction. For those individuals so honoured, it is especially gratifying to have Dr. MacEwan himself bestow this award. In essence it is also the day that recognizes Dr. MacEwan. In reference to Dr. MacEwan, former Board of Governors representative John McGee eloquently stated, "the College is a mirror of the man."[10] For everyone associated with Grant MacEwan Community College, there can be no greater compliment.

---

[1] G.O. Kelly, personal interview, July 7, 1993.

[2] *Perspectives*, February 28, 1979.

[3] *Perspectives*, March 31, 1977, p. 4.

[4] Ibid.

[5] *MacEwan Journalist*, March 20, 1985.

[6] Ibid.

[7] *Perspectives*, March 31, 1977, p. 4.

[8] Located at the Mill Woods campus.

[9] *Perspectives*, October 7, 1976.

[10] *MacEwan Today*, February 16, 1993, pp. 2–3.

Appendix B

GMCC Board Members

1969—Edmonton College—Planning Committee
W.D. Neal, Chair, University of Alberta
R.G. Fast, Alberta Colleges Commission
R.W. Jones, Edmonton Public School Board
W.A.B. Saunders, Northern Alberta Institute of Technology
E.D. Stack, Edmonton Separate School Board
P.J. Husby, Executive Assistant

1970—Edmonton College—Board of Governors
Barry Moore, Chair
Edward Stack
Winnifred Ferguson
Fred Kurylo
Robert Guebert

1971–1972
Barry Moore, Chair
John L. Haar, President
Keith Lang, Student Rep.
Hy Sheinin, Faculty Rep.
Fred Kurylo
Winnifred Ferguson
Robert Guebert
Edward Stack

1972–1973
Barry Moore, Chair
John L. Haar, President
Keith Lang, Student Rep.
Hy Sheinin, Faculty Rep.
Fred Kurylo
Winnifred Ferguson
Robert Guebert
Edward Stack

1973–1974
Edward Stack, Chair
John L. Haar, President
Pat Allison, Student Rep.
Robert Eggers, Faculty Rep.
Winnifred Ferguson
Fred Kurylo
Sally Stewart

1974–1975
Edward Stack, Chair
John L. Haar, President
Brian Keating, Student Rep.
Juliana Lazaruk, Faculty Rep.
Lionel Wood
Laura Scott Kilgour
Sally Stewart

1975–1976
Sally Stewart, Chair
John L. Haar, President
Juliana Lazaruk, Faculty Rep.
Lawrence Symon, Student Rep.
Enid Crockett
Laura Scott Kilgour
William Astle
Robert McLeod

1976–1977
Laura Scott Kilgour, Chair
John L. Haar, President
Karl Homann, Faculty Rep.
John Strauss, Student Rep.
Enid Crockett
Robert McLeod
Orest Mulka
William Astle

1977–1978
Laura Scott Kilgour, Chair
John L. Haar, President
Owen Smith, Student Rep.
Karl Homann, Faculty Rep.
Bill Lord
Bryan O'Donnell
Nick Porozni
Robert McLeod
Orest Mulka
Enid Crockett

1978–1979
Laura Scott Kilgour, Chair
John L. Haar, President
Colin Simpson, Student Rep.
Don Meen, Faculty Rep.
Bill Lord
Bryan O'Donnell
Nick Porozni
Robert McLeod
Orest Mulka
Enid Crockett

1979–1980
Robert McLeod, Chair
John L. Haar, President
Don Meen, Faculty Rep.
Ann Morin, Student Rep.
Bryan O'Donnell
Bill Lord
Tony Thibaudeau
Orest Mulka
Enid Crockett
Nick Porozni

1980–1981
Robert McLeod, Chair
John L. Haar, President
Don Meen, Faculty Rep.
Denise Germain, Student Rep.
Orest Mulka
Bryan O'Donnell
Nick Porozni
Irene Koziol
Bill Lord
Tony Thibaudeau

1981–1982
Bill Lord, Chair
Gerry Kelly, President
Steve Higgins, NASA
Peter Furstenau, Faculty Rep.
Pat Haidner, Student Rep.
Bryan O'Donnell
Tony Thibaudeau
Bev Mahood
Orest Mulka
Irene Koziol
Nick Porozni

1982–1983
Bill Lord, Chair
Gerry Kelly, President
Steve Higgins, NASA
Peter Furstenau, Faculty Rep.
John Prodon, Student Rep.
Bryan O'Donnell
Tony Thibaudeau
Bev Mahood
Irene Koziol
Nick Porozni
Orest Mulka

1983–1984

Peter Kossowan, Chair
Gerry Kelly, President
Steve Higgins, NAS Rep.
Bert Giles, Faculty Rep.
Peter Dent, Student Rep.
Bill Barry
Bev Mahood
Irene Koziol
Rose Marie Nicas
Ralph Young
Lorne Yacuk, NAS Rep.
John Steffensen

1984–1985

Peter Kossowan, Chair
Gerry Kelly, President
Lorne Yacuk, NAS Rep.
Bert Giles, Faculty Rep.
Robin Nering, Student Rep.
Bill Barry
Bev Mahood, Vice-Chair
Irene Koziol
Rose Marie Nicas
John Steffensen
Ralph Young

1985–1986

Peter Kossowan, Chair
Gerry Kelly, President
Lorne Yacuk, NAS Rep.
Bert Giles, Faculty Rep.
Kevin Sinnott, Student Rep.
Bill Barry
Bev Mahood, Vice-Chair
Irene Koziol
Rose Marie Nicas
John Steffensen
Ralph Young

1986–1987

Peter Kossowan, Chair
Gerry Kelly, President
Linda Wood, NAS Rep.
Bert Giles, Faculty Rep.
David V.L. Way, Student Rep.
Bill Barry
Bev Mahood, Vice-Chair
Irene Koziol
Rose Marie Nicas
John Steffensen
Ralph Young

1987–1988

Peter Kossowan, Chair
Gerry Kelly, President
Linda Wood, NAS Rep.
Pat Moffat, Student Rep.
Bev Mahood, Vice-Chair
Rose Marie Nicas
Rick Angus
John Steffensen
Ralph Young
Fred Singer
Werner Jappsen
Dave Milner, Faculty Rep.
John McGee

1988–1989

Peter Kossowan, Chair
Gerry Kelly, President
Linda Wood, NAS Rep.
Dave Milner, Faculty Rep.
Rose Marie, Nicas, Vice-Chair
Rick Angus
John McGee
John Steffensen
Ralph Young
Fred Singer
Werner Jappsen
Debbie Hughes, Student Rep.

1989–1990
John Ramsey, Chair
Gerry Kelly, President
Scott Rutherford, NAS Rep.
Jack Phelan, Faculty Rep.
Marc Tremblay, Student Rep.
Vi Becker
John McGee, Vice-Chair
John Steffensen, Vice-Chair
Phyllis Anderson
Fred Singer
Werner Jappsen
Betty Andrews
Pat Bentley

1990–1991
John Ramsey, Chair
Gerry Kelly, President
Scott Rutherford, NAS Rep.
Jack Phelan, Faculty Rep.
Mike Jenner, Student Rep.
Vi Becker
John McGee, Vice-Chair
Phyllis Anderson
Fred Singer
Werner Jappsen
Betty Andrews
Pat Bentley

1991–1992
John Ramsey, Chair
Gerry Kelly, President
Brian Brix, NAS Rep.
Brian Zwicker, Faculty Rep.
Rose Notenboom, Student Rep.
Vi Becker
John McGee, Vice-Chair
Phyllis Anderson
Fred Singer (Nov. 13, 1991)
Werner Jappsen
Betty Andrews
Pat Bentley
Gary Elliott

1992-1993
John Ramsey, Chair
Gerry Kelly, President
Brian Brix, NAS Member
Brian Zwicker, Faculty Member
Rocky Maddex, Student Member
Vi Becker, Vice-Chair
John McGee, Vice-Chair
Phyllis Anderson
Werner Jappsen
Betty Andrews
Pat Bentley
Gary Elliott
Ted Bosse

1993–1994
John Ramsey, Chair
Gerry Kelly, President
Brian Brix, NAS Member
Brian Zwicker, Fac. Member
Rocky Maddex, Stu. Member
Vi Becker, Vice-Chair
Phyllis Anderson
Betty Andrews
Dale Dowell
Brian Reid
Ted Bosse
Pat Bentley

1994–1995
John Ramsey, Chair
Gerry Kelly, President
Brian Brix, NAS Member
Brian Zwicker, Faculty Member
Greg Dexter, Student Member
Vi Becker, Vice-Chair
Ted Bosse
Dale Dowell
Brian Reid
Phyllis Anderson
Pat Bentley
Mary Cameron

Appendix C

GMCC Faculty Association
Executive Committee

Complete lists of Executive Committee members are not available until 1982, when Shirley Kniazky became the Administrative Assistant for the Faculty Association.

1971–1972
John Hart, President

1972–1974
Lorne Yacuk, President

1974–1976
Karl Homann, President

1976–1978
Jay Handel, President

1978–1980
Christy Nelson, President

1980–1982
Eric McCorkell, President

1982–1983
David Milner, President
Karl Homann
Don Patterson
Donna Mitchell
Barry Olsen
Dolf Ryks
Peter Furstenau

1983–1984
David Milner, President
Karl Homann
Paul Ancel
Donna Mitchell
Barry Olsen
Dolf Ryks
Bert Giles

1984–1985
Dolf Ryks, President
David Milner
Julie Lazaruk
Eric McCorkell
John Western
Barry Olsen
Bert Giles

1985–1986
Dolf Ryks, President
Julie Lazaruk
Eric McCorkell
Doug Rusu
Barry Olsen
Bert Giles
David Milner

1986–1987
Dolf Ryks, President
David Milner
Celia Smyth
Eric McCorkell
Doug Rusu
Al McQueen

1987–1988
Bert Giles, President
Dolf Ryks
Celia Smyth
Mavis Tingey
Brian Zwicker
Al McQueen
David Milner

1988–1989
Bert Giles, President
Julie Lazaruk
Mavis Tingey
Brian Zwicker
Eric McCorkell
David Milner

1989–1990
Bert Giles, President
Julie Lazaruk
Claire Kibbler
Brian Zwicker
Eric McCorkell
Jack Phelan

1990–1991
Bert Giles, President
Rick Garn
Claire Kibbler
Brian Zwicker
Randy Jenne
Jack Phelan

1991–1992
David Milner, President
Bert Giles
Rick Garn
Joanne Kemp
Larry Knechtel
Randy Jenne
Brian Zwicker
Pat Lloyd
Peter Mitchell

1992–1993
David Milner, President
Doug Ringrose
Joanne Kemp
Larry Knechtel
Randy Jenne
Brian Zwicker
Pat Lloyd
Peter Mitchell

1993–1994
David Milner, President
Doug Ringrose
Don Fisher
Barry Walker
Randy Jenne
Brian Zwicker
Pat Lloyd
Peter Mitchell

1994–1995
David Milner, President
Joan Patrick
Al McQueen,
Barry Walker
Kathryn Jones
Brian Zwicker
Joanne Christie
Jack Robinson

1995–1996
Kathryn Jones, President
David Milner
Lynn Sugden
Al McQueen
Barry Walker
Dolf Ryks
Joan Patrick
Joanne Christie
Jack Robinson

Appendix D

GMCC Non-Academic Staff Association
Executive Committee

1982–1983
Barrie White, President
Len Rust, Vice-President
Ilene Nessel, Treasurer
Madelaine Boston, Secretary
Barb Bech, Director
Peter Jenkins, Director
Sharon Schnell, Director
Joy Shaw, Director

1983–1984
Barrie White, President
Len Rust, Vice-President
Ilene Nessel, Treasurer
Madelaine Boston, Secretary
Barb Bech, Director
Peter Jenkins, Director
Sharon Schnell, Director
Joy Shaw, Director

1984–1985
Ric Johnsen, President
Pat Wilson, Vice-President
John Jaglal, Treasurer
Barb Bech, Director
Rosemarie Kneubuhler, Director
Anne Lavoy, Director
Sharon Schnell, Director

1985–1986
Ric Johnsen, President
Pat Wilson, Vice-President
Joyce Nethercote, Treasurer
Anne Lavoy, Secretary
John Jaglal, Director
Linda Robinson, Director
Scott Rutherford, Director

1986–1987
Tim Mechalski, President
Scott Rutherford, Vice-President
Joyce Nethercote, Treasurer
Brenda Pottle, Secretary
Elaine Kirschner, Director
Ilene Nessel, Director
Fred Sawka, Director
Ev Simpson, Director

1987–1988
Scott Rutherford, President
Fred Sawka, Vice-President
Joyce Nethercote, Treasurer
Betty Thibeault, Secretary
Natalie Dzioba, Director
Mike Mazza, Director
Ilene Nessel, Director
Ken Stachniak, Director

1988–1989
Scott Rutherford, President
Penny Bruce, Vice-President
Fran Hagland, Treasurer
Betty Thibeault, Secretary
Bernie Fritz, Director
Linda Robinson, Director
Ken Stachniak, Director
Janitt Strachan, Director

1989–1990
Lynne Wright, President
Fred Sawka, Vice-President
Fran Hagland, Treasurer
Bruce McIntosh, Secretary
Bernie Fritz, Director
Michelle Leveille, Director
Linda Robinson, Director
Ken Stachniak, Director

1990–1991
Sharon Schnell, President
Don Young, Vice-President
Virginia Harris, Treasurer
Monika Weber, Secretary
Lil Bartel, Director
Bernie Fritz, Director
Bruce McIntosh, Director
Nancy Ritchie, Director

1991–1992
Sharon Schnell, President
Don Young, Vice-President
Ilene Nessel, Treasurer
Monika Weber, Secretary
Lil Bartel, Director
Murray Birch, Director
Bruce McIntosh, Director
Nancy Ritchie, Director

1992–1993
Pat Wilson, President
Anne Lavoy, Vice-President
Monika Weber/Pat Pelech,
Treasurer
Lise Bourret, Secretary
Jill Day, Director
Anna Martin, Director
Leanna Price, Director
Jacque Service, Director

1993–1994
Pat Wilson, President
Anne Lavoy, Vice-President
Pat Pelech, Treasurer
Lise Bourret, Secretary
Cheryl Carbert, Director
Renata Kuhtz, Director
Judy Sandstrom, Director
Jacque Service, Director

1994–1995
Pat Wilson, President
Anne Lavoy, Vice-President
Glenda Yearley, Treasurer
Jean Anne Armstrong, Secretary
Lise Bourret, Director
Carlyn Ching, Director
Renata Kuhtz, Director
Judy Sandstrom, Director

Appendix E

GMCC Students' Association Executive Council

1978–1979
Carol Lynn Chilkowich, Chair
Diane Hart
Colin Simpson
Eldon Morrison
Anna Cristello
Carla Bit
John McGrath
Stephanie Massingham-Pearce
Garret Parsons
Vicki Spinks
Dave Anderson
Tim Paziuk
Mike Derbyshire
Carol Hayes

1979–1980
Lorrie Moore, Chair
Ann Morin
Kevin Golka
Wanda Buchanan
Ida Baril
Randy Martyshuk
Sandy Mills
Dave Johnston
Diane Reas
Christopher Foreman
Heather Stewart
Glen Gilchrist
Juli Hickson
Monique Dammer
Jolaine Ryckman
Michael Lessard
Jan Goodman
Mike Demers
Fran Auburn
Jack Anderson
Gail Kelly
Bev Nalesnik

1980–1981
Brad Switzer, President
Joanne Rice
Brenda Sian
Denise Germaine
Lin Wennerstrom
Lance Love
Olga Mandryk
Su Ross
Don Kew
Calvin Cairns
Tony Bohnenkemp
Pam Lavertu
Joyce Verstraete
Karen Hoskins
Linda Pratch
Kerry Pierson
Laura Lynn Shatz
Gail Neufeldt

1981–1982
David Wunker
Diane Hutchinson
Pat Haidner
John Prodan
Marilyn Tkachuk
Peter Christiansen
Randy Smith
Sandy O'Neil
Colleen Carney
Pam MacRae
Verna Nakonechny
Monica Tonn
Sue Kellock

1982–1983
Peter Christiansen, President
Derek Dick
Diane Hutchinson
John Prodan
Richard Bryce
Rhondda Hinch
Darrell Skidnuk
Kim Borystmayer
Colleen Carney
Karl Nord
Verna Nakonechny
Teresa Azevedo
Fred Mueller
Peter Dent
Treasure Ducharme
Diane MacNeill

1983–1984
Kent Quinn, President
Franco Sorgiovanni
Rebecca Butler
Peter Dent
Teresa Azevedo
Barbara Lynn Pollard
Neeraj Varma
Laurie Lefebvre
Doug Buxton
Mary Toronyi
Terri Murphy
Cindy Mappleback
Sandra Mayers
Adele Seguin
Brenda Schultz

1984–1985
Teresa Azevedo, President
Sandra Mayers
Kelly Tansem
Robin Nering
Deb Tworek
Paul Manuel
Ken MacLeod
Colleen Brennan
Robyn Drader
Loretta Watson
Terri Murphy
Jennifer Copp
Duane Seibel,
Kay Wilson
Alana Tiffen
Cindy Fast

1985–1986
Colleen Brennan, President
Ken Schultz
Kevin Sinnott
Gloria McKale
Jim Kavanagh
Tom Jones
Rhonda Belous
Susan Newbury
Cory Ratke
Tracy Jampolski
Mark Barron
Judy Daniels
Karen Lupul
Darrell Pacini
Diane Bourassa

1986–1987
Lona Cunningham, President
Greg Debogorski
Jed Goddard
David Way
Martin Brown
Blair MacSymetz
Peter Box
Kim King
Cordell Becker
Franc Grove
Rob Birse
Lawrence MacLean
Diane Bourassa
Twyla-Raie Gunette

1987–1988
Franc Grove, President
Robert Kaemingh
Pat Moffat
Dave Smith
Cheryl Katzmarzyk
Angi Cividino
Mike Kraus
Carol Stevenson
Robin Telasky
Rob Birse
Mark Laubman
Nancy Sward
Tracy Porter
Liane Cournoyer
Trish Lasouski

1988–1989
Pat Moffat, President
Paul Christiansen
Debbie Hughes
Dozan Ng
Kim Clegg
Kelly Leier
Lee Dreger
Clarence Randall
Shawn Deen
Darren McCullough
Dan Dragicevic
Kerry Harris
Heather Holtby

1989–1990
Lee Dreger, President
Len Bingham
Tracy Slemko
Marc Tremblay
Suzi Semchuk
Lynda Pelletier
Rosann Semchuk
Gary Monias
Sally Chambers
Darren McCullough
Chris Minchau
Jennifer Wallace
Tamara Thomas

1990–1991
Sally Chambers, President
Kurt Gosselin
Mike Jenner
Rob McKinley
Michelle van-der-Merwe
Andrea EngelLeah Dupont
Sherri Henderson,
John Foxall
Andrew Robertson
Marvin Woloshyniuk
Mike Keller

1991–1992
Kim Bowlby, President
Doug Markevich
Sandra Manchul
Rose Notenboom
Sandy Lawson
Paul Morstand
Illiki Bugej
Doug Choptiany
Dave Cochrane
Shirley-Ann Hannah
Hendriatta Wong
Kathy Nickerson
Mike McCaul
Keltey Ziegler

1992–1993
Kim Bowlby, President
Jeff Burgess
Trina Flodell

Rocky Maddex
Wade Staples
Dave Cameron
Penny Whitford
Paul Buchwald
Ngozi Odina
Sandy Romeo
Tracy Ford
Rob Peeling
Mike McCau

1993–1994
Jason Tetzlaff, President
Paul Buchwald
Lisa Ross
Rocky Maddex
Steve Francoeur
Alison Crawford
Dave Cameron
Terry Rhode
Carolyn Hooker
Andrea Rudolph
Bevin Bileski
Kelly Balanecki

1994–1995
Shauna Liber, President
Terry Rhode
Wendy Cooper
Greg Dexter
Mercedes Dizon
Jennifer Graham
Sean Connolly
Heather McKenzie
Mike Sokoluik
Dennette Schultz
Cory Soule
Fiona McNair
April Johnson
Melanie Owen
Glenn Melnychuk
Natasha Alexander
Steven Hoose

Appendix F

Honorary Diploma Recipients, Convocation Guest Speakers, and Distinguished Alumni Awards

YEAR	HONORARY DIPLOMA	GUEST SPEAKER	ALUMNI
1972	Hon. J. W. Grant MacEwan (Dr.)	Hon. J. W. Grant MacEwan	
1973	Dr. Henry Kolesar	Hon. James Foster (Mr.)	
1974	Mr. Jerome Robbins	Hon. Peter Lougheed (Mr.)	
1975		Judge E. D. (Ed) Stack	
1976	Judge E. D. (Ed) Stack	Dr. Max Wyman	
1977	Mrs. Ethel Marliss	Hon. Bert Hohol (Mr.)	
1978		Mr. John Haar	
1979	Dr. Tommy Banks	Hon. Doug Roche (Mr.)	
1980	Hon. Ralph Steinhauer	Mr. Warren Graves	
1981	Sister Therese Castonguay	Mr. Mel Hurtig	
1982	Dr. Dick Rice	Mr. Bob Clark	
1983	Mr. Conrad Bain *Theatre Arts*	Dr. Myer Horowitz	
1984	Dr. Charles Allard *Business Administration*	Hon. J. W. Grant MacEwan (Dr.)	
1985	Mr. Max Ward *Travel*	Mrs. June Sheppard	
	Mrs. Alice Makokis *General Arts & Science*		

YEAR	HONORARY DIPLOMA	GUEST SPEAKER	ALUMNI
1986	Dr. Joseph Shoctor *Arts Administration* Dr. Helen Hays *Extended Care Nursing*	Dr. Joseph Shoctor	Ms. Carol Lynn Chilkowich, 1979 *Travel Consultant.*
1987	Hon. Neil Crawford *Community Services*	Dr. John Paterson	Mrs. Sherri Makarewicz, 1983 *Volunteer* *Management*
1988	Dr. Harold Baker *General Arts & Science* Mr. David Foster, *Music*	Mr. Bill Smith	Mr. John Meston, 1976 *Youth* *Development*
1989	Hon. Dave Russell (Mr.) *Business* Dr. Francis G. Winspear *Community Services*	Hon. Dave Russell Dr. R. Gordon McIntosh	Ms. Linda Tyre, 1984 *Volunteer* *Management*
1990	Mrs. Peggy Holmes *Community Services* Mrs. Bettie Hewes *Community Services*	Mrs. Peggy Holmes Mrs. Bettie Hewes	Mrs. Sunita Kumar, 1988 *Arts* *Administration*
1991	Dr. Myer Horowitz *University Transfer* Dr. Randy Gregg *Community Services*	Dr. Myer Horowitz Dr. Randy Gregg	Mr. William Exelby, 1981 *Accounting*
1992	Mr. Bruce Hogle *Community Services* Mrs. Mary Burlie *Community Services*	Mr. Bruce Hogle Mrs. Mary Burlie	Ms. Stephanie Wilson, 1979 *Occupational* *Health Nursing*
1993	The Right Hon. Joe Clark *Community Services*	The Right Hon. Joe Clark	Ms. Margo Kane, 1975 *Dance*

Dr. Donald Stanley
Community Services

Dr. Donald Stanley

YEAR	HONORARY DIPLOMA	GUEST SPEAKER	ALUMNI
1994	Dr. Steve Ramsankar *Community Services*	Dr. Steve Ramsankar	Ms. Lynn Loos, 1987 *Interpreter Training*
	Mr. Robert Stollery *Business Administration*	Mr. Robert Stollery	
1995	Mr. Sigmund Sobolewski *Community Services*	Mr. Sigmund Sobolewski	Mr. Stephen Williams, 1990 *Voluntary Sector Management*
	Mr. Bill Comrie *Business Administration*	Mr. Bill Comrie	

Appendix G

Long-Serving Employees of
Grant MacEwan Community College

*I apologize for not having talked to everybody. There were so many.
Each week I would think, There, now I've finished with that section.
Now I know all there is to know about "that." And a few days later I
would learn of someone new or someone I had not thought of or
someone I never would have thought of, and he would have one more
window on the past for me to raise.*[1]

It is difficult to recognize, in the space of a short history, all of the
people who have contributed to the character and chronicle of Grant
MacEwan Community College. Unfortunately, not everyone deserving
mention can be acknowledged within a project of this nature. Their
employment, however, exemplifies the genuine history of the College.

Everyone, of course, who has worked for Grant MacEwan Community College is part of its history. This includes volunteers, sub-contrac-
tors, the various guest lecturers, and also the temporary employees who
"answered the call" during particularly busy times. The role that these
people have played is inestimable.

Approximately ten years after the establishment of Grant MacEwan
Community College, at the initiative of Dennis Larratt, Director of
Human Resources, employees of the College were recognized for their
long service to the institution. These employees are particularly noteworthy in that their longevity has supplied a continuity and bond for the
College. Those employees that have received recognition for long
service include:

Long Service Awards Recipients
1981 Ten Year Service

Jack Allen	Peter Brown
Donna Askin	Jack Cooper
Bill Besse	Chuck Day
Olga Eliuk	George Naylor
Bert Giles	Paul Otke
Vijay Gupta	Andi Pallas
John Haar	Len Rust
Joan Holt	Sharon Schnell

Caterina Loverso
Donna Mitchell

Allen Watson
Samuel Yakimishyn

1982 Ten Year Service

Laurie Allen
Bob Bennett
Danin Bodnar
Terry Flannigan
Peter Furstenau
Chery Hoffmeyer

George Knight
Myrna Maquera
Eric McCorkell
Wendy Muscroft
Laurene Park
Norma Young

1983 Ten Year Service

Richard Burtnik
Wesley Drager
Millard Evans
Kim Frandsen
Karl Homann
John Jaglal
Juliana Lazaruk
Duane Massing
Gordon Nicholson
Barry Olsen
Daniel Rafferty

Eva Roche
Ronald Rowswell
Dolf Ryks
Mildred Stefanick
Alice Switzer
Charlene Tarver
Rhoda Taylor
Patricia Wilson
Lorne Yacuk
Janice Zielinski

1984 Ten Year Service

Charlie Austin
Andy Blake
Terry Bonneau
Norma Carr
Keith Chapman
Bob Cowan
Kay Feehan
Fern Fleming

Carol Gardner
Mary Kachmar
Ruby Kinnear
Tim Mechalski
Josephine Moscardelli
Pati Russell
Lian Smith
Laurie Taschuk
Jennifer Wolfe

1985 Ten Year Service

Wendy Albrecht
Barbara Beeson
Bob Cairns
Wendy Campbell
Brian Ellis
Rick Garn
Isabel Golightly

Anne Gurney
Claire Kibbler
Doris Kniazky
Marie Middleton
Bill Mucklow
Barbara Myler
Bruce Vincent

1986 Ten Year Service

Lynda Bowes
Robert Chubb
Elizabeth Dawson
Doris Hunt

Ilene Nessel
Eugene Riel
Celia Smyth
Shirley Thuesen

Ellen Krytor
Mary Livojevic
Ralph Marshall

John Waddell
Joanne Wilde

1986 Fifteen Year Service

William Besse
Peter Brown
T. C. (Chuck) Day
Olga Eliuk
Bert Giles
Vijay Gupta
Joan Holt

George Naylor
Paul Otke
Andi Pallas
Len Rust
Sharon Schnell
Allen Watson
Samuel Yakimishyn

1987 Ten Year Service

Paul Ancel
Paul Byrne
Bert Beckman
Bob Gilligan
Adrian Kennedy
Judy Koch
Pat Lloyd
Hardip Mann
Stewart McDonald
Sheila McLeod

Allen McQueen
David Milner
Brenda Moore
Lawrence Peta
Peggy Quinney
Mike Rosanova
Joy Shaw
Theresa Tomaszewski
Bert Ward
Wally West

1987 Fifteen Year Service

Laurie Allen
Danin Bodnar
Terry Flannigan
Peter Furstenau
Chery Hoffmeyer

George Knight
Eric McCorkell
Wendy Muscroft
Laurene Park
Norma Young

1988 Ten Year Service

Diane Butcher
Suzanne Couture
Coleen Finlayson
Theresa Gagnon
Everett Gorman
Ross Hill
Dorothy Howard

Marian Kowler
Donald Patterson
Elly Schenkel
Janitt Strachan
Pamela Taylor
Valerie Walker
Dianne Yusep

1988 Fifteen Year Service

Donna Askin
Richard Burtnik
Millard Evans
Kim Frandsen
Karl Homann
John Jaglal

Daniel Rafferty
Eva Roche
Ronald Rowswell
Dolf Ryks
Mildred Stefanick
Alice Switzer

Juliana Lazaruk
Duane Massing
Gordon Nicholson
Barry Olsen

Charlene Tarver
Rhoda Taylor
Patricia Wilson

1989 Ten Year Service
Joyce Benders
Ron Campbell
Isabelle Darrah
Betty Downie
Patricia Fields
Dorothy Gray
Rosemarie Kneubuhler
Anna Kurnik
Rita Long
Robert Lysay
Marilyn Meyer
Gerri Nakonechny
Pat Picketts

Patricia Reeb
Shirley Reid
Pat Roddick
Camille Romaniuk
Tim Ryan
Anne-Marie Schrock
Elizabeth Sheppard
Barbara Sundal
Marina Vettergreen
Beverly Walker
Barry White
Jennie Wilting
Richard Zwicker

1989 Fifteen Year Service
Charlie Austin
Bob Bennett
Andy Blake
Theresa Bonneau
Norma Carr
Keith Chapman
Bob Cowan

Kay Feehan
Mary Kachmar
Tim Mechalski
Josephine Moscardelli
Lian Smith
Laurie Taschuk
Jennifer Wolfe

1990 Ten Year Service
Lillian Bennett
Rossana Bonanni
James Burke
Marianna Chmielewski
Diane Ewen
Anthony Fell
Philip Flannigan
Arlene Ford
Mary Lynne Gokiert
Liela Hastie
Bea Isfeld
Darlene James
Bruce Johnson

Joanne Kemp
Dennis Larratt
Raylene Manolescu
Wendy McLachlin
Kathlene Mene
David Morris
Gertrude Neumann
Marica Novogradac
Shirley Ochitwa
Teresa Panza
Helen Sterr
Deborah Ulan
Yvonne Walmsley
Brian Zwicker

1990 Fifteen Year Service
Barbara Ausman
Bob Cairns
Brian Ellis

Anne Gurney
Claire Kibbler
Bill Mucklow
Pati Russell

Isabel Golightly

1991 Ten Year Service
Louise Bennett
Calvin Bowal
Lynda Brown
Joanne Christie
Irene Collard
Hugh Cowley
Richard Day
Sandra Edwards
Barbara Gibeau
Pat Hall
Berni Holowach
Karen Hoskins
Glenna Hughes
Jim Humphries
Gerald Kelly
Gail Leonard

Bruce Vincent

Sharon Ludbrook
Karen MacKinnon
J. V. Mehta
Florence Mitchell
Cherie Moses
June Mowers
Jack Pleckaitis
Terry Reynolds
Nancy Roberts
Brenda Sallis
Gayle Shaw
Evelyn Simpson
Julie Stevens
Hazel Sutherland
Eugenia Van Eck
Susan Verhulst
Marianne Wright

1991 Fifteen Year Service
Liz Dawson
Rick Garn
Shirley Kniazky
Mary Livojevic

Ralph Marshall
Sheila McLeod
Ilene Nessel
Eugene Riel

1991 Twenty Year Service
Peter Brown
Chuck Day
Bert Giles
Vijay Gupta
George Naylor

Paul Otke
Andi Pallas
Sharon Schnell
Allen Watson
Samuel Yakimishyn

1992 Ten Year Service
Marilynn Berg
Michelle Bezenar
Carla Costuros
Tim Crisall
David Cuyler
Bill Dean
Jannie Edwards
Georgina Fysh
Ursula Hindle
Randy Jenne
Donna Lauritsen

Anne Lavoy
Chuck Lee
Betty Lucas
Joseph MacLellan
Carol Maranchuk
John McGrath
Alex Palamarek
Kingsley Payne
Adelle Rurka
Fred Sawka
Clayton Wright

1992 Fifteen Year Service
Paul Ancel

David Milner

Bert Beckman
Bob Gilligan
Adrian Kennedy
Pat Lloyd
Hardip Mann
Stewart McDonald
Allen McQueen
Marie Middleton

Brenda Moore
Lawrence Peta
Peggy Quinney
Mike Rosanova
Joy Shaw
Celia Smyth
Valerie Walker
Wally West

1992 Twenty Year Service
Danin Bodnar
Peter Furstenau
George Knight

Wendy Muscroft
Laurene Park
Norma Young

1993 Ten Year Service
Lillian Bartel
Keith Burgess
Julienne Colbow
Bernadette Fritz
Robert Gawreluck
Carolyn Graber
Kathryn Jones
Elaine Kirschner
Rosemarie Matwie
Sean O'Connell

Bonnie Overton
Patricia Pelech
John Phelan
MaryAnn Polack
Brenda Pottle
Frank Salopek
Paul Saturley
Mary Sullivan
Gloria Swanson
Donna-Mae Winquist

1993 Fifteen Year Service
Marian Allen
Diane Butcher
Robert Chubb
Suzanne Couture
Coleen Finlayson
Theresa Gagnon

Ross Hill
Marilyn Meyer
Donald Patterson
Elly Schenkel
Pamela Taylor
Theresa Tomaszewski

1993 Twenty Year Service
Millard Evans
Chery Hoffmeyer
Karl Homann
John Jaglal
Julie Lazaruk
Gordon Nicholson

Barry Olsen
Dan Rafferty
Eva Roche
Ron Rowswell
Dolf Ryks
Charlene Tarver
Pat Wilson

1994 Five Year Service
David Adams
Brenda Allan
Dianne Allen
Jean Anne Armstrong
Geoff Bacchus

Lynne Baker
Marlene Baltare
Butram Barnes
Brenda Barrett-Boisclair
Cindi Berg
Joyce Berreth
Joseph Birch
Pat Birch
Noreen Blue
Elmer Bly
Richard Boisvert
Carol Bolding
Madeleine Booth
Fred Bosgraaf
John Brittain
Brian Brix
Carol Brown
Glenn Budney
Louise Bureau
John Casey
Wes Caswell
Helen Chartrand
Alex Chaykowski
Diane Christensen
Carol Chrusch
Carol Clark
Gaston Clermont
Kevin Collard
Tom Collier
Malcolm Connell
Richard Cook
Pat Cooper
Bill Coppinger
Ann Cox
Marilyn Cromwell
Harry Davis
Karen Davis
Katherine Dawson
Mark Degner
Lisa Del Bove Orlandi
Pat Dober
Lee Dreger
Lois Drew
Jaswinder Kaur Dulai
Judith Dumont
Brenda Duncan
Natalie Dzioba
Elsie Elford

Lynda Ferguson
Don Fisher
Sylvia Flood
Margaret Ford
Karen Freiman
Dzidra Goor
Gwen Greanya
Mary Grubisa
Marcel Hamel
Chris Hancock
David Hannis
Virginia Harris
Doreen Haskell
Donna Hastings McGeady
Doug Heckbert
Cathryn Heslep
Barbara Hess
David Higgins
Kathy Higgins
Katherine Hildebrand
Bert Hoogewoonink
Marilyn Hooper
Jennifer-May Hunter
David Hynne
Craig Janke
Corinne Jeffery
Ray Jorritsma
Deanna Kenwell
Manjinder Khatra
Dianne Kittlitz
Renata Knos
Alan Knowles
Ken Kobly
Sandra Kostashuk
Chris Krozser
Shelagh Kubish
Pat Kuefler
Renata Kuhtz
Sylvie Labbe
Karen Lambert
Naomi Langlois
Terri Larson
Day Lepoole
Michelle Leveille
Richard Lewis
Patricia Lirette
Janine Loewan-Jackson
Janice Mackay

Rob Mackenzie
Irene Makar
Amin Malak
Shahram Manouchehri
Margo March
Wendy Martin
Carole Massing
John Matechuk
Eileen Matthews
Bruce McIntosh
Bernadette McNeil
Marg Melton
Barbara Migaj
Celine Miller
Daniel Mitchell
Peter Mitchell
Evelyn Mitton
Darlene Morrill
Lori Murray
Margaret Mykietyshyn
Susan Neiser
Janet Nichol
Renate Oddy
Josie O'Reilly
Dan Pagnucco
Eileen Passmore
Joan Patrick
Randall Paul
Roman Petryshyn
Lorna Phelan
LaRee Pickup
Karen Portas
Russell Powell
Cindy Pratt
Leanna Price
Kathaleen Quinn
Sue Rees
Faye Ripley
Oswald Reich
Nancy Ritchie
Jack Robinson
Louise Rolinger
Marilyn Romanyk
Linda Ross
Douglas Rusu
Valerie Rutherford
Dianne Ryan
Nancy Samuell

Judy Sandstrom
Janice Scammell
Merna Schmidt
Brian Schroter
Dorothy Semenchuk
Jacque Service
Beth Smith
Marian Jo-anne Smith
Reginald Smith
Margaret Sobchyshyn
Joseph Sombach
Monya Sonnleitner
Marian Sorensen
Mary Splawinski
T. Michael Stock
Jennifer Stevenson
Angela Stratiy
John Stropel
Robert Stroup
Patrick Sullivan
Ronald Szala
Sonia Taverner
Martha Taylor
Sushila Thomas
Lidija Thompson Ward
Brian Thurgood
Mavis Tingey
Sadie Tkachuk
Doris Van Andel
Edith Villarica
Daniel Villeneuve
Alan Vladicka
Mansoor Waljee
Donna Walton
Kathy Warner-Hudson
Malcolm Watt
Monika Weber
Alan Wesley
Dianne Westwood
Sharla White
Heather Williams
Judy Windsor
Judy Wizniuk
Kathy Wong
Maria Wong
Elaine Wowchuk
Lynne Wright
Terri Yaremko

Dorothy Yost
Donald Young
Annie Yu
Linda Zahacy
Theodore Zazula

1994 Ten Year Service

Bonnie Armstrong
Margaret-Anne Cameron
Viola Cerezke-Schooler
Helen Colbert
Cheryl Crocker
Shannon Dean
Cathy Dool
Joan Earle
Alex Hill
Shelly Hladun
Lucija Ivanc
Audrey Jeffery
Barbara Jones
Larry Knechtel
Sandra Kostashuk
Mark Lund
Mary Lynne Matheson

Michele Mazza
Joan McCullough
Heather Mechalski
Patricia Ness
Gertrude Neumann
Margaret Palichuk
Carol Peters
Scott Rutherford
Beverley Sochatsky
Jean St. Arnaud
Mary Sullivan
Carol Tackaberry
Betty Thibeault
Brian Webb
Edy Wong
Julie Younie

1994 Fifteen Year Service

Joyce Benders
Rossana Bonanni
Ron Campbell
Patricia Fields
Dorothy Gray
Dorothy Howard
Rosemarie Kneubuhler
Gerri Nakonechny
Barbara North

Patricia Picketts
Patricia Reeb
Camille Romaniuk
Tim Ryan
Anne-Marie Schrock
Marina Vettergreen
Beverly Walker
Barrie White
Richard Zwicker

1994 Twenty Year Service

Charlie Austin
Bob Bennett
Andy Blake
Keith Chapman
Bob Cowan

Kay Feehan
Mary Kachmar
Duane Massing
Laurie Taschuk
Jennifer Wolfe

---

[1] Robert W. Creamer, *Babe: The Legend Comes to Life* (Middlesex, England: Penguin Books, 1983), p. 13.

Appendix H

A Brief History of Tuition and Grading Policies

1970–1972

Tuition: $100 per program.

Grading: Four grades were approved by the Board of Governors, October 13, 1971: 1. Outstanding; 2. Completed Requirements; 3. Incomplete; and 4. Special Circumstances.

1972–1976

Tuition: A full program was assessed $100 per trimester for each program containing 12 to 18 trimester credit-hours, or $400 for a two-year program. Each single course containing 3 trimester credit hours was assessed a cost of $30.

Grading: The following grading system was in use:

OS = Outstanding

CR = Completed requirements

INC = Incomplete—must repeat course if credit desired (initiated in 1974-1975).

INCS = Incomplete—special circumstances—no credit granted. Student must complete requirements within following trimester.

AUD = Auditor—attended classes, no assignments or examinations completed.

1976–1979

Tuition: For a full program; a cost of $125 per trimester for each program containing 12 or more trimester credit hours. A single course cost $37.50 for each course containing 3 trimester credit-hours.

Grading: No changes.

1979–1980

Tuition: Fees were based on the number of credits a student was enroled in each trimester to a maximum $137.50 for a full course load of 10 or more credits. A differential foreign student fee was applied to all foreign students not registered at the college prior to September 1, 1977. Foreign students paid $220 for a full course load.

Grading: (Effective September 1978, the following grading system was employed. Grading was based on a 4-point system.)

A = excellent

B = very good

C = average

D = low pass

I = incomplete

F = failure

AUD = auditor

1980–1987

Tuition: Fees continued to be based on the number of credits a students was enroled in. In 1980, 10 credits cost $150 for Canadian students and $216 for foreign students; 12 credits and over cost $151.25 and $242 for Canadian and foreign students, respectively. By 1987, tuition for Canadian students was $212 and $318 for foreign students for 10 or more credits.

Grading: Grade of CR = completed requirements added for 1986–1987.

1988–1990

Tuition: Tuition was assessed based on the program in which the student was enroled. In 1988, approximate total costs, including tuition, per year varied from $775 (second year travel consultant program) to $3,270 (environmental graphic design, included materials).

Grading: No change.

1990–1992

Tuition: Continued to be assessed according to program of study. Approximate total costs, including tuition, per year, in 1991–1992 ranged from $1,012 (second year theatre production) to $4,395 (graphic design, included materials).

Grading: Grading continued to use a four-point system. In 1990-1991, the grading system was refined to include the additional grades, and grade point definitions, of: A- (3.7), B+ (3.3), B- (2.7), C+ (2.3), C- (1.7), and D+ (1.3). The grades of A, B, C, D, and F continued to be assigned values of 4.0, 3.0, 2.0, 1.0, and 0.0, respectively.

Appendix I

GMCC Full-time Equivalents and Facilities Requirements[1]

Year	FTE Enrol.	Area Required sq.ft.	sq.m.	Actual Area sq.ft.	sq.m.	notes	short
71-72	561	87,000	8,100	71,000	6,600	CT,Crom,Scona	1,500
72-73	1,327	206,000	19,200	143,000	13,300	Assumption	5,900
73-74	1,510	234,000	21,800	189,000	17,600	J.P.,St.Anthony's	4,200
74-75	1,982	308,000	28,700	189,000	17,600		11,100
75-76	2,422	377,000	35,100	196,000	18,300	Portables	16,800
76-77	2,650	413,000	38,400	306,000	28,500	MillWoods	9,900
77-78	2,547	397,000	36,900	306,000	28,500		8,400
78-79	2,452	381,000	35,500	306,000	28,500		7,000
79-80	2,406	374,000	34,800	418,000	38,900	Jasper Place	(4,100)
80-81	2,417	376,000	35,000	418,000	38,900		(3,900)
81-82	2,717	437,000	40,700	418,000	38,900		1,800
82-83	3,042	506,000	47,100	427,000	39,700	JP Annex	7,400
83-84	3,557	612,000	56,900	427,000	39,700		17,200
84-85	3,715	658,000	61,200	431,000	40,100	JP Annex	21,100
85-86	3,940	719,000	66,900	431,000	40,100		26,800
86-87	4,268	807,000	75,000	591,000	55,000	7th Street Plaza	20,000
87-88	4,485	850,000	79,000	591,000	55,000		24,000
88-89	4,750	893,000	83,000	591,000	55,000		28,000
89-90	5,025	936,000	87,000	591,000	55,000		32,000
90-91	5,300	968,000	90,000	591,000	55,000		35,000

	FTE	Area Required		Actual Area			
Year-	Enrol.	sq.ft.	sq.m.	sq.ft.	sq.m.	notes	short
91-92	5,575	1,011,000	94,000	591,000	6,600		39,000
92-93	5,850	1,054,000	98,000	1,183,000	110,000	City Centre Campus	(12,000)
93-94	6,100	1,097,000	102,000	1,183,000	110,000		(8,000)
94-95	6,400	1,140,000	106,000	1,183,000	110,000		(4,000)
95-96	6,650	1,183,000	110,000	1,183,000	110,000		0
96-97	6,800	1,215,000	113,000	1,183,000	110,000		3,000
97-98	6,950	1,237,000	115,000	1,183,000	110,000		5,000
98-99	7,050	1,258,000	117,000	1,183,000	110,000		7,000
1999-2000	7,125	1,269,000	118,000	1,183,000	110,000		8,000
2000-2001	17,175	1,280,000	119,000	1,183,000	110,000		9,000

¹ Source: B.Snowden, vice-president—administration, May 20, 1987.

Appendix J

GMCC Campus Development Chronology[1]
1970–1993

As of 1993, the history and development of physical facilities for Grant MacEwan Community College begins a new phase with the City Centre Campus. Unless the present economic and political conditions change dramatically, it is hard to envision any future involvement by the College with a project of the magnitude of the City Centre Campus. Nevertheless, the combination of creative leadership and "responsiveness to the community" will ensure that growth, in some form, of the physical facilities for Grant MacEwan Community College will continue.

While useful from a chronological perspective, a recapitulation of the College's physical facilities fails to reveal the rationale behind the property acquisitions and transactions. The initial growth period of the College addressed the facilities issue with a pragmatic, short term, "responding to need" philosophy. This resulted in space deficiencies that created the need for leasing arrangements based on a reactionary response. Long-range planning for facilities that anticipated growth was not a characteristic of the College's early planning process. Subsequently, new facilities such as the Mill Woods and Jasper Place campuses appeared to give the College additional space. Andi Pallas, GMCC facilities director, and the person responsible for all facilities development throughout the College's history, recalled the new facilities, "only replaced existing leased space" and, in reality, were, "a *catch-up* to existing space deficiencies."[2]

Thus, the construction of the City Centre Campus was a major break from the traditional philosophy employed by Grant MacEwan Community College regarding facilities.

Chronology of Development and Utilization of Grant MacEwan Community College Facilities

1970
- Leased office space in Confederation Building

1971
March:
- Terminated lease for Confederation Building

April:
- Leased Canada Trust building space for administrative offices.
- Leased old Workers' Compensation Building for student affairs offices.

June:
- Purchased Cromdale campus and renovated for classes by September 1971. Leased Old Scona campus from Edmonton Public School Board (EPSB) and renovated for classes by September 1971.

1972

April:
- Purchased 1,000 square-foot portable for Cromdale campus.

June:
- Leased Assumption Campus.

July:
- Leased space at Edmonton General Hospital for nursing program.

September:
- Leased storefront on 111 Avenue.

1973

June:
- Purchased 1,000 square-foot portable for Old Scona.
- Leased Jasper Place campus from EPSB.
- Leased St. Anthony's School from Edmonton Separate School Board (ESSB).

July:
- Gave up old Workmans' Compensation Building and relocated offices to Assumption.

August:
- Leased 6,000 square feet of warehouse space.

1974

April:
- Terminated lease of storefront on 111 Avenue.

May:
- Leased Azure Acres for equine studies program.

July:
- Purchased 2,000 square-foot portable classrooms for Jasper Place campus.

September:
- Leased storefront on 114 Street.
- Commenced construction of Mill Woods campus.

1975

July:
- Purchased 6,000 square feet of portable classrooms space for Jasper Place campus.
- Purchased Assumption Academy facilities and property.

1976

April:
- Completed construction of Mill Woods campus.

May:
- Gave up Old Scona, moved into Mill Woods campus.

June:
- Gave up St. Anthony's, moved to Mill Woods and Assumption campuses.
- Gave up Canada Trust Building and relocated to Assumption campus.

July:
- Purchased 6,000 square feet of portable classroom space for Jasper Place campus.
- Relocated Old Scona portable to Cromdale campus.
- Decreased size of leased facilities at Edmonton General Hospital.

September:
- Terminated lease of storefront on 114 Street.
- Terminated Warehouse lease, relocated at Mill Woods.

1977

April:
- Renewed lease of Azure Acres for two years to May 1979.

July:
- Purchased 1,500 square foot portable classrooms for Jasper Place campus.
- Purchased 3,000 square feet of portable classroom space for Cromdale campus.

September:
- Swapped properties with EPSB: their Jasper Place site for Assumption campus site.

November:
- Retained architect for Jasper Place project.

1978

April:
- Purchased 3,000 square feet of portable classrooms for Cromdale campus.

May:
- Terminated lease of Azure Acres.

June:
- Leased Whitemud Equine Centre from the City of Edmonton for five years.

July:
Leased space from Westmount School and Victoria Composite High School (EPSB) for design arts and theatre programs, respectively.

September:
- Leased space at Alberta Native Communications Society (ANCS).
- Relocated 3,400 square feet of portable classrooms from Jasper Place to Equine Centre.
- Relocated house trailer from Azure Acres to Equine Centre.

1978

November:
- Demolished south part of Jasper Place campus building.

December:
- Commenced excavation of Jasper Place project.

1979

April:
- Sold 5,500 square feet of portable classrooms from Jasper Place campus to Edmonton Separate School Board.

July:
- Gave up Westmount school space.
- Leased additional space at Victoria Composite High School for interim accommodation of design arts and theatre programs during Jasper Place campus construction.

August:
- Leased parking lot at 157 Street and 100 Avenue from City for interim Jasper Place parking.

November:
- Capital Cable installed satellite headend unit on Mill Woods campus building.

1980

January:
- Leased additional space for dance program at Alberta Academy of Dance.

April:
- Old Jasper Place campus torn down.
- Relocated all remaining portable classrooms from Jasper Place to Cromdale.
- Jasper Place staff, furniture and equipment accommodated at Victoria Composite High School, Mill Woods and Assumption campuses during interim period.

July:
- Took over Community Enrichment Project and leased Kingsway Avenue site.

August:
- Leased space from Edmonton Public School of Ballet for dance program.
- Staff, furniture and equipment moved out of Victoria Composite High School into west building of Jasper Place campus.

September:
- Classes for Music and Design Arts programs commenced in west wing of Jasper Place campus.

November:
- Started Yellowhead Regional Educational Consortium (YREC).

December:
- Moved into centre and east wing of Jasper Place campus.

1981

January:
- Returned Assumption campus to EPSB.

June:
- Jasper Place Theatre completed.
- Leased space for Drayton Valley Educational Consortium (DVEC).

1982

July:
- Terminated Equine Centre operation and lease.

August:
- Leased space for Bishop Sewing at Jasper Place.

September:
- Leased additional space for DVEC.

December:
- Gave up ANCS space.

1983

March:
- Leased new space for Native Communications Program (NCP).

May:
- Leased Annex space at Jasper Place.

September:
- Leased new space for YREC.

1984

July:
- Bishop Sewing space converted to Community Relations department office.

1985

January/June:
- Leased Winnifred Stewart School for English as a Second Language program (ESL).

January:
- Leased space in Edmonton Convention Centre.

July:
- Leased additional space in JP Annex.

August:
- Leased Stony Plain classroom ("Barn") for Community Relations–gave up former lease.
- Renewed lease of Kingsway Avenue sitefor Community Enrichment Project.
- Leased some warehouse space.

September:
- Request for City Centre Campus planning funds approved.

1986

March:
- Leased Seventh Street Plaza campus.

May:
- Terminated lease of Edmonton Convention Centre space.

August:
- Major alterations to existing facilities and program relocation from Cromdale to Jasper Place campus and Mill Woods and Jasper Place campuses to Seventh Street Plaza.

September:
- Commenced classes at Seventh Street Plaza campus.
- Leased 211 square-foot space, first floor, SSP building.
- Terminated lease on Native Communication Program space on 107 Avenue.

October:
- Relocated College executive officers to Seventh Street Plaza campus.

1987

July:
- Terminated lease, of Stony Plain classroom (Barn).

September:
- Leased additional space, 2nd level parkade, Seventh Street Plaza building.

October:
- Construction of gym storage addition completed, Mill Woods campus.

November:
- Leased additional space on 2nd floor, Seventh Street Plaza campus (formerly Dr. Ridgeway's space).
- Sub-leased second floor space at Seventh Street Plaza campus to Lakeland College.

1988
April:
- CCC project, $100 M budget approved by Province.

May:
- Commenced construction of new portable classroom/office complex, Mill Woods campus.

June:
- Leased 435 square-foot first floor storage space at Seventh Street Plaza building.

September:
- Reduced lease space at Edmonton General Hospital.
- Commenced operations in new portable classrooms and offices, Mill Woods campus.

1989
January:
- Leased first floor retail space at Seventh Street Plaza building.

July:
- Cancelled lease for first floor retail space at Seventh Street Plaza building.
- Leased new administrative office space at Donsdale Place.

September:
- Relocated administrative offices from Mill Woods and Jasper Place campuses to Donsdale Place.
- Converted vacated Mill Woods and Jasper Place space to teaching facilities.

1990
March:
- 65,250 square-meter project approved by Minister of Advanced Education.

June:
- Advanced Education Minister gives perrmission to proceed with CCC project working drawings.

September:
- Second floor space at Donsdale Place leased for *Job Search Strategy Project,* September 1, 1990 to August 31, 1991.

November:
- CCC project Contract Number One–*Site Services*–awarded November 21, 1990.

1991
June:
- CCC project Contract Number Two–*Foundations and Parkade Structure*–awarded June 4, 1991.

July:
- Jasper Place Annex lease expired.
- Exercised one year option for Seventh Street Plaza campus, July 1, 1992 to June 30, 1993.
- City Centre Campus property transferred to GMCC.

September:
- Renewed Donsdale Place *Job Search* project space, September 1, 1991 to March 31, 1992.

November:
- CCC project Contract Number Three–*Campus Buildings A & B plus site work components*–awarded November 21, 1991.

1992
January:
- Leased 1128 square-foot at Capilano Centre (January 1, 1992 to December 1992) for additional *Job Search* project space.

March:
- CCC project, Contract Number 4–*Building R*–awarded.

April:
- CCC project, Contract Number 5–*Building C*–awarded.

1993
January:
- Gave up Capilano Centre space.

March:
- Gave up *Job Search* project space, Donsdale.

May:
- Moved into Building R.

June:
- Moved into Building B.
- Took Mill Woods campus portable classrooms out of use.

July:
- Moved into Building A.

August:
- Gave up Community Enrichment Project space on Kingsway Avenue.
- Gave up Seventh Street Plaza campus.

September:
- Gave up Cromdale campus.
- Gave up Donsdale Place.
- Started Classes – City Centre Campus.

---

[1] The author wishes to acknowledge the contributin of Andi Pallas, the Director of the Facilities Division, for his assistance in supplying information and insight concerning the history of the College's physical facilities.

[2] A. Pallas, Board of Governor's Retreat, Red Deer, Alberta, November 16, 1984.

Appendix K

College Governance Principles[1]

Central Principle

Empowerment of Learners–Students and Employees Alike

GMCC will provide opportunities which enable learners to take responsibility for and have influence on their learning and the conditions in which it takes place, as preparation for a life-long process of independent learning. College employees must be similarly empowered in order to create such conditions for student learning.

Supporting Principles

• **Focus on the Human Dimension of GMCC**

Organizational development, interpersonal skills such as problem solving among college employees will be promoted in order to ensure that the process of collaborative governance works as smoothly as possible. Systems for employee support and recognition will also be a priority.

• **Intrinsic Value of Individuals' Work**

The college recognizes and affirms the potential of each employee to contribute to the mission of the college. To ensure that each employee is provided with an opportunity to excel, the college will provide jobs in which employees can experience intrinsic value in their work.

• **Clarity of Decision-Making**

The roles and mandates of individuals and groups (i.e., committees) with responsibility for decision-making in various areas must be clearly defined and widely understood.

• **Opportunity for Involvement**

College employees will have the opportunity to become involved, either directly or by representation, in decisions which affect them and their work units.

• Focus on Communications

Open sharing of information at all levels, and effective channels of communication (upward, downward and lateral) are essential to the process of collaborative governance. There must be ongoing emphasis on both written and verbal communication.

• Congruence: Classroom to Board Room

College operations, from the board and senior administration level to divisions and units, to classroom activities, will all reflect the principle of empowerment as appropriate to the situation.

• Values and Mission of GMCC

Development of and commitment to a common and well understood sense of college mission and guiding values as a framework within which staff are free to pursue objectives creatively. The cultivation of a common philosophy of purpose minimizes conflict and maximizes goal attainment.

• Responsible Use of Resources

Public funds will be utilized as efficiently as possible toward the effective fulfilment of the college mission and achievement of specific objectives.

• Policy Development vs. Administration

College governance must recognize distinctions between policy-setting functions, which require a particularly high degree of staff input and participation, and administrative functions, which require clear lines of authority and accountability to ensure leadership in the implementation of policies.

• Leadership and Management Styles

The styles of leadership and management practised within the college need to reflect the principle of empowering staff to achieve objectives within the general scope of the college mission and values.

• Adaptive Organization

The college will strive to be a flexible and responsive organization. The organizational structure will continue to evolve as the college adapts to internal and external change.

---

[1] *Task Force on College Governance: Statement of Principles and Recommendations,* Grant MacEwan Community College, June 1991.

Appendix L

MacEwan 2000: Forms for Thought

A Discussion Paper

November 1988

Prepared by Gerry Kelly, President

GMCC CITY CENTRE CAMPUS - A DESIGN PHILOSOPHY

The purpose of this discussion paper is to stimulate ideas about the general design of a new GMCC campus; a facility whose primary purpose will be to serve life long educational needs of Edmontonians in the 21st century.

Following input from the MacEwan community the philosophical statement and principles which emerge will provide a conceptual foundation upon which the actual campus design can be developed.

The concepts discussed in this paper encompass both form (the physical design) and function (the activity taking place in the structure), in the belief that the former should follow and be driven by the latter.

Buildings may speak a language which tells us about: the institution and organization; its values and priorities; its development and future; and its relationship to its community. What will our new campus say? How will a new campus look, how will it feel, how will its personality be reflected? How do we want Grant MacEwan Community College to be portrayed? From our experiences and philosophies as community college educators some ideas and questions begin to emerge.

1. Future Orientation

What should our future orientation be? The campus will accommodate today's students, but also children born today who will become students in 2010 and beyond. What are their needs likely to be? What are the implications for building facilities in the 1990's to serve current learners and learners fifty years hence.

What are the current and future, local, national, and international contexts within which our students will learn and work? What changes are taking place and what are their potential impacts on college education? How might these affect building design?

2. Flexibility for the Future

Although we can make educated guesses as to the educational ramifications of new technology and shifts in philosophy, we can't be sure and therefore we will need to be capable of adjusting as the future unfolds. In this case, it seems to make sense to build in as much flexibility in campus design as possible, so that alterations can be made over the years as the situation warrants.

But at what cost? What will we be prepared to sacrifice to achieve flexibility? On the other hand, what are the costs of inflexibility?

3. Program Philosophy

By and large, Grant MacEwan College programs have a practical orientation which should be reflected in the facility. Beyond this, to what extent can we ensure that the facility itself reflects the nature of the programs which give it life? The campus should reflect not only programs' practical needs, but where feasible, how should the educational philosophy of our creatively oriented Ad and P.R., Visual Arts, or Early Childhood programs be reflected in their facilities?

4. Learner Centred

Increasingly the College is orienting its curriculum and learning activities to the self-directed learner, and integrating part-time learning into the fabric of the College. What are the implications of this direction for facilities design? MacEwan's philosophy also speaks of the College being student centred. What does this mean for campus design? If we consider the entire campus, not just the classrooms, as a learning centre, what are the implications for the learning dimensions of all campus space - the learning resource centre, student services, physical education facilities, the student centre, etc.?

5. Open Learning

The image of learning as an open process is compatible with the philosophy of the community college. While instructional spaces (classrooms and laboratories) need, first and foremost, to be functional and aesthetically pleasing from the perspective of students and faculty, we may also want to adopt the concept of the community college actually "seeing learning taking place". One aspect of this design which we might consider further is the "glass walls" concept, of which we have examples on our Jasper Place Campus. What has been the experience of users? Is this an idea we can build on? What corrections would be required? The principle of "user group" input is essential to successful design here.

6. College & External Environment

The notion of reflecting Edmonton's and Alberta's physical environment in our campus design is compelling. How might the campus portray the grandeur of the province of Alberta - in form, materials, colour, etc.? Greenery, park like settings and the capability of seeing Alberta's sunny blue skies while working indoors come to mind. Bright offices and classrooms lit with natural light, and glass covered streets with roofs may provide a useful model.

Conceptually we want a campus which has a welcoming and warm environment compatible with the spacious and open feelings of Alberta. What blend of materials could be utilized to create a warm and inviting interior for the campus.

Also, Edmonton is a winter city. What can we do with our campus to make the sometimes inhospitable winter more palatable?

7. Community Access/Receptivity

We wish Edmontonians to feel as relaxed in entering the College campus as they would other public places. If the campus looks like a fortress from the outside that conveys one message; hopefully we want to convey the opposite. How can we design a campus (as well as the activities inside) so it is inviting, exciting and enticing?

8. Construction Quality

The public should expect this campus to be fully functional well into the 21st century. The campus will be built with public funds and we are obligated to utilize these funds in the most prudent manner. For a variety of reasons, MacEwan in the past built cheaply to gain additional space which in the long run has not proven to be an efficient use of resources. A challenge for us will be to ensure an appropriate balance between quality and quantity of space, utilizing standards generally applicable in Alberta post-secondary education.

9. Corporate Image

The College is a people place, a place for learning, and a community of service. How can we use the building's image to promote the benefits of community college education? Is it possible to have the structure convey the College's educational philosophy, its values, its corporate identity, its name and its colours?

We also hope that our new campus will be an attraction to visitors to downtown Edmonton. Might the design include a utilitarian but distinctive architectural feature that would come to symbolize GMCC in people's minds?

Our facilities, by themselves, cannot create good teaching and learning situations, but our people can. As educators, we cannot by ourselves create good facilities, but we have an opportunity to participate in their creation. The purpose of this paper is to stimulate thinking about facilities design, and to invite your input and feedback with respect to the concepts and ideas discussed above. This input can be provided in a variety of ways, but I will welcome receiving your suggestions directly. During the functional programming process, we will be refining a statement of design philosophy, from the College members' perspective, and your assistance in this vital activity will be greatly appreciated.

Appendix M

"2020 VISION"

**A Discussion Paper on Edmonton's
Community College Development: 1990–2020**

Gerald O. Kelly, President

August 13, 1990

Edmonton 1990–2020

It is now the year 2020. Over the past 30 years Edmonton's economy has continued to be based on services to natural resource industries and the agricultural sector, government services, and some manufacturing, but increased diversification has also taken place, into the areas of advanced technology, research and applications, and higher education. Additionally, responding to the demands of a global information based economy. Edmonton is becoming internationally recognized as a world centre for higher education.

During the early 21st century, Edmonton became acclaimed as one of the world's most habitable and hospitable cities both winter and summer. Edmonton's 1990 metropolitan population of 775,000 grew to 1,000,000 in 2010, and is now 1,115,000 in 2020.

In response to this growing population, based on the entrepreneurial initiative of Grant MacEwan Community College and the increasing participation rate of adults in higher education, enrolment (and accompanying facilities requirements) at Edmonton's community college continued to grow throughout this period. The college's facilities planning was guided initially by a development concept entitled "2020 Vision" prepared in 1990/91. In 1987/88 the Board's Long Range Facilities Development Report reviewed the history of GMCC facilities. Original plans for the College found in the 1969 "Edmonton College" report recommended a campus for about 10,000 students be built on 240 acres of land. However, this vision was not captured. Rather the College evolved in the 1970's and 80's on a series of small campuses and ad hoc buildings. Not only did MacEwan fail to keep pace with standards for College facility development found throughout Alberta, the multiple site locations proved to be inefficient, costly, and in many respects hampered the College's ability to fully respond to community needs. Nevertheless, the College did find the experience of locating campuses (of a minimum size) in various sectors of the city to be a viable and desirable facilities development concept. Building on this experience the 1987–88 Long Range Facilities Development report concluded that:

- Evolution to a single campus configuration is neither feasible nor desirable.

- The "main campus with satellites" model is a short range reality, but not a desirable long range campus configuration.

- A multi-campus configuration with each campus providing a relatively comprehensive range of programs, services, and facilities is an optimal model for long range facilities development.

Recommendations from the report adopted by the Board of Governors were:

- That the Board adopt, as the long-range facilities development strategy, a multi-campus configuration model.

- That permanent campuses be developed to sizes in the range of a minimum of 3,000 to 5,000 FTE.

Grant MacEwan Community College 1990—2020

The first campus of this range was the 4,500 FTE city centre campus, completed for opening in the fall of 1993. Although the College had gotten off to a rapid start in the early 70's, plateaued in the late 70's, and then doubled enrolments in the 80's, the 1993 city centre campus served as a springboard for GMCC to make an even more dramatic impact on its community. The new campus allowed the college to respond as demand for college courses soared, GMCC became a 'lighthouse' college in North America. Furthermore, the presence of the campus served as a catalyst to downtown revitalization. Over the past 30 years, due to its success as a community college, MacEwan's diverse mandate has become better known and supported within the Edmonton community. In particular its pride in adapting to changing societal needs has kept it in the forefront of responsive educational institutions.

Having retained and enhanced its strong vocationally oriented program base, the College's programs were also strengthened by implementation of the university transfer alternative during the 90's. Community development activity, known for its responsiveness to Edmontonians, adult upgrading formerly associated with another centre, and continued creative expansion of non-credit self-funding offerings have been the hall mark of our community college's programming. In addition, the college's emphasis on internationalization during the 1990's helped not only to make the college an early leader in addressing the educational requirements of our global society, but helped broaden its funding base to a point where MacEwan is now 50 percent self-funded.

During the late 90's and early part of the 2000's, several new college programs were added, some deleted, and many reconfigured to adjust to changing times.

The college, as indicated in their 1990 Ten Year Goals, kept abreast of changing educational technologies, and individualized learning activity was designed accordingly. Nevertheless, the basis of its educational complex remains group oriented, requiring classroom teaching/learning functions not unlike those associated with educational practice prevalent when the college started back in the 1970's.

MacEwan's programs and delivery have proved to be flexible and responsive to their environment. Consistent with the comprehensive role of a community college, in the early 2000's, the formerly government-run vocational centre in Edmonton was eventually incorporated into MacEwan's Community Education and Arts and Science Divisions. As well, by 2000 MacEwan had become established and well respected for university transfer programs in Edmonton. In fact for many in Edmonton, it became the preferred alternative. Grant MacEwan Community College offers, not only programs in the University of Alberta pattern, but distinctive and popular alternative delivery and study modes including the home based independent learning option, the highly acclaimed study abroad programs in world centres including, Moscow, Kiev, Rio, Berlin, etc., and the innovative societal issues based interdisciplinary program started at MacEwan, has now been adopted by the University of Western Canada as one of their most popular degrees.

Throughout the last 30 years, the driving force for the college's development has continued to be the high level of community demand for its programs and services, which in turn was nurtured by MacEwan's educational philosophy and initiative in developing programs responsive to community needs.

College Enrolment:

As Grant MacEwan continued to be responsive to educational needs in its growing community, enrolments continued to increase. In 1990 FTE credit figures were 5,300 FTE (4,500 FT and 4,250 PT) with another 18,000 taking non-credit activity. Corresponding figures for 2000, 2010 and 2020 are shown below:

	FTE	FT	PT	Non-credit	Community People
1990	5,300	3,500	5,500	16,000	25,000
1995	6,500	5,000	8,000	27,000	35,000
2000	10,000	7,500	12,500	30,000	50,000
2010	13,500	10,000	17,000	40,000	67,000
2020	17,000	12,000	22,000	50,000	84,000

College enrolment patterns over the past 30 years were influenced by the following factors:

- participation rates among adult Edmontonians nearly doubled by 2020;

- a shift towards more part-time enrolments, which reflected the college's emphasis on life-long learning in an information based economy;

- amalgamation of the former Alberta Vocational College with the Community College;

- expansion of diploma programs and increased university transfer responsibility.

College Campus Facilities

By the year 2020 MacEwan's facilities have expanded significantly in response to ever increasing demands for its programs, learning experiences and activities.

Following the construction of the City Centre Campus in the early 90's, the College continued its development as a multi-campus strategy adopted by the Board in the late 1980's, which identified a multi-campus configuration, with each campus providing a relatively comprehensive range of programs, services and facilities, as an optimal model for long range development. This strategy required that permanent campuses be developed to accommodate 3000 to 5000 FTE each.Although the multi-campus (actually a multi-site) model, with campuses of limited size and services, was established when the college began, the first comprehensive campus in the 3-5000 FTE range was the City Centre Campus which opened its doors on the former CN lands in 1993 for 4500 full time students.

Unlike previous campus locations, such as Jasper Place and Mill Woods, which were land poor and basically limited to 1000 students, the City Centre Campus and those we now have in 2020 are located on sites which allow for expansion or related development such as applied research as required.

Shortly after 2000, given the growth of the city and increasing requirements for community college education in the Edmonton area, citizen groups in the suburban localities of Fort Saskatchewan, St. Albert, Sherwood Park, Leduc and Devon/Riverbend were demanding separate community colleges be established there. The government of the day decided to continue development of all Edmonton area community colleges under the Grant MacEwan Community College Board, which was charged with the planning responsibility for future development. The system was not unlike that planned for Dallas, Texas, with its seven college campuses planned and established in the 1960's.

Fortunately, the Board of the day back in the early 90's also had the foresight to acquire several sites in the Edmonton area for future campuses. As indicated in the following facilities map, college campuses are now located in five sectors of the city, with land set aside in two more for future development.

To qualify as a campus development district, it was decided that a campus must draw from a population area of approximately 200,000 people and attract a minimum of 3000 FTE students.

In the early 1990's, the College Board, in pursuing its long term facilities plan, decided to identify sites with a minimum size of 1/4 section of land, if possible, and have these ear marked for future campus development. Acquisition of land and or buildings included approaching significant community members to serve as benefactors as well as having the city and/or the province designate future sites. MacEwan also negotiated with business, other educational agencies and government enabling the college to obtain future options on underutilized shopping malls, high schools and government sites.

Strategies over the past 30 years to obtain and develop college sites were as follows:

[*The paper ends at this point*].